Expert Service-Oriented Architecture in C#

Using the Web Services Enhancements 2.0

JEFFREY HASAN

Apress®

Expert Service-Oriented Architecture in C#: Using the Web Services
Enhancements 2.0
Copyright © 2004 by Jeffrey Hasan

ISBN (pbk): 1-59059-390-1

Printed and bound in the United States of America 9 8 7 6 5 4 3 2

Trademarked names may appear in this book. Rather than use a trademark symbol with every occurrence of a trademarked name, we use the names only in an editorial fashion and to the benefit of the trademark owner, with no intention of infringement of the trademark.

Lead Editor: Ewan Buckingham

Technical Reviewers: Mauricio Duran, Fernando Gutierrez

Editorial Board: Steve Anglin, Dan Appleman, Ewan Buckingham, Gary Cornell, Tony Davis, Jason Gilmore, Chris Mills, Dominic Shakeshaft, Jim Sumser, Karen Watterson, John Zukowski

Project Manager: Tracy Brown Collins

Copy Edit Manager: Nicole LeClerc

Copy Editor: Ami Knox

Production Manager: Kari Brooks

Compositor: Linda Weidemann, Wolf Creek Press

Proofreader: Sachi Guzman

Indexer: Rebecca Plunkett

Cover Designer: Kurt Krames

Manufacturing Manager: Tom Debolski

Distributed to the book trade in the United States by Springer-Verlag New York, LLC, 233 Spring Street, Sixth Floor, New York, NY 10013 and outside the United States by Springer-Verlag GmbH & Co. KG, Tiergartenstr. 17, 69112 Heidelberg, Germany.

In the United States: phone 1-800-SPRINGER, e-mail orders@springer-ny.com, or visit http://www.springer-ny.com. Outside the United States: fax +49 6221 345229, e-mail orders@springer.de, or visit http://www.springer.de.

For information on translations, please contact Apress directly at 2560 Ninth Street, Suite 219, Berkeley, CA 94710. Phone 510-549-5930, fax 510-549-5939, e-mail info@apress.com, or visit http://www.apress.com.

The information in this book is distributed on an "as is" basis, without warranty. Although every precaution has been taken in the preparation of this work, neither the author(s) nor Apress shall have any liability to any person or entity with respect to any loss or damage caused or alleged to be caused directly or indirectly by the information contained in this work.

The source code for this book is available to readers at http://www.apress.com in the Downloads section.

*Nothing is really work
unless you would rather be doing something else.*

JAMES BARRIE
SCOTTISH DRAMATIST
(1860–1937)

Contents at a Glance

Contents

Foreword

I HEAR MANY misconceptions about Web services. The phrase "Web services is for calling methods using XML" appears most often. It is true that Web services give developers a way to invoke code on a remote machine. And that code is encapsulated in a method. But that does not mean that the Web services architecture exists for remote method invocation. The Web services architecture offers an unprecedented level of freedom when building distributed applications.

Developer freedom takes many forms. To some it is the freedom to recompile their C++ code on another compiler. Others think of freedom as the ability to see and modify the source code of underlying libraries.

The portability of Java appeals to many. In distributed applications another freedom appeals: loose-coupling. Distributed applications are made up of multiple pieces running on multiple machines. Coordinating multiple versions of software, operating systems, and platform libraries can be a terrible burden.

The Web services architecture, service-orientation, offers a solution in the form of loosely-coupled services. The power of XML isn't that you can read it with Notepad. XML's gift comes from a structure that allows for growth and change in a backward-compatible fashion. The cool thing about XML is that it is everywhere. The architecture takes advantage of these fundamental tenets of XML and grows them up for use in distributed applications.

For instance, developers live in a versioning hell. If you want to upgrade one side of your application, you are taking your life (or at least your job) into your hands if you don't upgrade the rest of the application as well. Well-defined interfaces tend to melt when the infrastructure behind them change. Fragile software breaks. The Web services architecture helps with complimentary technologies like XML Schema's anyElement and anyAttribute features, SOAP's MustUnderstand, and the policy framework. Each of these address a particular versioning problem from changing user data to changes to underlying service capabilities.

Interoperability gives another form of freedom. Without interoperability, monolithic applications force themselves on developers. Businesses need to communicate with other businesses that run entirely different platforms. The cost and logistics of forcing one or both parties to install a platform they do not have any expertise using is immense. Web services deliver freedom from monoliths. I've personally spent tons of time working with developers of Java, Perl, C++, and other Web services platforms on testing interoperability and making sure it works. This is a work-in-progress, but each day it's better.

We designed Web Services Enhancements 2.0 for Microsoft .NET to give developers this freedom. You can build a service-oriented application without WSE, but with WSE you can build an advanced and secure service-oriented application. You are holding a book that describes how to use WSE to its fullest potential. Jeffrey Hasan's writing exceeds my expectations. Read this book and you will be well on your way to understanding the Web services architecture. You will be ready to use WSE to build a service-oriented application that will free you.

Keith Ballinger
Program Manager for Web Services Enhancements, Microsoft Corporation

About the Author

Jeffrey Hasan is the President of Bluestone Partners, Inc., a software development and consulting company based in Orange County, California (http://www.bluestonepartners.com). His company provides architectural design and software development services to businesses that implement advanced Microsoft technologies. Jeff is an experienced enterprise architect and .NET developer, and is the coauthor of several books and articles on .NET technology, including *Performance Tuning and Optimizing ASP.NET Applications* (Apress, 2003). Jeffrey has a master's degree from Duke University and is a Microsoft Certified Solution Developer (MCSD). When he is not working, Jeffrey likes to travel to far-flung corners of the world. His most recent travels have taken him from Southern Spain to Yosemite Valley and a few stops in between. You can contact Jeffrey at jeffh@bluestonepartners.com.

About the Technical Reviewers

Mauricio Duran is a software architect specialized in Microsoft technologies with more than six years of experience in custom software development. He is a co-founder of Sieena Software, a company based in Monterrey, Mexico, that provides technology services to US-based companies.

Fernando Gutierrez is a software architect and a co-founder of Sieena Software. He has expertise working with a wide variety of technologies, including web-development with J2EE and the .NET Framework.

Acknowledgments

THE BOOK YOU HOLD in your hands is the culmination of months of hard work and a passionate desire to create a high-quality, informative text on service-oriented architecture using Web Services Enhancements 2.0. Like all major projects, it would not have been possible without the hard work and dedication of a great many people. First and foremost I would like to thank the team at Apress: Gary Cornell, Ewan Buckingham, Tracy Brown Collins, Ami Knox, Grace Wong, Glenn Munlawin, Kari Brooks, and all of the editorial and production staff who worked on this book. In addition I am very grateful to Keith Ballinger for his reviews and comments, and for appreciating my book enough to write a foreword. A big thanks goes out to all of the people who spent time discussing the material with me and giving me new insights and ideas on how to approach it. Finally, I reserve my BIGGEST thanks of all to the hard work and dedication of my friends, colleagues, and technical reviewers: Mauricio Duran, Fernando Gutierrez, and Kenneth Tu. They rock. We roll. Together we rock 'n' roll!

Introduction

WE SOFTWARE ARCHITECTS and developers live in a fascinating time. With the release of the .NET Framework in 2000, Web services technology has swept into our programming toolset and into our collective consciousness. Web services are the killer application for XML. Web services are the "new way" to call distributed objects remotely. Web services will take all of our integration headaches away, and allow formerly incompatible systems to communicate again. What Microsoft developer has not recently thought to themselves, "Should I be building my application with Web services?"

What .NET developer has not recently thought to themselves, "I'm confused"?

Every tidal wave has a genesis, and a momentum, and a final destination where it typically crashes head-on into a stable landmass and causes havoc and confusion. Web services technology is a tidal wave.

The genesis is Microsoft's strategic decision to simplify SOAP-based Web services development using a seamless set of integrated classes in the .NET Framework. The momentum is provided by a relentless marketing machine that promotes Web services as the solution for many of our worst IT problems. One destination is us, the architects and the developers who must understand this technology and learn how to implement it. Another destination is the manager, who must make strategic decisions on how to put this technology to its best use.

The Web services technology tidal wave has created confusion for .NET developers because, quite simply, we do not know the best way to use it. We are wrapped up in misconceptions about what the technology is for, and this affects our judgment in using it properly. We will spend the first chapter clarifying these misconceptions, but let me reveal one:

Misconception: Web services are for making remote procedure calls to distributed objects.

Reality: Web services are not optimized for RPCs. This is not what they are best at. Web services work best when they respond to messages, not to instructions.

Until now, we could safely give developers time to absorb the new Web services technology. We needed time to play around with the .NET Framework and to get used to a new development approach. Web services development using the .NET Framework is stunning in its simplicity. It is equally stunning in its oversimplification of a deep and sophisticated technology. Play time is over, now it's time we grow up.

Web services play a key role in a greater whole known as service-oriented architecture (SOA). Quite simply, SOA is an architecture based on loosely coupled components that exchange messages. These components include the clients that make message-based service requests, and the distributed components that respond to them. In a service-oriented architecture, Web services are critically important because they consume and deliver messages.

It is difficult to tackle a topic like service-oriented architecture and Web services without invoking the ire of developers working on other platforms such as J2EE and IBM WebSphere. I have full respect for these platforms and for the efforts of the developers and architects who use them. These guys and girls "get it," and they have been doing it for longer than we Microsoft-oriented developers have. Let's give credit where credit is due, but then move on. *Because if you are reading this book, then it is a safe assumption that you are interested in SOA the Microsoft way.* If this describes you, then please buy this book and read on!

So why don't we Microsoft/.NET developers "get it"? It is not for lack of intelligence, nor is it for lack of an ability to understand sophisticated architectures. We don't get it because we have been mislead as to why Web services are important. Let me roughly restate my original assertion:

Web services work best with messages. They are not optimized to handle specific instructions (in the form of direct, remote procedure calls).

Most of us have been "trained" to this point to use Web services for implementing SOAP-based remote procedure calls. This is where we have been misled, because SOAP is about the worst protocol you could use for this purpose. It is verbose to the point where the response and request envelopes will likely exceed in size the actual input parameters and output response parameters that you are exchanging!

At this point, I hope I have left you with more questions than answers. I have stated things here that you can only take my word on, but why should you believe me?

This is exactly what I am trying to get at. I want to shake you out of your Web services comfort zone, and to help you rethink the technology and think of the bigger picture that is SOA. I devote the first part of this book to clearing up the misconceptions. And I devote the second part of this book to showing you how to implement Web services in a service-oriented architecture.

Free your mind.

Who This Book Is For

This book is a practical reference written for intermediate to advanced .NET solution developers and architects who are interested in SOA and Web services development. The book focuses on two key areas:

- How to build message-oriented and service-oriented Web services

- Web Services Enhancements (WSE) 2.0

Solution developers and architects alike will find a lot in this book to hold their interest. The material in the book provides detailed conceptual discussions on service-oriented architecture combined with in-depth C# code samples. The book avoids rehashing familiar concepts, and focuses instead on how to rethink your approach to Web services development using today's best tools and industry-standard specifications. The book was written using prerelease copies of WSE that were released after the Tech Preview, so you have the benefit of the latest and greatest developments with WSE.

What This Book Covers

This book covers service-oriented architecture and cutting-edge Web services development using the WS-Specifications and Web Services Enhancements 2.0. The first half of the book shows you how to think in terms of messages rather than procedure calls. It shows you how to design and build message- and service-oriented Web services that provide the security and the functionality that companies and businesses will require before they are ready to widely adopt Web services technology.

The second half of the book focuses on WSE 2.0, which provides infrastructure and developer support for implementing industry-standard Web service specifications, including

WS-Security: A wide-ranging specification that integrates a set of popular security technologies, including digital signing and encryption based on security tokens, including X.509 certificates.

WS-Policy: Allows Web services to document their requirements, preferences, and capabilities for a range of factors, though mostly focused on security. For example, a Web service policy will include its security requirements, such as encryption and digital signing based on an X.509 certificate.

WS-Addressing: Identifies service endpoints in a message and allows for these endpoints to remain updated as the message is passed along through two or more services. It largely replaces the earlier WS-Routing specification.

WS-Messaging: Provides support for alternate transport channel protocols besides HTTP, including TCP. It simplifies the development of messaging applications, including asynchronous applications that communicate using SOAP over HTTP.

WS-Secure Conversation: Establishes session-oriented trusted communication sessions using security tokens.

The WS-Specifications are constantly evolving as new specifications get submitted and existing specifications get refined. They address essential requirements for service-oriented applications. This book aims to get you up to speed with understanding the current WS-Specifications, how the WSE 2.0 toolkit works, and where Web services technology is headed for the next few years.

If you are interested in taking your Web services development to the next level, then you will find this book to be an invaluable reference.

Chapter Summary

This book is broken out into ten chapters, progressing from introductory conceptual information through to advanced discussions of the WS-Specifications, and their implementation using Web Services Enhancements (WSE) 2.0. You will get the most out of this book if you read at least the first five chapters in sequence. These chapters contain reference information and conceptual discussions that are essential to understanding the material in the second half of the book. The remaining chapters of the book cover all of the WS-Specifications that are implemented by WSE 2.0. Finally, the book closes with a chapter on Indigo, which is the code name for a future managed communications infrastructure for building service-oriented applications. The purpose of the Indigo chapter is to show you the direction that service-oriented application development is headed, and to show you how your work with WSE 2.0 will help you make the transition to Indigo very smoothly.

The summary of the chapters is as follows:

Chapter 1, "Introducing Service-Oriented Architecture": This chapter introduces the concepts behind service-oriented architecture, and the characteristics of a Web service from the perspective of SOA. This chapter reviews the following topics:

- SOA concepts and application architecture

- The WS-I Basic Profile

- The WS-Specifications

- Web Services Enhancements (WSE) 2.0 (an introduction)

Chapter 2, "The Web Services Description Language": This chapter reviews the WSDL 1.1 specification and the elements of a WSDL document. This information is essential to understanding what makes up a service. The concepts that are presented here will come up repeatedly throughout the book, so make sure you read this chapter! This chapter includes the following:

- The seven elements of the WSDL document (types, message, operation, portType, binding, port, and service), which together document abstract definitions and concrete implementation details for the Web service

- How to work with WSDL documents using Visual Studio .NET

- How to use WSDL documents

Chapter 3, "Design Patterns for Building Message-Oriented Web Services": This chapter shows you how to build message-oriented Web services, as opposed to RPC-style Web services, which most people end up building with ASP.NET even if they do not realize it. The goal of this chapter is to help you rethink your approach to Web services design so that you can start developing the type of message-oriented Web services that fit into a service-oriented architecture framework. This chapter covers the following:

- Definition of a message-oriented Web service

- The role of XML and XSD schemas in constructing messages

- How to build an XSD schema file using the Visual Studio .NET XML Designer

- Detailed review of a six-step process for building and consuming a message-oriented Web service. This discussion ties into the sample solutions that accompany the chapter.

Chapter 4, "Design Patterns for Building Service-Oriented Web Services": This chapter extends the discussion from Chapter 3 and shows you how to build Web services that operate within a service-oriented application. This chapter includes the following:

- A discussion on building separate type definition assemblies that are based on XSD schema files.

- How to build a business assembly for delegating service processing.

- Detailed review of a six-step process for building and consuming a service-oriented Web service. This discussion ties into the sample solutions that accompany the chapter.

- How to build a service agent, which is unique to service-oriented architecture.

Chapter 5, "Web Services Enhancements 2.0": This chapter provides a detailed overview of WSE 2.0. This chapter covers the following:

- Overview of the WS-Specifications.

- Introduction to WSE 2.0: what it contains, what it does, how it integrates with ASP.NET, and how to install it.

- Overview of X.509 certificates: The WSE sample digital certificates are used frequently throughout the sample applications. Certificate installation can be difficult, so this section shows you what you need to do.

Chapter 6, "Secure Web Services with WS-Security": This is the first of four chapters that provide detailed discussions on the WSE implementations of the WS-Specifications. "Security" typically refers to two things: authentication and authorization. The WS-Security specification provides authentication support, while WS-Policy (reviewed in Chapter 7) provides both authentication and authorization support. This chapter contains the following:

- Overview of the WS-Security specification

- How to implement WS-Security using WSE 2.0

- Overview of digital signatures and encryption, and how to implement using different security tokens, including X.509 digital certificates

- How to prevent replay attacks using timestamps, digital signatures, and message correlation

Chapter 7, "Use Policy Frameworks to Enforce Web Service Requirements with WS-Policy": This chapter discusses how to implement Web service policy frameworks using the WS-Policy family of specifications. Policy frameworks document the usage requirements and preferences for using a Web service. For example, you can specify authentication requirements, such as requiring that request messages be digitally signed using an X.509 certificate. The WSE 2.0 Toolkit automatically validates incoming and outgoing messages against the established policy frameworks, and automatically generates SOAP exceptions for invalid messages. This chapter covers the following:

- Overview of the policy framework specifications, including WS-Policy, WS-Policy Assertions, and WS-Security Policy.

- How to implement a policy framework using WSE 2.0.

- How to implement role-based authorization using WSE and the WS-Policy family of specifications. Authorization is the second part of what we refer to as "security" (in addition to authentication).

Chapter 8, "Establish Trusted Communication with WS-Secure Conversation": The WS-Secure Conversation specification provides a token-based, session-oriented, on-demand secure channel for communication between a Web service and client. WS-Secure Conversation is analogous to the Secure Sockets Layer (SSL) protocol that secures communications over HTTP. This chapter includes the following:

- Overview and definition of secure conversation using WS-Secure Conversation.

- How to implement a secure conversation between a Web service and its client, using a security token service provider. This section is code intensive, and reviews the sample solution that accompanies the chapter.

Chapter 9, "Design Patterns for SOAP Messaging with WS-Addressing and Routing": This chapter covers several WS-Specifications that work together to provide a new messaging framework for Web services. Traditional Web services are built on the HTTP Request/Response model. WSE 2.0 provides a messaging framework that expands the supported transport protocols to include TCP and an optimized in-process transport protocol, in addition to HTTP. These protocols are not natively tied to a request/response communications model, so you can implement alternative models, such as asynchronous messaging solutions. This chapter also reviews the WS-Addressing specification, which enables messages to store their own addressing and endpoint reference information. This chapter includes the following:

- Overview of communication models for Web services

- Overview of the WS-Addressing specification, including a discussion of message information headers versus endpoint references

- Overview of how WSE implements the WS-Addressing specification

- Overview of the WS-Messaging specification, and the WSE implementation, which provides support for alternate message transport protocols and communication models

- How to implement a TCP-based Web service using SOAP sender and receiver components

- Overview of the WS-Routing and WS-Referral specifications, which allow messages to be redirected between multiple endpoints

- How to build a SOAP-based router using WSE, WS-Routing, and WS-Referral

- How to integrate MSMQ with Web services in order to implement one form of reliable messaging

Chapter 10, "Beyond WSE 2.0: Looking Ahead to Indigo": Indigo provides infrastructure and programming support for service-oriented applications. Indigo will be released as part of the future Longhorn operating system. It is focused on messages, and provides support for creating messages, for delivering messages, and for processing messages. With Indigo, there is less ambiguity in your services: The infrastructure forces you to be message oriented, and to work with well-qualified XML-based data types. WSE 2.0 and its future revisions will provide you with excellent preparation for working with Indigo in the future. This chapter contains the following:

- Overview of Indigo architecture, including the Indigo service layer, the Indigo connector, hosting environments, messaging services, and system services

- Understanding Indigo Web services

- Understanding Indigo applications and infrastructure

- How to get ready for Indigo

- WSE 2.0 and Indigo

Code Samples and Updates

This book is accompanied by a rich and varied set of example solutions. The sample solutions were built using the WSE v2.0 Pre-Release bits that were released on 1/23/2004. The code examples are chosen to illustrate complicated concepts clearly. Although Web Services Enhancements are conceptually complicated, this does not mean that they translate into complex code. In fact, the situation is quite the opposite. I guarantee that you will be surprised at how clear and straightforward the code examples are.

NOTE *The sample solutions are available for download at* `http://www.apress.com.`

Visit `http://www.bluestonepartners.com/soa` for updates to the book and sample solutions, and for errata corrections. Check back here often, because WSE is expected to undergo several revisions between now and the release of Indigo. In addition, the topic of service-oriented architecture continues to evolve rapidly, and every month brings new, interesting developments.

And now, once more into the breach, dear friends, once more . . .

CHAPTER 1

Introducing Service-Oriented Architecture

SERVICE-ORIENTED ARCHITECTURE (SOA) represents a new and evolving model for building distributed applications. *Services* are distributed components, which provide well-defined interfaces that process and deliver XML messages. A service-based approach makes sense for building solutions that cross organizational, departmental, and corporate domain boundaries. A business with multiple systems and applications on different platforms can use SOA to build a loosely coupled integration solution that implements unified workflows.

The concept of services is familiar to anyone who shops online at an eCommerce web site. Once you have placed your order, you have to supply your credit card information, which is typically authorized and charged by an outside service vendor. Once the order has been committed, the eCommerce company then coordinates with a shipping service vendor directly to deliver your purchase. ECommerce applications provide another perfect illustration of the need for a service-oriented architecture: If the credit card billing component is offline or unresponsive, then you do not want the sales order collection process to fail. Instead, you want the order collected and the billing operation to proceed at a later time. Figure 1-1 provides a conceptual workflow for an eCommerce business that uses multiple services to process orders.

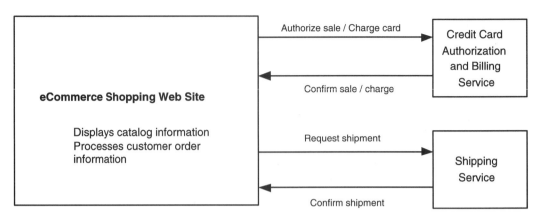

Figure 1-1. Service-based workflow for an eCommerce business

SOA is like other distributed architectures in that it enables you to build applications that use components across separate domain boundaries. SOA uses Web services as application entry points, which are conceptually equivalent to the proxy and stub components of traditional component-based distributed systems, except that the interactions between the Web service provider and consumer are more loosely coupled. SOA is also unique in that it incorporates those factors that are critically important to business: service reliability, message integrity, transactional integrity, and message security. In the real world, business cannot rely on services that *may* process requests *if* they receive a request that they can understand. Businesses require more certainty than this. It is a given that disparate systems may be up or down at various times, or that different systems may differ in their responsiveness due to varying loads. However, none of this is an excuse for allowing service request messages to simply drop away into the void, or to go unanswered. Furthermore, there can be no ambiguity as to how a service must be called. If a system publishes its capabilities as a Web-enabled service, then it needs to clearly document how the service must be called.

SOA will address many of the availability and scalability issues in today's applications. Most applications implement a rigid synchronous communication model with a linear workflow model that is highly susceptible to failures at any point in the workflow. SOA assumes that errors can and will occur, and so it implements strategies for handling them. For example, if a service fails to accept a message request the first time, the architecture is designed to retry the delivery. And if the service is entirely unavailable (which should never occur in a robust SOA), then the architecture is designed to avoid possible catastrophic failures that may disrupt the entire service request. SOA improves reliability because temporary failure in one part of the workflow will not bring down the entire business process.

In a broader sense, SOA represents a maturing process, that is, the "growing up" of Web services and integration technologies. SOA recognizes that mission-critical systems built on distributed technology must provide certain guarantees: They must ensure that service requests will be routed correctly, that they will be answered in a timely fashion, and that they will clearly publish their communication policies and interfaces.

Welcome to the grown-up world of SOA.

Overview of Service-Oriented Architecture

In an SOA solution, the distributed application uses service components that reside in separate domains. Service components operate inside their own trust boundary, encapsulate their own data, and are maintained and updated independently of, though loosely coupled with, the applications that use them.

Figure 1-2 shows a conceptual service-oriented architecture that summarizes the three main entities in a typical SOA solution. They are

- Service providers

- Service consumers

- Service directories

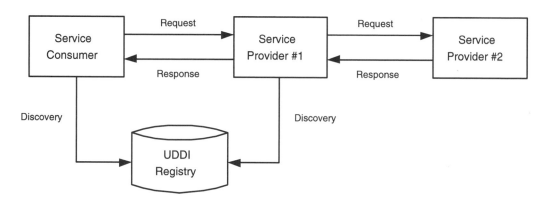

Figure 1-2. A conceptual service-oriented architecture solution

The interesting point to note is that the consumer can use a Universal Discovery, Description, and Integration (UDDI) registry to discover, or reference, the description information for a service provider. Interestingly, Service #1 references a service provider (Service #2). In this role, Service #1 is equivalent to a service consumer as well, and can reference the UDDI registry for information about Service #2.

The communication between the services and the consumer is in the form of XML messages that are qualified according to defined XSD schemas. XML messages are discrete entities that may be transported, rerouted, and referenced at any point along the business workflow. Messages promote higher levels of reliability and scalability because they can be stored, and the services that process the messages can append additional information, which provides for a clear and unambiguous chain of custody across the business workflow. In addition, messages can be queued in the event that a service is temporarily unavailable or backlogged. XML messages are unlike traditional Remote Procedure Calls (RPCs), which do not provide a discrete structure for encapsulating a method "request." Traditional RPCs cannot typically be cached or held in a queue to wait for a better time to service the request. Instead, traditional RPCs typically timeout if the receiving component does not respond within the expected length of time. In addition, RPCs are not qualified to a reference schema (although they must conform to type libraries for custom data types). Here lies the first important lesson for developing SOA solutions: The Web services in the solution must be designed to be message-oriented, rather than RPC-oriented. This topic is the exclusive focus of Chapter 3.

What Are Web Services, Really?

Many of us are so familiar with current Web services technology that we often do not stop to think about what services really are. However, you will need to if you are going to fully understand what makes SOA so significant. Let's pull out four definitions that collectively describe what a service is:

- Services are autonomous components that process well-defined XML messages.

- Services provide a well-defined interface that is described by an XML-based document called the *Web Service Description Language (WSDL) document*, otherwise known as the *WSDL contract*. This documents the operations (methods) that the service supports, including data type information, and binding information for locating and communicating with the Web service operations.

- Services provide endpoints that consumers and other services can bind to, based on the service's port address (typically a URL).

- Services are analogous to traditional object-oriented (OO), type-based components in that they provide a defined interface and they execute one or more operations. However, a key difference is that service consumers can flexibly bind to a service, whereas OO component consumers must set more rigid references. Service consumers can respond flexibly to changes in a service provider interface because it is easy to regenerate the proxy class using the updated WSDL document. However, if a traditional component changes its interface, then the consumer itself must be recompiled in order to avoid type mismatch errors. Components are tightly integrated to their consumers, and can break them. Service consumers, however, do not have to recompile if their service changes. Instead, they simply have to rebind to the updated WSDL document. This is what is known as *loose coupling*, or *loosely coupled services*.

Of course, if the service drastically changes its method signatures, then problems may result in the consumer. For example, the consumer may not currently have the ability to supply new and modified input parameters for the updated methods. But as with any kind of interface-based programming, it is understood that you cannot make significant changes to an existing method signature, especially in terms of dropping existing input parameters, or changing the type definitions for existing input or output parameters. And just as with traditional components, services should remain backward compatible as their interfaces evolve. Still, it is a significant advantage that service consumers are autonomous from their services. This promotes better stability in the SOA solution as the member services evolve.

There are five important properties of services in contrast to traditional type-based components:

Services are described by a WSDL contract, not by type libraries: The WSDL contract fully describes every aspect of the service, including its operations, its types, and its binding information. WSDL is fully described in Chapter 2. In this sense it is much more complete than traditional type libraries.

Service descriptions can be easily extended: The WSDL contract is based on an extensible document structure that readily incorporates additional information beyond the core service description. For example, security and policy information may be stored within the WSDL document as custom SOAP elements. In fact, all of the Web services enhancements that implement SOA infrastructure support can be documented as custom SOAP elements. At its most basic level, SOAP is a stateless, one-way messaging protocol. But it is also highly extensible, which makes it an excellent medium for storing and transporting Web service enhancement information.

Services provide a service guarantee: Traditional type definitions provide no guarantees. They are what they are, and you simply use them. But what happens if the type definition gets out of sync with the component it is supposed to describe? This happens all the time in the COM+ world, which relies on the Windows registry to store associated references between registered components and their type libraries. Every developer has experienced so-called DLL Hell, in which successive installations and removals of upgraded components cause incorrect type information to be retained in the registry. There is no service guarantee in the world of type libraries. You just have to hope that the component is registered with the correct type library.

Services, on the other hand, can implement a service guarantee in the form of a policy description that is contained within the WSDL contract. So-called policy assertions are published with the contract to describe what level of service the consumer can expect, and how the service operations can be expected to respond. There are many advantages to policy assertions, not the least of which is that you could implement code in your consumer so that it will only work with a service that enforces a minimum policy guarantee. Should this policy ever change, then your consumer is designed not to use the service any longer. In a very sophisticated application, you could design your consumer to auto-discover an alternate service using the UDDI registry.

Services allow for things to go wrong: When you call a method on a traditional type-based component, you are making a leap of faith that the call will execute successfully. The reality is that the vast majority of calls do go through, so we have been lulled into a sense of complacency that this is always the case. But in the service-oriented world, where the supporting infrastructure is vastly more intricate and decoupled, you cannot have such a high level of faith that calls will always go through. Recall that XML messages are the gold currency of service requests. Messages can experience trouble at many steps along the way. Trouble in the transport channel can prevent them from being delivered. Trouble in the service's server or firewall can prevent the service from ever responding to a received message. Furthermore, messages may be tampered with, so that they are malformed or suspect when they do reach their intended target.

SOA accommodates all of these many potential problems using a set of technologies that maintain the integrity of a service request even if things go wrong along the way. These include reliable messaging, transaction support, and authentication mechanisms to ensure that only trusted parties are involved in the service request (including certificate-based mechanisms).

Services provide flexible binding: Services fully describe themselves using the WSDL contract. This information includes documentation of the service operations as well as data type information, referenced by well-defined XML schemas. This enables clear and unambiguous qualified references. The best part is that a consumer does not have to have any prior knowledge of a data type, as long as its XML namespace is documented by, or referenced by, the WSDL contract. For example, consider a consumer that calls a stock quote service. This service provides a RequestQuote method that returns a custom complex data type called Quote (including current and previous share price information, as well as 52-week high and low values). The consumer has no advanced knowledge of how the Quote data type is structured, but it does not need to as long as it can reference the qualified associated XSD schema.

Services can also be registered in a UDDI registry, which enables them to be searched for by consumers and other services. The UDDI registry is very thorough, and includes a reference to the WSDL contract information, as well as a summary of supported messages, in a search-efficient format. This is useful for many reasons. For example, a consumer may only wish to call services that utilize a specific set of XSD schemas (such as industry-specific standard schemas). The UDDI registry enables that consumer to search for services that conform to this requirement.

Components of Web Service Architecture

Experienced developers are comfortable with *n-tier application architecture*, in which the components of an application are broken out across separate layers, or tiers. At a minimum, this includes the three classic layers: user interface (front end), business layer (middle tier), and data layer (back end).

Now let's consider how an SOA solution is broken out in terms of layers and constituent components. Figure 1-3 illustrates a basic SOA solution architecture.

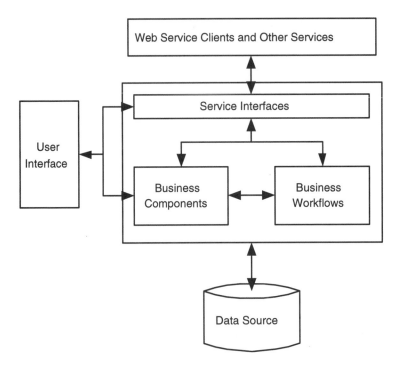

Figure 1-3. Basic service-oriented architecture

The large bounding box around service interfaces, business components, and business workflows represents the conceptual business layer (middle tier). This layer encapsulates the service interfaces, which in .NET terms are the .asmx Web service files and the code-behind that directly relates to verifying and relaying incoming messages (but which excludes actual business logic). The .asmx files should delegate the business processing to dedicated business components and/or a business workflow process (essentially a sequenced chain of components in a workflow). This is a different approach to Web services coding than most of us are used to taking, because typically we place all processing code directly in the code-behind file of the .asmx Web service. But in a service-oriented architecture, it is important to design the Web service components themselves so that they truly act as gateways to dedicated business components or workflows.

The service interface has the following properties:

- It supports the communication requirements that the service specifies in its WSDL contract (specifically, in its binding information). This includes the format and transport protocols that the service responds to (e.g., SOAP over HTTP).

- It supports the security requirements that the service specifies. In .NET terms, the .asmx code-behind can implement code that verifies incoming XML messages to ensure that they contain the required security tokens or headers.

- It supports the methods (operations) that the service specifies in its WSDL contract. In .NET terms, the .asmx file provides methods that correspond to the service operations, but the actual business processing should be handed off to dedicated components and workflow.

Figure 1-3 also shows that there are two categories of service consumers that have entry points into the business layer. The first is a traditional user interface, on the left of the diagram, such as a Windows form or ASP.NET Web page. This type of user interface is part of the same domain where the service components reside. The second category of front-end consumers is the external Web service clients and other services, shown at the top of the diagram. These two categories are well-known to developers: If you develop a Web service for external use, you can just as easily call it internally within its application domain. Of course, it is more efficient to call the Web service's delegated business components, because when you are internal to the domain, you do not need to route requests through the .asmx gateway using special transport and messaging protocols (HTTP and SOAP, for example). This is yet another reason all Web services logic should be abstracted out to dedicated business components.

The architecture in Figure 1-3 is a good start, but it quickly breaks down under the demand of more sophisticated SOA applications. Figure 1-4 provides one example of a more complex SOA solution architecture.

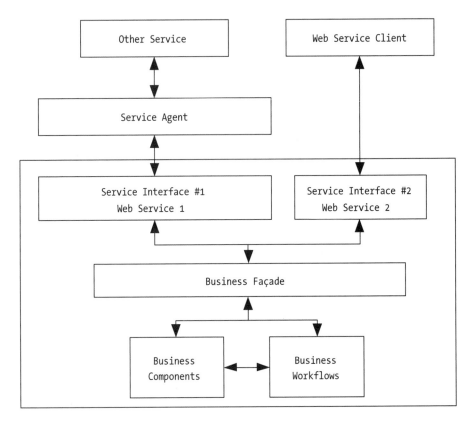

Figure 1-4. Complex service-oriented architecture

Figure 1-4 illustrates an architecture in which two separate Web services access the same back-end business components. Each Web service provides a distinct service interface, each of which is suitable for a different type of client. For example, Web service 1 may provide access to a public, unsecured subset of functions, whereas Web service 2 provides access to a restricted, secured subset of functions. In addition, Figure 1-4 introduces two new entities that play an important role in complex SOA solutions:

Service agent: The service agent manages communications between one service and another, or between a business object and an external service. In doing so, it simplifies those interactions by shielding translation quirks between the consumer and the provider.

Business façade: The business façade acts as a trust boundary between incoming service requests (from a client, another service, or a service agent) and the middle-tier business components that service those requests.

Let's consider each of these in turn.

Service Agent

Business components are the engines of applications because they contain the logic to make the application work. In addition, business components know where to find information, whether it comes from a back-end database or from an external data source. In classic Windows-based n-tier architecture, we are used to thinking of business components as self-sufficient. But sometimes business components need to retrieve information from external sources in order to do their work. In SOA terms, sometimes business components need to call external services.

The service agent is responsible for managing communications between a business object and an external service. Service agents are extremely important because they simplify the amount of work that a business object has to do when it needs to use an external service. A service agent is a locally installed assembly that provides a well-known interface to the business object. Service agents do the manual legwork of communicating with external services and implementing whatever infrastructure is required to do so. This is useful for two important reasons:

- Business objects do not have to implement the infrastructure that is required to communicate with an external service. Instead, they communicate their requests to a local assembly (the service agent) using a mutually understood interface.

- Business objects avoid the maintenance work that is required to keep service interactions up to date. For example, if an external Web service interface changes, the service agent takes care of updating its proxy class and reworking the code implementation as needed. The business object can continue to communicate with the service agent in the same manner, even as the underlying communication details change.

I cannot resist using a travel analogy to describe the role that service agents play. Let's say you and a friend are traveling in Madrid. Your friend is fluent in both English and Spanish, but is too lazy to read the guidebook and has no idea what to see in the city. You only speak English, but you read the guidebook cover to cover, and you know that the Prado Museum cannot be missed . . . if only you knew how to get there from your hotel. So you need to ask directions, but cannot communicate with the locals. Your friend can ask for directions, but needs to know from you where you are trying to go. The analogy is hopefully clear! You are the business component, your friend is the service agent, and the friendly locals act as the external service.

Business Façade

The business façade is not as intuitive as the service agent because it has no analogy in traditional component-based development. Essentially, the business façade is a trust boundary that sits between middle-tier business components and the service interfaces that call them. The business façade plays the roles of both a service agent and a service interface, and it only applies in situations where there are two or more service interfaces associated with the middle tier. It provides a common interface for multiple service interfaces to interact with. In addition, the business façade may provide additional security, authentication, or screening on incoming service requests.

Figure 1-5 provides another SOA solution architecture that illustrates the usefulness of the business façade.

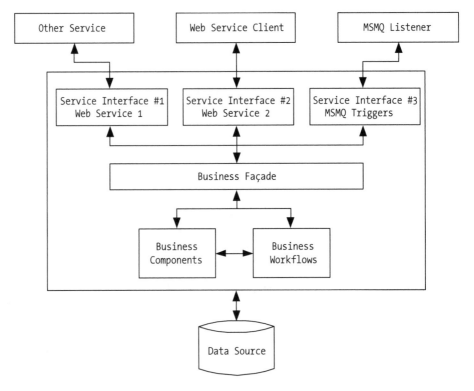

Figure 1-5. Service-oriented architecture illustrating the business façade

In this example, the service layer must handle requests from a wide variety of different services, and it must support three separate service interfaces. A business façade is necessary to manage requests from several incoming service interfaces and to ensure that the requests get communicated to the business components in a consistent fashion.

> **NOTE** *The concept of a business façade follows the well-known session façade design pattern. For an overview of this design pattern, please consult the article "Java Modeling: A UML Workbook" at* http://www-106.ibm.com/ developerworks/java/library/j-jmod0604/.

The Web Services Specifications and the WS-I Basic Profile

Recall the difference between Web services technology today versus service-oriented architecture: The difference is in the level of infrastructure support. Infrastructure in this context refers to the helper technologies and assemblies that support the implementation of an SOA solution. Stand-alone Web services require very little additional infrastructure support beyond what they already get from the .NET Web services assemblies and the built-in HTTP handlers. However, as you have seen in the conceptual overview, SOA requires a lot of infrastructure support, including multiple transport options, security infrastructure, and support for reliable messaging, to name a few. Different companies, including Microsoft and IBM, are working together to establish standard specifications that cover the full range of supporting technologies for SOA infrastructure.

It is an unfortunate reality that Web service specifications are developed and advanced in a politically charged environment where companies are often rivals, rather than partners. Corporate animosity causes companies to disagree on the right specifications. Sometimes, different groups of companies pursue separate specifications that apply to the same purpose. Nonprofit organizations such as OASIS provide a forum for companies to cooperate in the advancement and development of Web service specifications. Read more about OASIS at http://www.oasis-open.org.

Introducing the WS-I Basic Profile

The Web Services Interoperability (WS-I) organization has one primary goal: to establish standard specifications so that Web services can be interoperable across different platforms. In other words, the organization wants Web services to be able to work together, no matter which platform they reside on, or which development tool they were created with. The specifications cover a wide range of areas, from transport protocols to security, and are collectively grouped together as the *WS-I Basic Profile.*

> **NOTE** *The WS-I Basic Profile is the first in what are expected to be several future and evolving profiles. The Basic Profile specifies exact version numbers for its compliant specifications. For example, it includes SOAP 1.1, WSDL 1.1, and XML 1.0. Future profiles will use updated versions, but it takes a long time to establish new specifications, so do not expect new profiles very frequently! View the WS-I Basic Profile Version 1.0 at* `http://www.ws-i.org/Profiles/Basic/2003-08/BasicProfile-1.0a.html`.

Figure 1-6 illustrates the high-level grouping of interoperable Web services specifications that have been published jointly by Microsoft, IBM, and others. The WS-I Basic Profile covers most of the specifications in the bottom three layers of the diagram, namely the specifications for Transport, Messaging, and Description. The additional layers are covered by the various WS-Specifications, including WS-Security, WS-Reliable Messaging, and WS-Transactions, to name just a few. Some of the WS-Specifications fall within the lower three layers as well, including WS-Addressing for the Messaging layer, and WS-Policy for the Description layer. Note that this figure is adapted directly from a joint Microsoft-IBM white paper titled "Secure, Reliable, Transacted Web Services: Architecture and Composition" (September, 2003). Please see the "References" section in the Appendix for more information.

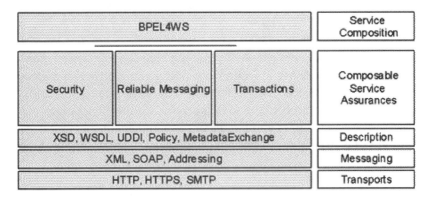

Figure 1-6. Interoperable Web Services specifications, including the WS-I Basic Profile

The high-level groupings of Web specifications fall into these categories:

Transport: This group defines the communications protocols for moving raw data between Web services. It includes HTTP, HTTPS, and SMTP.

Messaging: This group defines how to format the XML messages that Web services exchange. It includes the SOAP specification for encoding messages, and the XML and XSD specifications for the message vocabulary. The specifications are independent of a particular transport protocol. The Messaging group also includes the WS-Addressing specification, which decouples destination information for the request from the underlying transport protocol. WS-Addressing can, for example, be used to define multiple destinations for an XML message.

Description: This group defines specifications that allow a Web service to describe itself. The core specifications are WSDL (for the service contract) and XSD (for defining data type schemas). It also includes the WS-Policy specification, which describes the policy that a Web service enforces when it communicates with a client. For example, a Web service may have specific requirements for how its interface operations are called. The WS-Policy specification allows the Web service to tell prospective clients what rules to follow in order to execute a successful service request. Finally, this group includes the UDDI specification for discovering and describing Web services.

Service Assurances: Web services cannot simply exchange XML messages. They must also provide the client with some assurance that the messages will be transmitted in a secure way, and that the client can expect some kind of response, even if something goes wrong at some point in the workflow. This group of specifications includes WS-Security (which provides authentication mechanisms), WS-Reliable Messaging (to ensure the delivery of messages over unreliable networks), and several transaction-related specifications.

Service Composition: The wide array of specifications in the WS-I Basic Profile cannot all be implemented in every Web service. Developers must pick and choose which specifications are important for a particular Web service. To enable this, Web services support service composition, which allows developers to selectively pick specifications and to aggregate them and record them in the WSDL document.

Introducing the WS-Specifications

I introduce you to the WS-Specifications again in Chapter 5, and then cover them in detail in the remaining chapters of the book. Briefly, here is a summary of the most important WS-Specifications and their purpose:

WS-Security: A wide-ranging specification that integrates a set of popular security technologies, including digital signing and encryption based on security tokens, including X.509 certificates.

WS-Policy: Allows Web services to document their requirements, preferences, and capabilities for a range of factors, though mostly focused on security. For example, a Web service policy will include its security requirements, such as encryption and digital signing based on an X.509 certificate.

WS-Addressing: Identifies service endpoints in a message and allows for these endpoints to remain updated as the message is passed along through two or more services. It largely replaces the earlier WS-Routing specification.

WS-Messaging: Provides support for alternate transport channel protocols besides HTTP, including TCP. It simplifies the development of messaging applications, including asynchronous applications that communicate using SOAP over HTTP.

WS-Secure Conversation: Establishes session-oriented trusted communication sessions using security tokens.

WS-Reliable Messaging: Provides mechanisms to help ensure the reliable delivery of messages, even when one or more services in the chain are unavailable. This specification includes message delivery notifications so that a sender knows whether a receiver has successfully obtained a sent message.

The WS-Specifications are constantly evolving as new specifications get submitted and existing specifications get refined. However, the core set of specifications presented here will likely continue to form the cornerstone of specifications for some time to come, since they address essential requirements for service-oriented applications.

Introducing Web Services Enhancements

Web Services Enhancements (WSE) provides developers with .NET managed assemblies for implementing the WS-Specifications in conformance with the WS-I Basic Profile. WSE is an evolving product and does not currently support all of the Web service specifications, but it does support many important ones, such as WS-Security and WS-Policy. Keep in mind, though, that even currently supported specifications will continue to evolve in future releases of WSE. In some cases, this is because the specification is currently only partially implemented in WSE.

At a more conceptual level, WSE currently exists to provide additional infra-structure support for SOA solutions, beyond what is already provided by the .NET Framework. Microsoft chose to put WSE on a different release cycle than its .NET Framework releases, so that it would have the flexibility to vary the release schedule. Recall that SOA is governed by a number of technology standards and specifications that are themselves going through changes. WSE has to be on a flexi-ble release cycle in order to keep up with the newer versions of these technology standards.

WSE is introduced again in Chapter 5, and is also the focus of the second half of the book, where I will cover the various WS-Specifications in detail. WSE is what allows you to code several of the WS-Specifications in message-oriented, service-oriented .NET applications.

Summary

This chapter introduced the main concepts behind service-oriented architecture (SOA), which refers to distributed applications based on Web services technology. I defined what a Web service actually is, within the context of SOA, and reviewed the main aspects of SOA architecture. I briefly introduced the WS-I Basic Profile, the WS-Specifications, and Web Services Enhancements (WSE), all of which are covered in detail in the second half of the book starting with Chapter 5.

CHAPTER 2

The Web Services Description Language

WEB SERVICES are formally and fully described using an XML-based document called the *Web Service Description Language (WSDL) document*. The WSDL document communicates metadata information about the Web service to potential clients and shows them what operations (methods) the Web service supports and how to bind to them.

Visual Studio .NET automatically generates WSDL documents for your XML Web services and uses them behind the scenes, although it conveniently allows you to avoid opening the actual WSDL documents. WSDL documents are, for example, used by Visual Studio .NET when you select the Add Web Reference menu option, to allow your project to use the methods of an outside Web service.

In a service-oriented architecture (SOA), the WSDL document is a critically important document, and one that you will need to understand in detail so that you can exert tighter control over the Web services that you develop. This is because development tools such as Visual Studio .NET create the most generic WSDL documents with bindings for the SOAP protocol only. Web services can exchange messages over several different protocols in addition to SOAP, including HTTP POST, HTTP GET, and SMTP. However, keep in mind that SOAP is the most suitable protocol for exchanging complex XML-based messages. If you have built a true service-oriented Web service, then these messages cannot, for example, be represented using simple URL arguments as are used by the HTTP GET protocol. You can use the HTTP POST protocol to exchange XML messages, but XML is not qualified with namespaces, nor does it provide the organized SOAP structure that is so critical to technologies such as WSE 2.0. You can see a comparison between the messages exchanged over SOAP versus HTTP POST by browsing a Web service directly. Visual Studio .NET generates a generic input page for each Web method that shows you how the exchanged input and output messages will be generated.

WSDL documents fully describe a Web service, including the operations that it supports, the messages that it exchanges, and the data types that these messages use (both intrinsic and custom). The best way to approach a WSDL document is to understand that different XML elements take responsibility for describing different levels of detail. For example, the <messages> element is a detailed listing of the types that factor into a given message. On the other hand, the <operation> element simply lists the messages that factor into a given operation, without going into any detail as to what these messages look like. This additional information would be unnecessary because the <messages> element already does an excellent job of documenting the types that factor into a given message. This division of responsibility makes the WSDL document very efficient, but at the same time hard to read because you have to look in several places to assemble the full details of the documented Web service. But if you keep in mind that this is the approach that the WSDL document is following, then you will find the document much easier to understand.

In this chapter, I will describe the elements of a WSDL document so that you can understand how this document fully describes a Web service. I will also show you those aspects of the WSDL document that you may wish to edit manually.

Elements of the WSDL Document

The WSDL document is itself an XML document, so it obeys the rules that you expect for any well-formed XML document. This begins with schema namespace definitions, which are included as a root element in the WSDL document using the <definitions> element. A typical WSDL document includes several schema definitions, but the most important one is the following:

```
<definitions xmlns="http://schemas.xmlsoap.org/wsdl/">
```

The <definitions> root element encloses the contents of the WSDL document entirely. All of the elements presented next are child elements of the <definitions> root element.

The WSDL document contains seven primary XML elements (in addition to the <definitions> root element), all of which belong to the schema just listed. The seven XML elements fall into two main groups:

- **Abstract description:** XML elements that document the Web service interface, including the methods that it supports, the input parameters, and the return types.

- **Concrete implementation:** XML elements that show the client how to physically bind to the Web service and to use its supported operations.

The XML elements for abstract description are as follows:

<types>: This element lists all of the data types that are exchanged by the XML messages as input parameters or return types. The <types> element is equivalent to an embedded XSD schema definition file.

<message>: This element describes a SOAP message, which may be an input, output, or fault message for a Web service operation. A SOAP message is subdivided into parts, which are represented by <part> child elements and which document the types that are included in the SOAP message.

<operation>: This element is analogous to a method definition; however, it only allows you to define input, output, and fault messages that are associated with the operation. You can then consult the individual message details to determine what input parameters and return types are involved.

<portType>: This element lists all of the operations that a Web service supports. The <port> element (described later) corresponds to a single Web service, while the <portType> element describes the available operations. The previous three elements (<types>, <message>, and <operation>) all describe granular, individual pieces of the Web service operations and its types. The <portType> element avoids many of these lower-level details and instead provides a high-level summary of the operations (and associated input, output, and fault messages) that the Web service provides. The <portType> element provides a single location for a client to browse the offerings of a particular Web service.

The XML elements for concrete implementation are as listed here:

<binding>: This element links the abstract and concrete elements together within a WSDL document. The <binding> element is associated with a specific <portType> element, and it also lists the address of the Web service that is associated with the <portType> element. Finally, the <binding> element lists the protocol that is used to communicate with the Web service.

<port>: This element defines the Uniform Resource Indicator (URI) where the Web service is located, and it also implements a <binding> element.

<service>: This element encloses one or more <port> elements.

Figure 2-1 shows the high-level structure of a WSDL document and how the various XML elements relate to each other within the document.

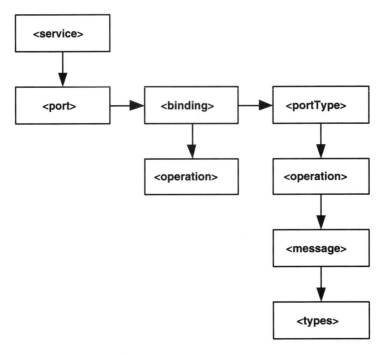

Figure 2-1. WSDL document structure

Let's look at each of the seven elements in further detail.

The *<types>* Element

The <types> element lists all of the data types that are exchanged by the XML messages as input parameters or return types. The <types> element is equivalent to an embedded XSD schema definition file. For design purposes, it is useful to separate out your XSD schema definitions into a separate file. This allows you to reference type information independently of the WSDL document, which is important because it provides a central reference point for validating XML documents against a single source. You can then import the XSD schema file into the WSDL document using a separate <import> root element as follows:

```
<import namespace="http://www.bluestonepartners.com/schemas/StockTrader/"
    location="http://www.bluestonepartners.com/schemas/StockTrader.xsd" />
```

With this approach the <types> element is no longer needed, so you can just include it as an empty element as follows:

```
<types/>
```

Having shown you this approach, I need to immediately point out that it does not conform to the WS-I Basic Profile, which states that the <import> element may only be used to import another WSDL document, not an external XSD schema file. You will still need to design and build XSD schema files separately from the WSDL document; however, once this task is complete, you will need to embed the XSD elements directly within the WSDL documents <types> section. The <import> element must not appear within a WSDL document for XSD schema information.

You cannot omit the <types> element, even if it is unused, because this will generate parsing errors in the WSDL document.

> **NOTE**   *XSD schema definition files are described in detail in Chapter 3. They are essential documents for describing the data types of XML messages in a service-oriented architecture. The discussion in Chapter 3 shows you how to build XSD schema files manually and then incorporate them into a WSDL document. You will also use XSD schema files to auto-generate code-based type definitions.*

The <message> Element

The <message> element describes a SOAP message, which may be an input, output, or fault message for a Web service operation. A SOAP message is subdivided into parts, which are represented by <part> child elements and which document the types that are included in the SOAP message.

For example, consider a Web method called RequestQuote. It accepts a stock ticker symbol and returns a complex XML Quote message, which contains multiple levels of detail, including the opening and closing prices of the stock, as well as long-term statistics such as 52-week high and low values. A client that expects to use the RequestQuote method does not care how this Web method is implemented. However, the client does need to know the structure of the messages for communicating with the Web method (or operation, as it is referred to in WSDL).

The RequestQuote operation uses a request (input) message and a response (output) message. The input message looks like this:

```
<message name="RequestQuoteSoapIn">
  <part name="Symbol" element="s0:Symbol" />
</message>
```

The output message looks like this:

```
<message name="RequestQuoteSoapOut">
  <part name="RequestQuoteResult" element="s0:Quote" />
</message>
```

Both messages use types from a namespace called StockTrader, which is referenced in the <definitions> element of the WSDL document. The <message> element does not need to document what these types look like; it simply needs to reference them. Notice that the operation's parameters are documented within the <message> root element using <part> child elements. If the RequestQuote operation required five input parameters, then the corresponding input <message> element would include five corresponding <part> child elements.

The <operation> Element

The <operation> element is analogous to a method definition; however, it only allows you to define input, output, and fault messages that are associated with the operation. You can then consult the individual message details to determine what input parameters and return types are involved.

In the previous section, I described the <message> element using an example operation called RequestQuote. I presented the input and output messages, but observant readers will notice that I did not formally associate these messages to the same operation beyond verbally stating that they were associated. This is what the <operation> element is for. It is responsible for formally associating messages with a given operation. The <message> element is a root element, so in theory you can define a message within the WSDL document and then use it across multiple operations. This is perfectly legal within the WSDL document.

Here is what the <operation> element looks like for the RequestQuote operation:

```
<operation name="RequestQuote">
  <input message="tns:RequestQuoteSoapIn" />
  <output message="tns:RequestQuoteSoapOut" />
  <fault message="tns:ExceptionMessage" />
</operation>
```

Notice that no additional description is provided for the messages beyond their names. For more details, you must reference the corresponding <message> elements.

Operations can be defined in one of four modes:

- **Request/Response:** The client sends a request message to the Web service, and the Web service returns a response message.

- **One Way:** The client sends a request message to the Web service, but receives no response message in return.

- **Solicit/Response:** The reverse of Request/Response. The Web service sends a message to the client, and then the client sends a response message to the Web service.

- **Notification:** The reverse of One Way. The Web service sends a message to the client, but receives no response message in return.

The WSDL document does not contain special attributes for describing how an operation is called. Instead, you must infer this information by the arrangement and inclusion (or exclusion) of input and output messages. Although I have used the concept of request and response messages to describe the interaction between Web service and client, this model does not really apply in a WSDL document. Instead, I refer to input and output messages. The difference may be semantic, but in a WSDL document, Web services never make requests, or send input messages to a client. Any message that originates from a Web service is referred to as an *output message*, even in Solicit/Response or Notification mode. Accordingly, here is how you define each of the four modes in WSDL:

- **Request/Response:** The client sends a request message to the Web service, and the Web service returns a response message.

```
<operation name="MyOperation">
  <input message="MyInputMessage" />
  <output message=" MyOutputMessage" />
</operation>
```

- **One Way:** The client sends a request message to the Web service, but receives no response message in return.

```
<operation name="MyOperation">
  <input message="MyInputMessage" />
</operation>
```

- **Solicit/Response:** The reverse of Request/Response. The Web service sends a message to the client, and then the client sends a response message to the Web service. The <operation> element lists the output and input messages in reverse order.

```
<operation name="MyOperation">
  <output message=" MyOutputMessage" />
  <input message="MyInputMessage" />
</operation>
```

- **Notification:** The reverse of One Way. The Web service sends a message to the client, but receives no response message in return.

```
<operation name="MyOperation">
  <output message=" MyOutputMessage" />
</operation>
```

The <portType> Element

The <portType> element lists all of the operations that a Web service supports. The <port> element (described later in this chapter) corresponds to a single Web service, while the <portType> element describes the available operations. The previous three elements (<types>, <message>, and <operation>) all describe granular, individual pieces of the Web service operations and its types. The <portType> element avoids many of these lower-level details and instead provides a high-level summary of the operations (and associated input, output, and fault messages) that the Web service provides. The <portType> element provides a single location for a client to browse the offerings of a particular Web service.

The four elements that I have discussed so far are presented in order of decreasing granularity. Whereas an <operation> element lists a collection of <message> elements (which in turn list a collection of <types> elements), a <portType> element lists a collection of <operation> elements.

For example, here is the <portType> element (named StockTraderServiceSoap) for a Web service that supports two operations, RequestQuote and PlaceTrade:

```
<portType name="StockTraderServiceSoap">
  <operation name="RequestQuote">
    <input message="tns:RequestQuoteSoapIn" />
    <output message="tns:RequestQuoteSoapOut" />
    <fault message=" tns:ExceptionMessage" />
  </operation>
  <operation name="PlaceTrade">
    <input message="tns:PlaceTradeSoapIn" />
    <output message="tns:PlaceTradeSoapOut" />
  </operation>
</portType>
```

You may be surprised to see the <portType> listing like this. I have pointed out on several occasions how the WSDL document is designed for efficiency. If this were entirely the case, then you would expect the <portType> element to look more like this:

```
<portType name="StockTraderServiceSoap">>
  <operation name="RequestQuote" />
  <operation name="PlaceTrade" />
</portType>
```

There is no easy explanation as to why the WSDL document takes a less effi-cient approach with the <portType> element other than to speculate that it is designed to be a one-stop location for a client to retrieve a summary of the oper-ations that the Web service supports.

The <binding> Element

The <binding> element links the abstract and concrete elements together within a WSDL document. The <binding> element is associated with a specific <portType> element, and it also lists the address of the Web service that is associated with the <portType> element. Finally, the <binding> element lists the protocol that is used to communicate with the Web service.

Keep in mind that the <portType> element is nothing more than an abstract definition for a Web service, which is a concrete entity that implements a set of operations. The <binding> element simply formalizes the association between a <portType> and a Web service.

Here is what the <binding> element looks like for a Web service that sup-ports a single operation called RequestQuote, and which communicates using the SOAP protocol:

```
<binding name="StockTraderServiceSoap" type="tns:StockTraderServiceSoap">
  <soap:binding transport="http://schemas.xmlsoap.org/soap/http"
        style="document" />
    <operation name="RequestQuote">
     <soap:operation
     soapAction="http://www.bluestonepartners.com/schemas/StockTrader/RequestQuote"
          style="document" />
    <input>
     <soap:body use="literal" />
    </input>
    <output>
     <soap:body use="literal" />
    </output>
  </operation>
</binding>
```

There is no new abstract information here that you do not already know from the discussion so far. For example, you already know the name of the <portType>, which is StockTraderServiceSoap. And you already know that it includes an <operation> element named RequestQuote. But the concrete information is new. The <binding> element informs you that the Web service uses the SOAP transport protocol. The <soap:operation> element tells you the name of the Web method that is associated with the RequestQuote operation, but it does not reveal the physical location of the Web service. (The soapAction attribute includes the namespace for the RequestQuote schema element, which appears to resemble a physical URL path.) Finally, you learned that the Web method uses literal encoding and a document style, which are both required settings for exchanging SOAP messages.

The <port> Element

The <port> element defines the URL where the Web service is located, and it also implements a <binding> element. As you know, I have already defined a <binding> element for the Web service, but it does not indicate the physical location of the Web service. This is what the <port> element is for.

Here is what the <port> element looks like for the StockTraderServiceSoap <binding> element:

```
<port name="StockTraderServiceSoap" binding="tns:StockTraderServiceSoap">
  <soap:address location="http://localhost/StockTrader/StockTrader.asmx" />
</port>
```

Finally you learned the physical location of the Web service, via the <soap:address> element.

The <service> Element

The <service> element encloses one or more <port> elements. It is essentially a collection of one or more Web service bindings. In most cases, your WSDL document will describe one Web service only, and so the <service> element itself will provide no additional value. However, the WSDL specification requires that all <port> elements be contained within the <service> element. The listing in the prior section actually appears within a <service> element called StockTraderService as follows:

```
<service name="StockTraderService">
  <port name="StockTraderServiceSoap" binding="tns:StockTraderServiceSoap">
    <soap:address location="http://localhost/StockTrader/StockTrader.asmx" />
  </port>
</service>
```

The WSDL 1.1 Specification

The WSDL 1.1 specification that describes the complete document structure can be found at http://www.w3.org/TR/wsdl. It is worth looking at the original specification because you will find useful elements that you can use even though they are not widely known or even generated using GUI tools such as Visual Studio .NET. For example, the <operation> element contains a child element called <documentation> that allows you to insert an English-language description of what the operation does. Here is an example:

```
<operation name="RequestQuote">
   <documentation>
        Returns a delayed 30-minute quote for a given stock ticker symbol.
        This operation returns a Quote XML type as defined in the XSD schema at:
        http://www.bluestonepartners.com/schemas/StockTrader.xsd
   </documentation>
   <input message="s0:RequestQuoteSoapIn" />
   <output message="s0:RequestQuoteSoapOut" />
</operation>
```

The <documentation> element adds a welcome level of readability to the WSDL document, which is challenging at best to read with human eyes.

If you were to distill a WSDL document down to its most basic set of associated elements, it would look like this:

```
<definitions>
     <types />
     <message />
     <operation>
          <message />
     </operation>
     <portType>
          <operation />
     </portType>
     <binding>
          <operation />
     </binding>
     <service>
          <port>
               <binding />
          </port>
     </service>
</definitions>
```

Listing 2-1 shows the actual WSDL document for the StockTrader Web service that we will be working with in detail in the following chapters. You do not need to read the document line-by-line, but try scanning it, and notice how much information you can get about the Web service without having seen any other documentation about it.

Listing 2-1. The WSDL Document for the StockTrader Web Service

```xml
<?xml version="1.0" encoding="utf-8" ?>
<definitions xmlns:http="http://schemas.xmlsoap.org/wsdl/http/"
    xmlns:soap="http://schemas.xmlsoap.org/wsdl/soap/"
    xmlns:s="http://www.w3.org/2001/XMLSchema"
    xmlns:s0="http://www.bluestonepartners.com/schemas/StockTrader/"
    xmlns:soapenc="http://schemas.xmlsoap.org/soap/encoding/"
    xmlns:tns="http://www.bluestonepartners.com/schemas/StockTrader"
    xmlns:tm="http://microsoft.com/wsdl/mime/textMatching/"
    xmlns:mime="http://schemas.xmlsoap.org/wsdl/mime/"
    targetNamespace="http://www.bluestonepartners.com/schemas/StockTrader"
    xmlns="http://schemas.xmlsoap.org/wsdl/">
<import namespace="http://www.bluestonepartners.com/schemas/StockTrader/"
    location="http://www.bluestonepartners.com/schemas/StockTrader.xsd" />
<types/>
<message name="RequestAllTradesSummarySoapIn">
    <part name="Account" element="s0:Account" />
</message>
<message name="RequestAllTradesSummarySoapOut">
    <part name="RequestAllTradesSummaryResult" element="s0:Trades" />
</message>
<message name="RequestTradeDetailsSoapIn">
    <part name="Account" element="s0:Account" />
    <part name="TradeID" element="s0:TradeID" />
</message>
<message name="RequestTradeDetailsSoapOut">
    <part name="RequestTradeDetailsResult" element="s0:Trade" />
</message>
<message name="PlaceTradeSoapIn">
    <part name="Account" element="s0:Account" />
    <part name="Symbol" element="s0:Symbol" />
    <part name="Shares" element="s0:Shares" />
    <part name="Price" element="s0:Price" />
    <part name="tradeType" element="s0:tradeType" />
</message>
<message name="PlaceTradeSoapOut">
    <part name="PlaceTradeResult" element="s0:Trade" />
```

```
</message>
<message name="RequestQuoteSoapIn">
    <part name="Symbol" element="s0:Symbol" />
</message>
<message name="RequestQuoteSoapOut">
    <part name="RequestQuoteResult" element="s0:Quote" />
</message>
<portType name="StockTraderServiceSoap">
    <operation name="RequestAllTradesSummary">
        <input message="tns:RequestAllTradesSummarySoapIn" />
        <output message="tns:RequestAllTradesSummarySoapOut" />
    </operation>
    <operation name="RequestTradeDetails">
        <input message="tns:RequestTradeDetailsSoapIn" />
        <output message="tns:RequestTradeDetailsSoapOut" />
    </operation>
    <operation name="PlaceTrade">
        <input message="tns:PlaceTradeSoapIn" />
        <output message="tns:PlaceTradeSoapOut" />
    </operation>
    <operation name="RequestQuote">
        <input message="tns:RequestQuoteSoapIn" />
        <output message="tns:RequestQuoteSoapOut" />
    </operation>
</portType>
<binding name="StockTraderServiceSoap" type="tns:StockTraderServiceSoap">
    <soap:binding transport="http://schemas.xmlsoap.org/soap/http"
        style="document" />
    <operation name="RequestAllTradesSummary">
        <soap:operation
            soapAction="http://www.bluestonepartners.com/schemas/StockTrader/➥
                RequestAllTradesSummary" style="document" />
        <input>
            <soap:body use="literal" />
        </input>
        <output>
            <soap:body use="literal" />
        </output>
    </operation>
    <operation name="RequestTradeDetails">
        <soap:operation
            soapAction="http://www.bluestonepartners.com/schemas/StockTrader/➥
                RequestTradeDetails" style="document" />
        <input>
```

```
                <soap:body use="literal" />
        </input>
        <output>
                <soap:body use="literal" />
        </output>
    </operation>
    <operation name="PlaceTrade">
        <soap:operation soapAction="http://www.bluestonepartners.com/schemas/↩
            /StockTrader/PlaceTrade" style="document" />
    <input>
    <soap:body use="literal" />
    </input>
    <output>
    <soap:body use="literal" />
    </output>
    </operation>
    <operation name="RequestQuote">
        <soap:operation
            soapAction="http://www.bluestonepartners.com/schemas/StockTrader/↩
                RequestQuote" style="document" />
        <input>
                <soap:body use="literal" />
        </input>
        <output>
                <soap:body use="literal" />
        </output>
    </operation>
</binding>
<service name="StockTraderService">
    <port name="StockTraderServiceSoap" binding="tns:StockTraderServiceSoap">
        <soap:address location="http:// www.bluestonepartners.com/StockTrader.asmx" />
    </port>
</service>
</definitions>
```

This concludes the overview of the elements that make up a WSDL document. You can reference the complete WSDL document for this Web service in the sample code (available from the Downloads section of the Apress Web site at http://www.apress.com), under Chapter 2\WSDL Documents\. You may find the file easier to read if you open it in Visual Studio .NET or from within XML document editing software.

Working with WSDL Documents

Now that you understand the structure of a WSDL document, the next questions are how to actually generate one, and what to do with it once you have it generated. These are not trivial questions, because the WSDL document is complex, and you will want to keep your manual alterations of the document to a minimum. Parsing errors are very easy to generate in a WSDL document from even the smallest of misapplied edits.

How to Generate a WSDL Document

The easiest way to generate a WSDL document is using a tool like Visual Studio .NET. There is very much a chicken-and-the-egg relationship between a WSDL document and the Web service implementation that it describes. That is, you can write the code first, and generate the WSDL document later. Or, you can manually write the WSDL document first, and then use it to auto-generate the code definition. Because it is very difficult to generate a WSDL document by hand, you are better off writing the code implementation first, and then using Visual Studio .NET to generate the WSDL document for you.

> **NOTE**   *Web services must be message-oriented if they are to be of any use in a service-oriented architecture. Chapters 3 and 4 provide a detailed discussion of how to build message-oriented Web services. The WSDL document will not improve or detract from the quality of the Web service implementation. It is essential that you follow good design patterns and practices when building Web services for a service-oriented architecture.*

Assuming that you have built a message-oriented Web service according to the best patterns and practices (as discussed in the following chapters), you can generate a WSDL document by browsing the .asmx file of your Web service, and then clicking the Service Description link in the default client page. This link simply appends ?WSDL to the URL of the .asmx file. Figure 2-2 shows the default client page for the StockTraderService Web service and the corresponding Service Description link.

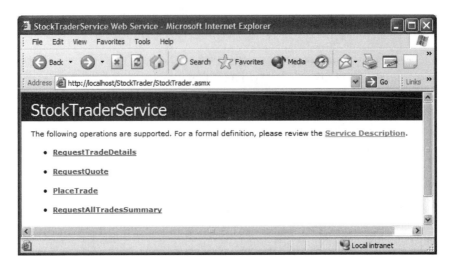

Figure 2-2. The default client page for the StockTraderService Web service

The Service Description link will display the WSDL document in a tree view–like format, wherein you can collapse and expand individual elements. This format is very useful for working your way through the document and learning how it is structured. Alternatively, you can copy the WSDL document from the browser window and then view it in an XML document editing application.

What to Do with the WSDL Document

Once you have auto-generated the WSDL document, there are two main things that you will want to do with the generated document. First, you will need to abstract out the data type information from the embedded <types> element into a separate XSD schema file. This is essential in a service-oriented architecture so that other Web services and clients can have access to the same centralized schema definition file of the custom data types.

Second, you can now use a command-line tool called wsdl.exe to auto-generate proxy classes that clients can use to interact with the Web service. You can replicate the same feature in Visual Studio .NET by adding a Web reference from a client project to a Web service. As you become a more sophisticated Web services developer, you will end up spending more time developing outside of the comfortable environment of Visual Studio .NET. This is because you will grow to need a higher level of control over your Web services development than Visual Studio .NET can currently provide.

I conclude the chapter here, but I will extend this material in greater detail in the following two chapters.

Summary

In this chapter, you studied the structure of a WSDL document and found that it contains seven XML elements in addition to a root element called <definitions>. The seven additional elements are divided into two groups: one set provides an abstract description of the Web service, while the other set provides concrete implementation details that associate the abstract descriptions with the physical Web service.

The XML elements for abstract description are

<types>: This element lists all of the data types that are exchanged by the XML messages as input parameters or return types.

<message>: This element describes a SOAP message, which may be an input, output, or fault message for a Web service operation.

<operation>: This element is analogous to a method definition; however, it only allows you to define input, output, and fault messages that are associated with the operation.

<portType>: This element lists all of the operations that a Web service supports.

The XML elements for concrete implementation are

<binding>: This element links the abstract and concrete elements together within a WSDL document.

<port>: This element defines the URL where the Web service is located, and it also implements a <binding> element.

<service>: This element encloses one or more <port> elements.

The chapter concluded with a brief look at how to generate and work with WSDL documents. In the following two chapters, I will give you a detailed look at how to build message-oriented Web services and how to work with WSDL documents and XSD schema definition files.

CHAPTER 3

Design Patterns for Building Message-Oriented Web Services

IN A SERVICE-ORIENTED ARCHITECTURE (SOA), the purpose of Web services is to exchange and process XML messages, not simply to act as hosts for Remote Procedure Call (RPC) style methods. The difference is that messages are bound to rich and complex operations, whereas RPC-style methods simply return a discrete result that is directly correlated to a specific set of input parameters. For example, a message-oriented Web method will accept a stock ticker symbol and will return a detailed stock quote in response. In contrast, an RPC-style Web method will return a simple output value.

Unfortunately, development tools such as Visual Studio .NET place a method-centric focus on Web services that causes you to lose sight of the bigger design picture and to take the underlying infrastructure for granted. It is very easy to build a Web service by creating an .asmx file and then throwing together several loosely related RPC-style Web method implementations. However, this is the wrong design approach because such a Web service fails to provide an integrated set of message endpoints. In simpler terms, the Web service fails to provide a service. The right design approach is always to think in terms of operations and XML messages, and to consider how the Web service methods work together to provide a service.

This chapter begins with a challenge for you to set aside what you have learned about Web services development until now, and to open your mind to a different design approach—one that is based on integrated XML messages, not on RPC-style methods.

How to Build Message-Oriented Web Services

There are six steps involved in building a message-oriented Web service, as described in the following sections.

Step 1: Design the Messages and the Data Types

Conceptually design what the messages and data types will look like. UML class diagrams are the best way to capture this information.

Step 2: Build the XSD Schema File for the Data Types

Use an XML designer tool to build the XSD schema file for all of the data types that are exchanged by the Web service methods. Visual Studio .NET's XML Designer is a good tool, but you can use any XML Designer tool that you are comfortable working with.

Step 3: Create a Class File of Interface Definitions for the Messages and Data Types

The interface definition class file provides the abstract definitions of the Web service methods and its data types. This class file derives from the System.Web.Services.WebService class, so it can be readily implemented in a Web services code-behind file. The .NET Framework provides a command-line tool called xsd.exe for generating an interface definition class file based on an XSD schema file. This will manually generate class definitions for the data types. You can add this class file to your Web service project and then manually insert abstract definitions for the Web methods.

Optional Step 3A: Generate the WSDL Document Manually

If you are brave enough, you can generate the WSDL document manually once you have built the XSD schema file. However, the only real benefit you gain from this step is you are then able to fully generate the interface definition file using the wsdl.exe command-line tool. It is easier to follow Step 3 (explained previously) using xsd.exe combined with manual coding of the abstract method definitions. The syntax of WSDL documents is very difficult to build correctly by hand. (However, Chapter 2, which reviews the structure of WSDL documents, is essential reading so that you can understand how the WSDL document is structured and how it relays Web service metadata to Web service clients.)

Step 4: Implement the Interface in the Web Service Code-Behind File

Your hard work in Steps 1 through 3 pays off, and you are now ready to implement code for the Web methods. The Web service .asmx code-behind class derives from the System.Web.Services.WebService class by default, as does the interface definition class file from Step 3. So you can derive the .asmx code-behind class directly from the interface definition class instead, and then implement code for each of the methods.

Step 5: Generate a Proxy Class File for Clients Based on the WSDL Document

Web services have no reason to exist unless they are being used by clients. In this step, you generate a proxy class file based on the Web service WSDL document so that clients know how to call your Web service, and what messages and data types will be exchanged. The wsdl.exe command-line tool will automatically generate this proxy class for you based on the WSDL document. And Visual Studio .NET will automatically generate the WSDL document for you, so no manual work is required.

You can actually skip this step if you are developing with Visual Studio .NET, because it will dynamically generate the proxy class file for you when you add a Web reference (for your Web service) to a client project. However, I prefer to manually generate the proxy class file so that I can either alter it or have it ready for clients who are using a development tool without code generating wizards.

Step 6: Implement a Web Service Client Using a Proxy Class File

This final step hooks a client to your Web service. If you are using Visual Studio .NET, then you simply add a (dynamic) Web reference to the Web service in your client project, and this will automatically generate the proxy class file for you. This wizard will also make the necessary adjustments to your application configuration file to record the location of the Web service. Alternatively, you can manually add the proxy class file from Step 5 to your project, update the configuration file, and begin coding. The client essentially does nothing more than delegate method calls out to the Web service. Valid clients include Web applications, Windows Forms applications, console applications, or even other Web services.

Next Steps

This process is obviously more involved than simply creating a new .asmx file and immediately implementing code. But it is the right way to do things because it abstracts out the Web service definitions and the code implementations. Visual Studio .NET and the .NET Framework provide all of the tools that you need to auto-generate the XML-based files and the code, so the amount of manual work is kept to a minimum.

The rest of this chapter dissects the various moving parts that make up a message-oriented Web service. You will gain a precise understanding of how multiple files and tools work together to define and implement a message-oriented Web service. I will also provide selective implementation examples that collectively show you how to build this type of Web service from scratch.

What Are Design Patterns?

Design patterns are loosely described as time-tested, established solutions to recurring design problems. Formal design patterns are highly structured and follow strict templates. The design patterns that are presented in this book do not follow this rigorous format, but they are in keeping with the spirit of design patterns because they factor in industry-accepted practices for approaching recurring design problems.

Design and Build a Message-Oriented Web Service

This section provides the information that you need in order to build a message-oriented Web service. It is organized along the same six steps presented earlier and provides both conceptual information and implementation information.

The Role of XML Messages and XSD Schemas

The starting point in designing a Web service is to determine what XML messages it will exchange—specifically, what messages it will respond to, and what messages it will return. Figure 3-1 shows the standard architecture for a client that interacts with a Web service via a proxy class. This architecture is based on the principle that the client and the Web service both have a common understanding of the messages and data types that are exchanged between them. This understanding can only be achieved if the Web service publishes a clear document of the operations that it supports, the messages it exchanges, and the types that it uses. This document is the Web Services Description Language (WSDL) document (described in Chapter 2). The WSDL document is the main reference for describing a Web service, and it includes embedded type definitions and message definitions among other things.

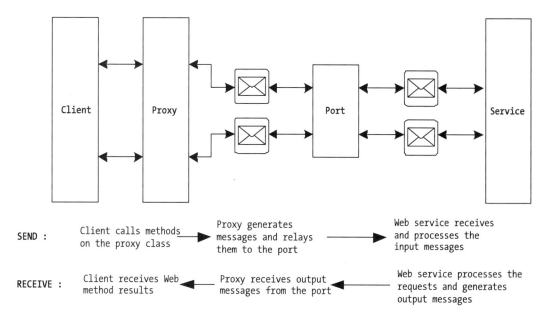

Figure 3-1. Web services architecture showing communication between the client and service

Consider an example Web service called StockTrader that provides methods for retrieving stock quotes and placing trades. Listing 3-1 presents one of the Web methods called RequestQuote that accepts a stock ticker symbol and returns a detailed stock quote.

Listing 3-1. Pseudo-Code for the RequestQuote Web Method

```
[WebMethod]
public Quote RequestQuote(string Symbol)
{
    // implementation code
}
```

```
public class Quote
    {
        public string Symbol;
        public string Company;
        public string DateTime;
        public System.Double High;
        public System.Double Low;
        public System.Double Open;
        public System.Double Last;
        public System.Double Change;
        public System.Double PercentChange;
        public System.Double Previous_Close;
        public string High_52_Week;
        public string Low_52_Week;
    }
```

This code listing represents a Quote type object and a method called RequestQuote that returns a Quote object. The RequestQuote method actually represents two messages: an input, or request, message that includes a stock ticker symbol, and an output, or response, message that provides a detailed stock quote. A client can only use the RequestQuote method if it can also understand the response. In other words, the client has to fully understand the definition of the Quote type in order to make use of the RequestQuote method. This is exactly the kind of information that WSDL documents and XSD schema files document.

Listing 3-2 shows what the RequestQuote input and output messages look like in WSDL.

Listing 3-2. WSDL for the RequestQuote Input and Output Messages

```
<message name="RequestQuoteSoapIn">
    <part name="Symbol" element="s0:Symbol" />
</message>
<message name="RequestQuoteSoapOut">
    <part name="RequestQuoteResult" element="s0:Quote" />
</message>

<portType name="StockTraderServiceSoap">
    <operation name="RequestQuote">
        <input message="tns:RequestQuoteSoapIn" />
        <output message="tns:RequestQuoteSoapOut" />
    </operation>
</portType>
```

And Listing 3-3 shows what the Quote type and Symbol type look like in an XSD schema file.

Listing 3-3. XSD Schema for the Quote and Symbol Types

```
<?xml version="1.0" encoding="utf-8" ?>
<xs:schema id="StockTrader"
    targetNamespace="http://www.bluestonepartners.com/Schemas/StockTrader/"
    elementFormDefault="qualified"
    xmlns="http://www.bluestonepartners.com/Schemas/StockTrader/"
    xmlns:mstns="http://www.bluestonepartners.com/Schemas/StockTrader/"
    xmlns:xs="http://www.w3.org/2001/XMLSchema" version="1.0">
    <xs:complexType name="Quote">
        <xs:sequence>
            <xs:element name="Symbol" type="xs:string" />
            <xs:element name="Company" type="xs:string" />
            <xs:element name="DateTime" type="xs:string" />
            <xs:element name="High" type="xs:double" />
            <xs:element name="Low" type="xs:double" />
            <xs:element name="Open" type="xs:double" />
            <xs:element name="Last" type="xs:double" />
            <xs:element name="Change" type="xs:double" />
            <xs:element name="PercentChange" type="xs:double" />
            <xs:element name="High_52_Week" type="xs:double" />
            <xs:element name="Low_52_Week" type="xs:double" />
        </xs:sequence>
    </xs:complexType>
    <xs:element name="Symbol" type="xs:string"></xs:element>
</xs:schema>
```

This schema representation of the Quote type is significant because it qualifies the type definition based on a specific target namespace, in this case http://www.bluestonepartners.com/schemas/StockTrader/. Although there may be many variations of the Quote type in the world, this specific qualified definition is unique. The Symbol type is nothing more than a standard string type element, but it is qualified to a specific namespace and therefore becomes more than just a standard element. Schema files are essential to ensuring that a Web service and its clients are absolutely clear on the messages and type definitions that are being exchanged between them. Schema files are how you define messages.

> **NOTE** *XSD schema files should always define types using nested elements rather than attributes. This makes the file easier to read and reduces the possibility of errors during processing.*

The Quote and Symbol types looks very similar if they are embedded directly in the WSDL document within the <types> section, and you should always assign qualified namespace information to embedded types. In addition, you should always abstract type definitions out to a separate XSD schema file for reference purposes, even though it is redundant to the embedded type information contained within the WSDL document. Separate XSD schema files are useful for lots of reasons. Most importantly, they allow different Web services to use the same qualified types, and to reference them based on a single XSD schema file in a single physical location. Life would get very confusing if you had multiple embedded definitions of the same qualified data type floating around in cyberspace. In addition, dedicated XSD schema files help you validate XML messages. In .NET, you can load an XSD file into an XmlValidatingReader object, and use it to validate XML messages. You can also use schema files with the xsd.exe command-line utility to generate class file definitions for types.

> **NOTE** *The target namespace is typically expressed as a Uniform Resource Identifier (URI), but it is not required to resolve to an actual location. The schema definitions that are presented in this book happen to be stored as XSD files at* http://www.bluestonepartners.com/schemas/. *For your convenience, they are also included in the sample code downloads (available from the Downloads section on the Apress Web site at* http://www.apress.com*).*

Design the XML Messages and XSD Schemas (Step 1)

XML messages represent the operations that your Web service supports, and they correlate to implemented Web methods. XML messages do not contain implementation logic. Instead, they simply document the name of an operation and its input and output types. XML messages must be designed in conjunction with XSD schema files. The best starting point is to construct a UML diagram for the operation. Figure 3-2 shows a UML class diagram for the RequestQuote operation and its associated input and output data types.

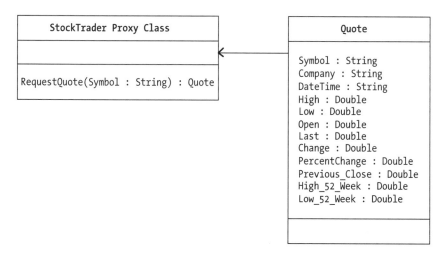

Figure 3-2. UML class diagram for the RequestQuote operation

The UML class diagrams will map conceptually to XSD schemas, so you do not have to sketch out any XML during the design phase unless it helps you to better visualize the XML messages and types. For example, here is what the Quote type will look like within a SOAP response (with the embedded namespaces omitted for clarity):

```
<Quote>
    <Symbol>MSFT</Symbol>
    <Company>Microsoft Corporation</Company>
    <DateTime>11/17/2003 16:00:00</DateTime>
    <High>26.12</High>
    <Low>24.68</Low>
    <Open>25.49</Open>
    <Last>25.15</Last>
    <Change>-0.36</Change>
    <PercentChange>-0.0137</PercentChange>
    <Previous_Close>25.49</Previous_Close>
    <High_52_Week>35</High_52_Week>
    <Low_52_Week>22</Low_52_Week>
</Quote>
```

For design purposes, you can simplify the XML down to this:

```
<Quote>
    <Symbol />
    <Company />
    <DateTime />
    <High />
    <Low />
    <Open />
    <Last />
    <Change />
    <PercentChange />
    <Previous_Close />
    <High_52_Week />
    <Low_52_Week />
</Quote>
```

Clearly, it is a lot of work to sketch out even this simplified XML by hand, and it does not provide any additional value beyond what the UML diagram provides. In fact, it provides less because this sketched out XML provides no type information. So the message here is that for efficiency you should design your XML messages using UML or any appropriate shorthand notation. This is the extent of the design work that is minimally required, and you should never shortcut this step.

Build the XSD Schema File (Step 2)

Once you have established what your XML messages and data types will look like, it is time to start building them. XSD schema files are the building blocks for XML messages, so you need to design the schema files first. XSD schema files may be coded by hand, but it is easier to use a visual designer tool, such as Visual Studio .NET's XML Designer. To access the designer, you simply add a new XSD schema file to a project. Visual Studio provides both a visual design view and an XML design view. Figure 3-3 illustrates the visual design view for StockTrader.xsd, which defines all of the data types for this chapter's StockTrader sample application.

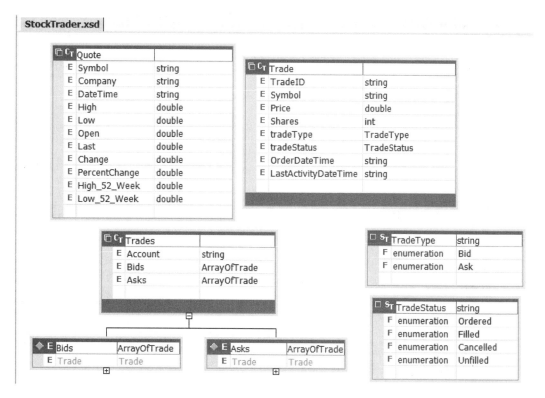

Figure 3-3. The Visual Studio .NET XML Designer, showing the StockTrader XSD schema

The XML Designer includes toolbox elements that you can drag onto the surface of the designer and then fill in, as shown in Figure 3-4. For example, it provides a toolbox element for XML complex types. Simply drag this element onto the designer and provide a name for the complex type. Then start specifying the included types by their name and type. Once you are finished defining all of the types, switch to the XML view to view the resulting XML. You can then copy and paste the XML into a notepad file, and save it with an .xsd extension.

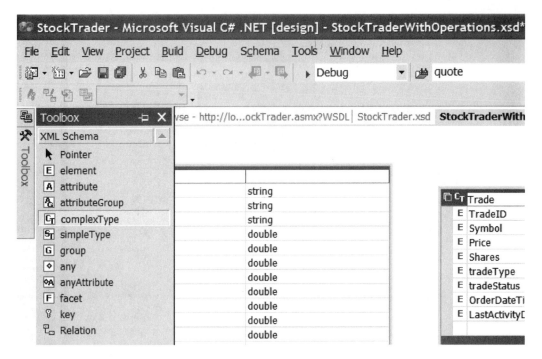

Figure 3-4. The Visual Studio .NET XML Designer Toolbox

You do not need to build the XML message documents by hand because they are created as part of the WSDL document, which Visual Studio .NET will automatically generate. But you will need to code the abstract method definitions in an interface definition file so that the WSDL generator knows what XML messages to create. The interface definition file contains type definitions and abstract method definitions.

The Role of the Interface Definition Class File

The interface definition class file contains two important sets of information:

- Class definitions for all custom types that are exchanged by the Web service

- Abstract class definitions for each operation that the Web service supports

Listing 3-4 provides the code for an interface definition class file for the RequestQuote operation and its associated types.

Listing 3-4. The Interface Definition Class File for the RequestQuote Operation and Its Associated Types

```
using System;
using System.Web.Services;
using System.Web.Services.Description;
using System.Web.Services.Protocols;
using System.Xml.Serialization;

namespace StockTrader
{

    public abstract class StockTraderStub : System.Web.Services.WebService
    {
        public abstract Quote RequestQuote(string Symbol);
    }

    [XmlTypeAttribute(Namespace=
      "http://www.bluestonepartners.com/schemas/StockTrader/")]
    public class Quote
    {
        public string Symbol;
        public string Company;
        public string DateTime;
        public System.Double High;
        public System.Double Low;
        public System.Double Open;
        public System.Double Last;
        public System.Double Change;
        public System.Double PercentChange;
        public System.Double Previous_Close;
        public System.Double High_52_Week;
        public System.Double Low_52_Week;
        }

}
```

Notice the following important points:

The definition file includes one stub class that encapsulates all operations, and then any number of additional classes for the data types.

The interface definitions for the operations are enclosed within an abstract class called StockTraderStub. The stub class derives from the System.Web.Services.WebService class, so it can be implemented in a Web service. In this listing it contains a single abstract function definition for the RequestQuote operation.

The definition file contains a separate class definition for the Quote type. This is how you are able to reference the Quote type from code-behind.

The definition file only contains class definitions for custom types (such as Quote), not for simple elements such as Symbol, which is a standard string (as qualified in the http://www.w3.org/2001/XMLSchema namespace). I make special mention of this because it may appear inconsistent with our earlier XSD schema file that includes an element definition for Symbol. But it is not inconsistent because the xsd.exe compiler resolves the Symbol element to a standard string, which therefore requires no special entry in the interface definition file.

> **NOTE** *You may be confused by the difference between abstract classes versus interfaces. An* interface *is a completely abstract set of members with no implementation logic. However, an* abstract class *supports implementations in its methods (although it is not required). Abstract classes are useful because they provide the benefits of interfaces combined with the convenience of reusable code.*

XML Serialization Attributes

The interface definition classes are decorated with XML serialization attributes that bind the classes to specific namespaces, attributes, and elements in the XSD schema file. Consider, for example, the following:

```
[return: XmlElement("Quote",
    Namespace = "http://www.bluestonepartners.com/schemas/StockTrader/")]
public abstract Quote RequestQuote(string Symbol);
```

This unambiguously states that the RequestQuote operation returns an object of type Quote, as qualified in the http://www.bluestonepartners.com/schemas/StockTrader/ namespace. In fact, this namespace is documented liberally throughout the interface definition file. It can never appear too often because XML messages must be as unambiguous as possible.

XML and SOAP serialization attributes give you direct control over the way in which the XML messages get serialized within the request and response SOAP messages. You should always set the SoapDocumentMethod reflection attribute to use bare encoding for parameters. This ensures that complex types (such as Quote) remain serialized as elements within the SOAP message:

```
[WebMethod()]
[SoapDocumentMethod(Use=SoapBindingUse.Literal,
    ParameterStyle=SoapParameterStyle.Bare)]
public abstract Quote RequestQuote(string Symbol);
```

If you do not use bare encoding, then complex types may end up serialized as attributes, which may interfere with schema validation. This is known as *wrapped encoding*. Bare encoding looks like this:

```
<Quote>
    <Symbol>MSFT</Symbol>
</Quote>
```

While wrapped encoding looks like this:

```
<Quote Symbol="MSFT" />
```

Wrapped encoding will generate fewer XML characters and a smaller SOAP payload, but it may create big problems if custom types cannot be validated against their XSD schema files.

Table 3-1 summarizes important properties of the serialization attribute, including how certain property values influence the processing behavior of a Web service.

> **NOTE** *Reflection attributes allow you to add additional metadata to a wide variety of code elements including classes and methods. Attributes modify the way that the element is processed. For example, the [WebMethod] attribute designates a standard method or function as capable of accepting serialized XML messages. Of course, reflection attributes must have meaning to the processing code in order to be applied. Reflection attributes may include properties that provide additional metadata information. For more on reflection attributes, consult the MSDN online article on attributes, located at MSDN Home ➤ MSDN Library ➤ .NET Development ➤ Visual Studio .NET ➤ Visual Basic and Visual C# ➤ Reference ➤ Visual C# Language ➤ C# Language Specification.*

Table 3-1. The SoapDocumentMethod Serialization Attribute and Selected Properties

Attribute Property	Description
Use	Specifies the encoding style of the messages. The options are Literal and Encoded. (The options are specified in code using the System.Web.Services.Description.SoapBindingUse enumeration.)
ParameterStyle	Specifies whether the parameters are wrapped in a single element within the body of the SOAP message, or whether they are unwrapped. (The options are specified in code using the System.Web.Services.Protocols.SoapParameterStyle enumeration.)
OneWay	Specifies whether the Web service client will receive a response to their request, or whether the request will be one-way only (without a response).
Binding	Associates a Web method with a specific operation within the binding that is specified for the Web service. The Web service binding is set at the Web service level using the WebServiceBinding serialization attribute. For example: [System.Web.Services.WebServiceBindingAttribute(Name= "StockTraderServiceSoap", Namespace="http:// www.bluestonepartners.com/schemas/StockTrader")] public class StockTraderProxy : System.Web.Services .Protocols.SoapHttpClientProtocol {}
RequestNamespace	The namespace URI that defines the request elements.
RequestElementName	The name of the request element as it is defined in the applicable XSD schema file.
ResponseNamespace	The namespace URI that defines the response elements.
ResponseElementName	The name of the response element as it is defined in the applicable XSD schema file.

Generate an Interface Definition File (Step 3)

Interface definition files (IDFs) can be generated in two ways:

wsdl.exe: This command-line tool generates a full interface definition file (including abstract classes and types) based on a WSDL document. Table 3-2 summarizes selected command-line switches for the wsdl.xe utility.

xsd.exe: This command-line tool generates the type section only for the interface definition file based on an XSD schema file. You can use this auto-generated file as a starting point and then manually insert the abstract class definitions for each of the Web service operations. Table 3-3 summarizes selected command-line switches for the xsd.exe utility.

Table 3-2. wsdl.exe Selected Command-Line Switches

Switch	Description
wsdl.exe <url or path> <options>	General usage of the wsdl.exe utility, which is a utility to generate code for XML Web service clients and XML Web services using ASP.NET from WSDL contract files, XSD schemas, and .discomap discovery documents. (Switch descriptions follow.)
<url or path>	A URL or path to a WSDL contract, an XSD schema, or .discomap document.
/server	Generate an abstract class for an XML Web service implementation using ASP.NET based on the contracts. The default is to generate client proxy classes.
/out:<filename>	The file name for the generated proxy code. The default name is derived from the service name. Short form is /o:.

Table 3-3. xsd.exe Selected Command-Line Switches

Switch	Description
xsd.exe <schema>.xsd /classes: dataset [/o:]	General usage of the xsd.exe utility, which is a utility to generate schema or class files from given source. (Switch descriptions follow.)
<schema>.xsd	The name of a schema containing the elements to import.
/classes	Generate classes for this schema. Short form is /c.
/dataset	Generate subclassed DataSet for this schema. Short form is /d.
/out:<directoryName>	The output directory to create files in. The default is the current directory. Short form is /o.

Here is how you generate an IDF using wsdl.exe:

```
C:\> wsdl /server /o:StockTraderStub.cs StockTrader.wsdl StockTrader.xsd
```

Here is how you generate an IDF using xsd.exe:

```
C:\> xsd StockTrader.xsd /c
```

> **NOTE** *In order to use the wsdl.exe and xsd.exe command-line tools from any directory location on your computer, you will probably need to set an environment variable that points to the directory location of the utilities. On my computer I created a user environment variable called PATH with a value of c:\Program Files\Microsoft Visual Studio .NET 2003\SDK\v1.1\ BIN. Alternatively, if you are using Visual Studio .NET, then from the Programs menu group you can select Visual Studio .NET Tools ➤ Visual Studio .NET Command Prompt.*

If you are following the steps in this chapter, then your only option for generating an interface definition file at this point is to partially generate it using xsd.exe and the XSD schema file. You have not yet defined the operations anywhere other than by design in the initial UML diagram in Step 1. So your next step is to use the UML diagram to manually add abstract class definitions to the auto-generated IDF. This is the approach I always take because it is far easier than the alternative, which is to generate WSDL by hand. Generating WSDL manually is prone to errors and takes far longer than it will take you to update a few lines in code, as is the case with the partially generated interface definition file.

Implement the Interface Definition in the Web Service (Step 4)

Once the interface definitions are in place, the last remaining step is to implement them in the Web service code-behind. The first step is to derive the Web service class file from the interface definition, and the second step is to override the abstract methods, as shown in Listing 3-5.

Listing 3-5. Derive the Web Service .asmx Code-Behind Class from the Generated Interface Definition Class (StockTraderStub)

```
// Step 1 (Before View): Implement the StockTraderStub class
[WebService(Namespace = "http://www.bluestonepartners.com/schemas/StockTrader")]
public class StockTraderService : StockTraderStub
{
    // Contains abstract methods (not shown)
}
```

```
// Step 2 (After View): Override and implement each of the abstract class methods
[WebService(Namespace = "http://www.bluestonepartners.com/schemas/StockTrader")]
public class StockTraderService : StockTraderStub
{
    public override Quote RequestQuote(string Symbol)
    {
        // Implementation code goes here
    }
}
```

You need to set namespace names for both the Web service class and the interface definition classes. I usually include all classes within the same namespace, but there is no rule about this. If you do use different namespaces, then in the Web service class file you will need to import the namespace for the interface definition classes.

At this point everything is in place to complete the implementation of the Web service methods. All operations and types are fully described and ready to be referenced from the Web service class file. Listing 3-6 shows an example implementation of the PlaceTrade Web method, which places a trade order and returns the trade details in a custom object type called Trade.

Listing 3-6. The PlaceTrade Web Method

```
[WebMethod()]
[SoapDocumentMethod(RequestNamespace=
    "http://www.bluestonepartners.com/schemas/StockTrader/",
    ResponseNamespace="http://www.bluestonepartners.com/schemas/StockTrader/",
    Use=SoapBindingUse.Literal, ParameterStyle=SoapParameterStyle.Bare)]
[return: XmlElement("Trade", Namespace=
    "http://www.bluestonepartners.com/schemas/StockTrader/")]
public override Trade PlaceTrade(string Account, string Symbol, int Shares, ➥
    System.Double Price, TradeType tradeType)
{
    Trade t = new Trade();
    t.TradeID = System.Guid.NewGuid().ToString();
    t.OrderDateTime = DateTime.Now.ToLongDateString();
    t.Symbol = Symbol;
    t.Shares = Shares;
    t.Price = Price;
    t.tradeType = tradeType;
    // Initialize the Trade to Ordered, using the TradeStatus enumeration
    t.tradeStatus = TradeStatus.Ordered;
    // Code Not Shown: Persist trade details to the database by account number
    // and trade ID, or to a message queue for later processing
    // Code goes here
    return t; // Return the Trade object
}
```

Notice that I have reapplied all of the XML and SOAP serialization attributes that were included in the interface definition file. You need to do this to ensure that they take effect. Also notice the use of several custom types, including Trade (a complex type that stores the trade details), TradeType (an enumeration for the type of trade being executed), and TradeStatus (an enumeration for the current status of the trade).

Assuming that you have followed the steps so far, your Visual Studio .NET Solution Explorer will look like Figure 3-5.

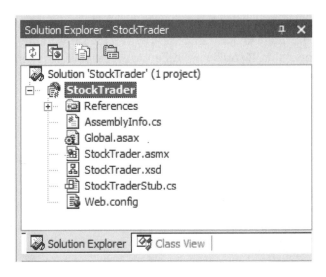

Figure 3-5. The Visual Studio .NET Solution Explorer showing the StockTrader Web service

Messages vs. Types

The discussion so far has drawn a distinction between messages and types. For example, Figure 3-2 outlines a message called RequestQuote that returns a type called Quote. This begs the question as to why they are different. Why can't the interface definition file treat the RequestQuote message as just another custom data type? This means you would need to include a custom class to represent RequestQuote, just as you create one to represent Quote.

This is not a trick question. The answer is that you can. There is no reason you cannot add a RequestQuote data type as its own custom class in the proxy stub file. To illustrate the distinction, Listing 3-7 shows you what this would look like. The listing is based on the shell of an autogenerated proxy stub file, with different class signatures for RequestQuote and Quote. In addition, I have added new custom data type for RequestQuote, shown in bold.

Listing 3-7. A Proxy Stub File That Includes the RequestQuote Message As a Custom Data Type

```
public abstract class StockTraderService : System.Web.Services.WebService
{
    public abstract Quote RequestQuote(string Symbol);
}

public class Quote
{
    // Quote properties not shown (e.g., Symbol, Open, Last, etc.)
}

public class RequestQuote
{
    public string Symbol;
}
```

Notice that the class signature for the RequestQuote operation contains no mention of the Quote object, which as you know is the output data type of the operation. It is not mentioned because the class signature reflects the input parameters only. Figure 3-6 shows a partial view of the StockTraderWithOperations.xsd schema file, which adds four additional complex types for each of the four supported Web service operations.

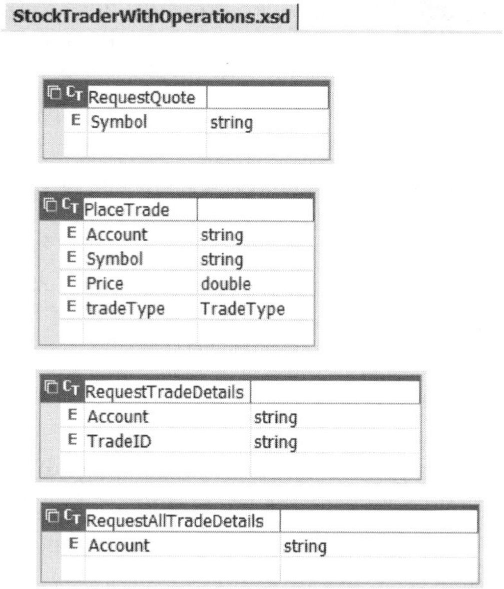

Figure 3-6. The Visual Studio .NET XML Designer, showing the StockTraderWithOperations XSD schema

Not only is it legal to include separate class signatures for the Web service operations, but you will need to do so if you have to manually retrieve the SOAP message body for a requested operation. Chapter 9 reviews services that use the TCP protocol and a specialized class called the SoapReceiver, which manually deserializes an incoming SOAP request message. The deserialized message body is mapped to an instance of the RequestQuote class, so you need to have a defined class signature. (Otherwise, you will need to write custom XPath queries to extract the operation name and input parameter values.)

Chapter 9 is many pages and concepts away, so until we reach there, it will not be necessary to create separate class signatures for the Web service operations. And unfortunately, the .NET Framework's WSDL generator will not be able to differentiate a message from a data type, unless you have implemented RequestQuote as a Web method in a .asmx file (to use just one example of a Web service operation). So for no other reason than convenience, you should continue creating .asmx code for each of the supported Web service operations. You can also start adding the operations to the associated XML schema file, so that they are there when you need them in the future. (The sample project for this chapter includes two versions of the StockTrader XML schema file: StockTrader.xsd and StockTraderWithOperations.xsd.)

Consume the Web Service

The hard part of the development is done, as is much of the value-added material in this chapter. By now you should have a good understanding of how to approach the development process for message-oriented Web services. Hopefully this chapter opened your eyes to the variety of moving parts that work together to power a Web service. Visual Studio .NET allows you to take shortcuts in the development process, but you need to avoid temptation and do the manual work that is required to create well-documented Web services.

I will close out this chapter with the final step of hooking the Web service to a client consumer.

Generate the Client Proxy Class File (Step 5)

You have done a lot of manual work to get to this point: You have manually created schema files and interface definitions, and you have implemented the operations as Web service methods. To generate a client proxy file, you can rely on the wsdl.exe utility to do the work for you in generating the proxy stub. The proxy file is similar to the interface definition file in that it includes class definitions for types and operations. But it is derived from the System.Web.Services.Protocols.SoapHttpClientProtocol namespace, and its purpose is to provide a programmatic interface between the client and the

Web service. The proxy class works with the underlying Web services infrastructure to make requests and receive responses using SOAP.

> **NOTE** *You can ignore the material in this section if you use Visual Studio .NET and work with the Add Web Reference Wizard. This wizard will automatically generate the proxy file for you, and you will not need to work directly with the Web service WSDL document. Read this section only if you want to know what happens under the hood when you create a client proxy class file.*

Assuming that you have completed the previous development steps correctly, your WSDL document will be in good shape, and you can trust that it accurately represents the messages and types that your Web service exchanges. You can use Visual Studio .NET to generate the WSDL file.

To generate the WSDL document, right-click the StockTrader.asmx file and select the View in Browser menu option. Append ?WSDL to the end of the URI, as in

```
http://localhost/StockTrader.asmx?WSDL
```

The WSDL document will open in a new browser window. You can copy and paste the XML into Notepad, and save it with a .wsdl file extension. You will need to edit this file in three ways:

- Remove dash characters from the WSDL browser view.

- Verify that the embedded type information (within the <types> tags) matches the type definitions within the XSD schema file you generated earlier.

- Remove the <service> element, which will bind the proxy to a static Web service location. (Instead, you will add a dynamic location to the client's configuration file.)

Listing 3-8 shows what the processed WSDL document will look like, assuming that RequestQuote is the only operation that the Web service supports.

Listing 3-8. The WSDL Document for the StockTrader Web Service Filtered to Show All Elements Related to the RequestQuote Web Method

```
<?xml version="1.0" encoding="utf-8" ?>
<definitions xmlns:http="http://schemas.xmlsoap.org/wsdl/http/"
    xmlns:soap="http://schemas.xmlsoap.org/wsdl/soap/"
    xmlns:s="http://www.w3.org/2001/XMLSchema"
    xmlns:s0="http://www.bluestonepartners.com/schemas/StockTrader/"
```

```
            xmlns:soapenc="http://schemas.xmlsoap.org/soap/encoding/"
            xmlns:tns="http://www.bluestonepartners.com/schemas/StockTrader"
            xmlns:tm="http://microsoft.com/wsdl/mime/textMatching/"
            xmlns:mime="http://schemas.xmlsoap.org/wsdl/mime/"
            targetNamespace="http://www.bluestonepartners.com/schemas/StockTrader"
            xmlns="http://schemas.xmlsoap.org/wsdl/">
<import namespace="http://www.bluestonepartners.com/schemas/StockTrader/"
        location="http://www.bluestonepartners.com/schemas/StockTrader.xsd" />
<types />
<message name="RequestQuoteSoapIn">
        <part name="Symbol" element="s0:Symbol" />
</message>
<message name="RequestQuoteSoapOut">
        <part name="RequestQuoteResult" element="s0:Quote" />
</message>
<portType name="StockTraderServiceSoap">
        <operation name="RequestQuote">
            <input message="tns:RequestQuoteSoapIn" />
            <output message="tns:RequestQuoteSoapOut" />
        </operation>
</portType>
<binding name="StockTraderServiceSoap" type="tns:StockTraderServiceSoap">
        <soap:binding transport="http://schemas.xmlsoap.org/soap/http"
          style="document" />
        <operation name="RequestQuote">
        <soap:operation

soapAction="http://www.bluestonepartners.com/schemas/StockTrader/RequestQuote"
            style="document" />
            <input>
                <soap:body use="literal" />
            </input>
            <output>
                <soap:body use="literal" />
            </output>
        </operation>
</binding>
</definitions>
```

Notice that I am using the <import> tag to pull in the type definitions from the reference XSD schema file, which is qualified at http://www.bluestonepartners .com/schemas/, and which is physically located at http://www.bluestonepartners .com/schemas/StockTrader.xsd. I am using this tag in order to avoid reprinting the lengthy embedded type information. This approach does not technically invalidate the WSDL file, although it does put the file out of compliance with the WS-I Basic Profile, Rule R2001, which disallows the import of external XSD schema files as a substitute for embedded type information.

Next, run the wsdl.exe command-line utility to generate a client proxy file:

```
C:\> wsdl /o:StockTraderProxy.cs StockTrader.wsdl StockTrader.xsd
```

You can then add the proxy class file to the Web service consumer's project, as I will discuss in the next section.

Build the Web Service Consumer

The proxy class file provides synchronous and asynchronous invocation mechanisms for each of the Web service operations, and derives from System.Web.Services.Protocols.SoapHttpClientProtocol. It also provides class definitions for the Web service types, just like the interface definition file. The proxy file does not include abstract methods, it only includes implemented methods. So you do not have to implement every method that the proxy class file provides. In addition, the consumer class does not need to derive from the service proxy class. You simply create instances of the proxy class as needed.

Implement the Web Service Consumer (Step 6)

Listing 3-9 shows a sample of the auto-generated service proxy class.

Listing 3-9. The Auto-Generated Service Proxy Class

```
[System.Web.Services.WebServiceBindingAttribute(Name="StockTraderServiceSoap",
    Namespace="http://www.bluestonepartners.com/schemas/StockTrader")]
public class StockTraderProxy : ➥
    System.Web.Services.Protocols.SoapHttpClientProtocol {

    public StockTraderProxy() {}

    [System.Web.Services.Protocols.SoapDocumentMethodAttribute(
        "http://www.bluestonepartners.com/schemas/StockTrader/RequestQuote",
        Use=System.Web.Services.Description.SoapBindingUse.Literal,
        ParameterStyle=System.Web.Services.Protocols.SoapParameterStyle.Bare)]
    [return: System.Xml.Serialization.XmlElementAttribute("Quote",
```

```
        Namespace="http://www.bluestonepartners.com/schemas/StockTrader/")]
    public Quote RequestQuote([System.Xml.Serialization.XmlElementAttribute(
        Namespace="http://www.bluestonepartners.com/schemas/StockTrader/")]
        string Symbol)
    {
        object[] results = this.Invoke("RequestQuote", new object[] {Symbol});
        return ((Quote)(results[0]));
    }

    public System.IAsyncResult BeginRequestQuote(string Symbol, ➥
        System.AsyncCallback callback, object asyncState)
    {
        return this.BeginInvoke("RequestQuote", new object[] { ➥
                    Symbol}, callback, asyncState);
    }

    public Quote EndRequestQuote(System.IAsyncResult asyncResult)
    {
        object[] results = this.EndInvoke(asyncResult);
        return ((Quote)(results[0]));
    }
}

[System.Xml.Serialization.XmlTypeAttribute(
    Namespace="http://www.bluestonepartners.com/schemas/StockTrader/")]
public class Quote
{
    string Symbol;
    // Additional type definitions go here (not shown)
}
```

This class was entirely auto-generated by the wsdl.exe utility. The only modification I made was to change the auto-generated name of the proxy class from StockTraderService to my preferred name of StockTraderProxy.

Figure 3-7 shows the Visual Studio .NET Solution Explorer as it appears when you add a consumer project to the same solution file as the StockTrader Web service. Note that this is done for convenience, to make debugging the projects simpler. In reality, the Web service and the consumer projects would be located on separate servers and likely in different domains.

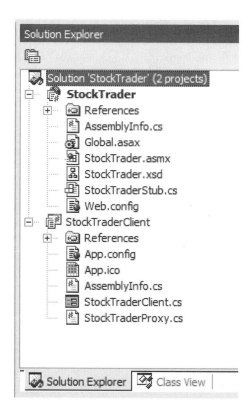

Figure 3-7. The Visual Studio .NET Solution Explorer showing the StockTrader Web service and the Web service consumer project

NOTE *This chapter does not provide specific instructions for how to create the consumer project, so please refer directly to the code samples that accompany this chapter.*

Figure 3-8 shows a form-based implementation of the consumer that allows you to receive stock quotes and place trades.

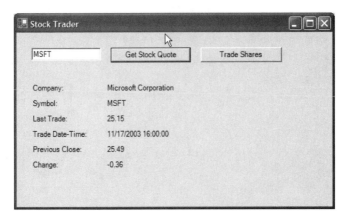

Figure 3-8. A consumer application for the StockTrader Web service

Listing 3-10 shows a sample of the implementation code behind the Request Quote button.

Listing 3-10. Web Service Consumer Code

```
private void btnQuote_Click(object sender, System.EventArgs e)
{
    // Create an instance of the Web service proxy
    StockTraderProxy serviceProxy = new StockTraderProxy();

    // Retrieve the Web Service URI from app.config
    serviceProxy.Url = ConfigurationSettings.AppSettings["remoteHost"];

    // Call the Web service to request a quote
    Quote q = serviceProxy.RequestQuote(this.txtSymbol.Text);

    // Display the Quote results in the form
    this.lblCompany.Text = q.Company;
    this.lblSymbol.Text = q.Symbol;
    this.lblTradeDateTime.Text = q.DateTime;
    this.lblLastTrade.Text = q.Last.ToString();
    this.lblPreviousClose.Text = q.Previous_Close.ToString();
    this.lblChange.Text = q.Change.ToString();
}
```

Notice that the client code references a configuration element called <remoteHost> that provides the URI for the StockTrader Web service. It should be entered into the project's .config file as shown in Listing 3-11.

Listing 3-11. The Web.config File for the Web Service Consumer

```
<?xml version="1.0" encoding="utf-8" ?>
<configuration>
    <appSettings>
      <add key="remoteHost"
value="http://localhost/StockTrader/StockTrader.asmx"/>
    </appSettings>
</configuration>
```

This concludes the discussion of how to build a basic message-oriented Web service.

Summary

The purpose of Web services is to exchange and process XML messages, not to act as simple endpoints for remote procedure calls. In this chapter, you learned a six-step process for designing and building a message-oriented Web service from scratch:

Step 1: Design the messages and the data types.

Step 2: Build the XSD schema file for the data types.

Step 3: Create a class file of interface definitions for the messages and data types.

Step 4: Implement the interface in the Web service code-behind file.

Step 5: Generate a proxy class file (for clients) based on the WSDL.

Step 6: Implement a Web service client using a proxy class file.

The goal of this chapter is to help you rethink your approach to Web services design so that you can start developing the type of message-oriented Web services that fit into a service-oriented architecture framework.

CHAPTER 4

Design Patterns for Building Service-Oriented Web Services

MESSAGE-ORIENTED WEB SERVICES are the building blocks for service-oriented applications. In the previous chapter, you learned how message-oriented Web services are constructed, and what sets them apart from traditional Remote Procedure Call (RPC) style Web services. The main difference is that messages typically include complex types that are defined using custom XML schema files. Message-oriented Web services are effective at executing operations, whereby the input parameters feed into a process rather than dictating the process. In contrast, procedure-style method calls are straightforward operations with a strong dependency on the input arguments. For example, the message-oriented StockTrader Web service provides a PlaceTrade operation that accepts the trade specifications, executes a complex trade operation, and then returns the details of the trade encapsulated in a complex data type (the Trade object). The simple input parameters trigger a complex operation and cause a complex type to be returned. There is no direct correlation between the input parameters and the complexity of the operation. In contrast, one example of a procedure-style Web method is a simple arithmetic Add operation that accepts two numeric input parameters. This Web method has nothing complicated happening internally, nor does it require that a complex data type be returned. What you get out of the method is directly correlated to what you send into it.

In this chapter, we need to make another conceptual leap, this time from message-oriented Web services to service-oriented Web services. Messages do not go away in this new architecture; they are just as important as ever. What is different is that Web services are not the central player in the architecture. Service-oriented Web services act more as smart gateways for incoming service requests than as destinations in and of themselves. Let's revisit the complex service-oriented architecture diagram from Chapter 1, reprinted here as Figure 4-1.

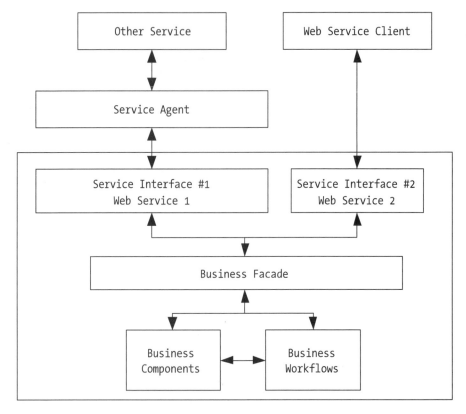

Figure 4-1. Complex service-oriented architecture

Notice that Web services are not the ultimate endpoint destinations in this architecture. Instead, their purpose is to authenticate and authorize incoming service requests, and then to relay the request details to back-end business components and workflows for processing. This fact by no means diminishes the importance of their role; it just switches perspectives. Web services have certain unique properties that make them essential to this architecture, namely

- Web services process SOAP messages.

- Web services provide publicly accessible (and discoverable) endpoints for service requests.

- Web services authenticate and authorize incoming service requests. In this role they selectively filter incoming service requests and keep out unauthorized requests.

In contrast, other components in the architecture, such as the business components, do not have any of these properties. They do not expose publicly accessible endpoints. They do not process SOAP requests directly. And they do not have the same ability to filter out incoming service requests based on security tokens.

So we have established that Web services play a unique role in service-oriented architecture, one where they are an important support player rather than the ultimate destination endpoint. But what does this translate to in practical terms, and how is it different from before? The implication is that you need to build Web services differently to maximize the effectiveness of their role in service-oriented architecture (SOA) applications. This includes

A renewed emphasis on breaking out Web service code-behind into separate class files and assemblies: This includes abstract interface definition files (based on the applicable WSDL document). It also includes generating a dedicated assembly for encapsulating custom data type definitions (so that common data types may be used across multiple services and components using a common reference assembly).

Delegation of all business process logic to back-end business components: The Web service code-behind should be focused exclusively on preprocessing incoming request messages and then relaying the request details to the appropriate back-end business component. The Web service code-behind should not handle any business processing directly.

A focus on new kinds of service-oriented components: SOA architecture creates a need for different kinds of service components that may have no equivalent in other architectures. For example, SOA applications rely heavily on service agent components, which act as the middleman between separate Web services and which relay all communications between them. (You will learn how to build a service agent component later in this chapter.)

Be forewarned: Some of the material in this chapter may strike you as unusual or unorthodox and certainly more complex than you are used to seeing with Web services development. This is not surprising given that SOA applications are still relatively new. Recall that it took several years for the n-tier architecture model to become fully formed and to gain wide acceptance as a standard. SOA will also go through an evolution. Some ideas will gain acceptance, while others will fall by the wayside. This chapter quite likely contains some of both, so read the chapter, absorb the material, and take with you as much or as little as you like.

How to Build Service-Oriented Web Services

The primary requirement that SOA imposes on a system is that its business functionality must be accessible through more than one type of interface and through more than one kind of transport protocol. Enterprise developers have long understood the need to separate out business functionality into a dedicated set of components. In the previous chapter, the StockTrader Web service implemented its business logic directly, based on an interface definition file (defined in a separate, though embedded, class file). This approach is incorrect from an SOA perspective for two reasons:

Web services should not implement business logic directly in their methods: They should delegate this processing to dedicated business assemblies. This is because you cannot assume that the business logic will always be accessed through a Web service. What happens, for example, when a new requirement comes through asking you to implement an alternate interface that cannot or will not interact with a Web service? You need to have a separate, ready-to-use assembly for the business logic.

Web services and their associated WSDL documents should not be the original reference points for interface definitions: Certainly, a WSDL document must conform to an established interface definition, but it should not be establishing what that definition is. This information belongs in a dedicated reference assembly, and should be stored as an interface definition that can be implemented in different kinds of components.

The previous StockTrader Web service is not compatible with SOA architecture because it prevents common functionality from being accessible via multiple interfaces. To put it in blunt terms, the StockTrader Web service is simply incompatible with SOA architecture because it is not abstract enough. What it needs to do instead is to act as a trusted interface to a back-end StockTrader business component. It cannot directly contain implementation for the StockTrader functions (such as getting quotes and placing trades). Instead, it must delegate this functionality to a back-end business component and focus on its primary role of authentication, authorizing and relaying incoming service requests (and sending out responses).

Consider another aspect to this architecture (as presented in Figure 4-1): type definitions. If you separate out common functionality across multiple components, how do they maintain a common understanding of type definitions? For example, how does every component maintain the same understanding of the Quote and Trade data types? XML Web services and their clients can share XSD schema information for custom data types via the service's published WSDL document. But this is not an efficient way to share type information between a middle-tier business component and a Web service, especially when the Web service is delegating requests to the business component. The more efficient approach is to generate a dedicated assembly that encapsulates the data type definitions as custom classes, and to include a reference to this assembly from wherever the custom data types are needed.

I have covered several challenging conceptual points, so now let's move on to code, and actually build a service-oriented Web service. Figure 4-2 is an architecture (and pseudo-UML diagram) that provides an alternate architecture for the original StockTrader Web service, one that will enable it to participate better in a larger service-oriented architecture. Notice that the type definitions and interface definitions have been broken out into a separate assembly called StockTraderTypes, which is referenced by several components in the architecture.

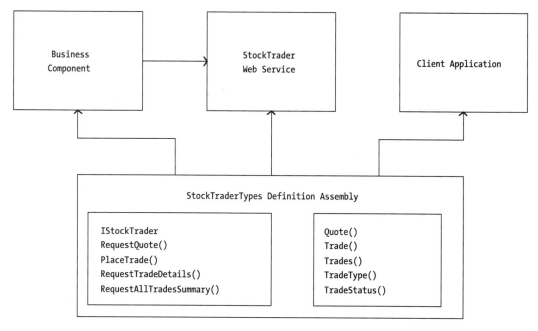

Figure 4-2. Revised architecture for the StockTrader Web service showing how several components reference the common StockTraderTypes definition assembly

Based on this UML diagram, there are six steps involved in building a message-oriented Web service that is compatible with SOA, as discussed next.

Step 1: Create a Dedicated Type Definition Assembly

Create a dedicated definition assembly for interfaces and type definitions. This assembly will be referenced by any component, service, or application that needs to use the interfaces or types.

Step 2: Create a Dedicated Business Assembly

Create a dedicated business assembly that implements logic for established interfaces and type definitions. This business assembly must reference the definition assembly from Step 1. This ensures that the business assembly implements every available method definition.

Once this step is complete, you now have the flexibility to build any kind of n-tier solution using the definition and business assemblies. This chapter focuses on building a service-oriented application that includes a Web service. But you could just as easily go a different route and build any kind of n-tier solution using the definition and business assemblies developed so far.

This point underscores the fact that in a service-oriented architecture, Web services are simply a gateway to a set of methods and types that are controlled by other assemblies. The Web service itself merely provides a set of SOAP-enabled endpoints that are accessible over one or more transport protocols.

Step 3: Create the Web Service Based on the Type Definition Assembly

In the previous version of the StockTrader Web service, the definition information for the Web method implementations came from a dedicated interface definition file, which provided abstract class definitions and class-based type definitions. But now this file is no longer needed because you have a dedicated definition assembly. The new Web service simply needs to import the definition assembly to have access to the required types and to the required interface.

Step 4: Implement the Business Interface in the Web Service

The Web service needs to import the business assembly so that it can delegate incoming service requests. Remember, the current architecture calls for a different level of abstraction, whereby the Web service itself does not control its interface, its data types, or the processing of business logic. Instead, it relies on other assemblies for this reference information and for this processing capability.

By implementing the interface, you are ensured not to miss any methods because the project will not compile unless every interface method is implemented in the Web service. So, the definition assembly provides the interface definition, while the business assembly provides the processing capability for each method. All incoming Web service requests should be delegated to the business component, rather than implementing the business logic directly in the Web service.

The methods in this class file must be decorated with any required reflection attributes, such as WebMethod and SoapDocumentMethod. You always had to do this, so this is not new. But there is added importance now because many of these attributes will be not be decorated elsewhere. Or, if they are, they will not propagate to your class file. For example, the SoapDocumentMethod attributes are not included in the interface definition assembly (although the XML serialization attributes are). These attributes are not automatically carried over to the class file when it implements the definition assembly. As a matter of practice, I make sure that the interface definition assembly is decorated with the required serialization attributes, but I leave out attributes that relate to WebService and WebMethod attributes. This approach is implementation agnostic, meaning that it makes no assumptions about what kind of class file will implement the interface definition assembly.

> **NOTE** *Reflection attributes provide additional metadata for your code. The .NET runtime uses this metadata for executing the code. Class members are said to be decorated with attributes. Reflection attributes are a powerful tool because they enable the same code listing to be processed in different ways, depending on how it is decorated. Chapter 3 has a more complete discussion of reflection attributes, and Table 3-1 (in Chapter 3) provides detailed property descriptions for the SoapDocumentMethod attribute.*

Step 5: Generate a Web Service Proxy Class File for Clients Based on the WSDL Document

Proxy class files can still be generated directly from the Web service WSDL document, so this step does not have to change with a revised architecture in order to still work. However, the auto-generated proxy class file will not automatically utilize the dedicated definition assembly. This creates a significant issue because the proxy class file maintains its own type and interface definitions. Your goal is to have a central repository for this information. So in the interest of type fidelity, you need to modify the auto-generated proxy file to utilize the definition assembly rather than a separate copy of the same information.

Separate copies can be modified, and there is nothing to stop you from altering a proxy file so that it can no longer call the Web service it is intended for. This is why it is good to derive all types and interfaces from a common source.

Step 6: Create a Web Service Client

The Web service client uses the generated proxy class file from Step 5 to set a reference to the new Web service. The client must also reference the type definition assembly from Step 1, so that they have a common understanding of the data types that are used by the Web services and its associated business assembly.

Some readers may see a red flag here because this approach creates a very tight coupling between the client and the Web service due to their mutual dependence on the same reference assembly. In contrast, it would be much easier to create a loosely coupled client that auto-generates a proxy file itself, using the Web service WSDL document. This auto-generated proxy file would include both methods and data types, so it would deviate from the more abstract approach that I am presenting here—namely, the approach of separating type definitions and method definitions into a dedicated assembly.

I am not advocating that you should always enforce this level of tight coupling between a Web service and its client. In some cases, this will not even be feasible because the client may not have access to a dedicated assembly. But this approach may be warranted in other cases, particularly when you have a sensitive business workflow, and you want to prevent any kind of miscommunication between a service and a client.

So, as with all the material in this book, absorb the information; consider the different approaches; but then decide which approach is most appropriate for your business requirements.

Design and Build a Service-Oriented Web Service

This section provides the information that you need to understand in order to build a message-oriented Web service for use in a service-oriented architecture. It is organized along the same six steps presented earlier and provides both conceptual information and implementation information.

Create the Definition Assembly (Step 1)

The definition assembly provides two important sets of information:

- Class definitions for all custom types that are exchanged in the system

- Interface definitions for each operation that the system supports

In this sense it is not unlike the auto-generated interface definition file from the last chapter. Recall that the type information in this file (StockTraderStub.cs) is auto-generated from an XSD schema file using the xsd.exe tool. The operations are manually inserted as abstract class methods that must be overridden by whatever class implements this file.

There are two differences between the definition assembly and the previous interface definition file:

The operations are documented as interfaces rather than abstract class methods. This is because a given class can only derive from one other class at a time. Web service classes, for example, must derive either directly or indirectly from the System.Web.Services.WebService class. The Web service class cannot implement an additional interface unless it is provided as an invariant interface.

The definition assembly does not include Web service and SOAP-related attribute decorations. This is because it will be referenced from a variety of different assemblies, some of which have nothing to do with Web services. However, the definition assembly can still include XML serialization attributes.

Figure 4-3 shows a UML class diagram for the definition assembly. Notice the following two important points:

1. The type definitions are encapsulated in dedicated classes (for example, Quote).

2. The method definitions are contained within an interface class called IStockTrader.

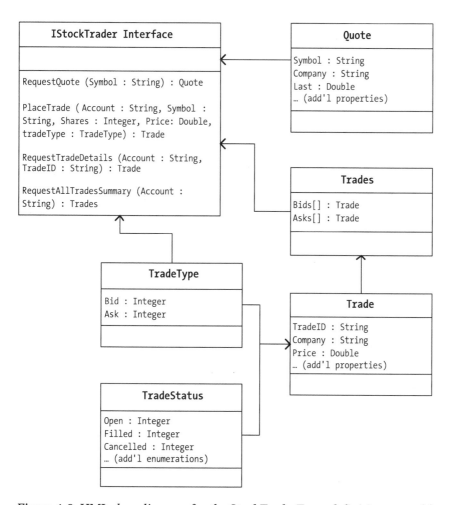

Figure 4-3. UML class diagram for the StockTraderTypes definition assembly

It is possible for a client project to reference the StockTraderTypes assembly solely for the purpose of accessing the custom data type definitions. The client does need to implement the interface class, just because it is included in the assembly. But of course if they do, then they will be required to implement every member of the interface.

To create the definition assembly, start by creating a new Class Library project in Visual Studio .NET called StockTraderTypes, and add to it a single class file also called StockTraderTypes.

Listing 4-1 shows high-level pseudo-code for the StockTraderTypes definition assembly.

Listing 4-1. Pseudo-Code Listing for the StockTraderTypes Definition Assembly

```
namespace StockTraderTypes
{
    public interface IStockTrader {}
    public class Quote {}
    public class Trade {}
    public class Trades {}
    public enum TradeStatus {}
    public enum TradeTypes {}
}
```

Listing 4-2 presents a more detailed code listing, excluding XML serialization attributes. These attributes are important because they directly relate the code elements to XML elements in the associated XSD schema (which is assigned to a qualified namespace at http://www.bluestonepartners.com/schemas/StockTrader/).

Listing 4-2. Detail Code Listing for the StockTraderTypes Definition Assembly

```
using System;
using System.Xml.Serialization;

namespace StockTraderTypes
  {
  public interface IStockTrader
  {
    Quote RequestQuote(string Symbol);
    Trade PlaceTrade(string Account, string Symbol, int Shares,  ➡
        System.Double   Price, TradeType tradeType);
    Trade RequestTradeDetails(string Account, string TradeID);
    Trades RequestAllTradesSummary(string Account);
  }
```

```
public class Quote
{
  public string Symbol;
  public string Company; // Additional type members not shown
}

public class Trade
{
  public string TradeID;
  public string Symbol; // Additional type members not shown
}

public class Trades
{
  public string Account;
  public Trade[] Bids;
  public Trade[] Asks;
}

public enum TradeStatus
{
  Ordered,
  Filled, // Additional type members not shown
}

public enum TradeType
{
  Bid,
  Ask
}

}
```

This is all the work that is required to create a definition assembly that can be reused across other components, services, and applications.

Create the Business Assembly (Step 2)

The business assembly implements the IStockTrader interface that is defined in the StockTraderTypes definition assembly. This logic was previously implemented directly in the Web service class file. But this design is very limiting because it isolates the business logic inside a specialized class file. The business assembly provides a standard middle-tier component that can be referenced and invoked by a wide variety of consumers, not just Web services.

Creating the business assembly requires three steps:

1. Create a new Class Library project in Visual Studio .NET called StockTraderBusiness, and add to it a single class file also called StockTraderBusiness.

2. Set a reference to the StockTraderTypes assembly. For now you can create all projects in the same solution, and then set a reference to the StockTraderTypes project (from the Projects tab in the Add Reference dialog box).

3. Import the StockTraderTypes namespace into the StockTraderBusiness class file and implement the IStockTrader class. Implement code for each of the interface operations. You will get compiler errors if you attempt to build the solution without implementing all of the operations.

Listing 4-3 displays the pseudo-code listing for the StockTraderBusiness business assembly.

Listing 4-3. Pseudo-Code Listing for the StockTraderBusiness Business Assembly

```
using System;
using StockTraderTypes;

namespace StockTraderBusiness
{

  public class StockTraderBusiness : StockTraderTypes.IStockTrader
  {
    public Quote RequestQuote(string Symbol)
    {
        // Implementation code not shown
    }
    public Trade PlaceTrade(string Account, string Symbol, int Shares, ➥
        System.Double Price, TradeType tradeType)
    {
        // Implementation code not shown
    }
    public Trade RequestTradeDetails(string Account, string TradeID)
    {
        // Implementation code not shown
    }
    public Trades RequestAllTradesSummary(string Account)
    {
        // Implementation code not shown
    }
  }

}
```

The business assembly is the sole location for implemented business logic and the final destination for incoming service requests. The previous listing looks very spare because it does not show the implementation code for any of the methods. You can refer to the sample project to view the full code listing. Very little implementation code is shown in this chapter because it is of secondary importance. It is more important that you feel comfortable with the interfaces and the architecture of the components.

Create the Web Service (Steps 3-5)

The previous version of the StockTrader Web service implemented an interface definition file for operations and types. This file is no longer needed because the same information is now provided by the definition assembly.

Create a new Web service project named StockTraderContracts in the Visual Studio .NET solution, and rename the .asmx file to StockTraderContracts. Use the Add Reference dialog box to set references to the StockTraderBusiness and StockTraderTypes assemblies.

Listing 4-4 displays the pseudo-code listing for the StockTraderContracts Web service.

Listing 4-4. Pseudo-Code Listing for the StockTraderContracts Web Service

```
using System.Web;
using System.Web.Services;
using System.Web.Services.Protocols;
using System.Web.Services.Description;

using StockTraderTypes;
using StockTraderBusiness;

namespace StockTrader
{

    public class StockTrader : System.Web.Services.WebService, ➡
        StockTraderTypes.IStockTrader
    {

    [WebMethod()]
    [SoapDocumentMethod(RequestNamespace=➡
        "http://www.bluestonepartners.com/schemas/StockTrader/",
        ResponseNamespace="http://www.bluestonepartners.com/schemas/StockTrader/",
        Use=SoapBindingUse.Literal, ParameterStyle=SoapParameterStyle.Bare)]
    [return: System.Xml.Serialization.XmlElement("Quote", Namespace=
        "http://www.bluestonepartners.com/schemas/StockTrader/")]
```

```
public Quote RequestQuote(string Symbol)
{
    // Implementation code not shown
}
 [WebMethod()]
//XML and SOAP serialization attributes not shown
public Trade PlaceTrade(string Account, string Symbol, int Shares, ➥
    System.Double Price, TradeType tradeType)
{
    // Implementation code not shown
}
 [WebMethod()]
//XML and SOAP serialization attributes not shown
public Trade RequestTradeDetails(string Account, string TradeID)
{
    // Implementation code not shown
}
 [WebMethod()]
//XML and SOAP serialization attributes not shown
public Trades RequestAllTradesSummary(string Account)
{
    // Implementation code not shown
}

}

}
```

The Web service methods no longer implement their own business logic. Instead, every method must delegate incoming requests to the business assembly. For example, Listing 4-5 shows how the RequestQuote Web method delegates an incoming service request to the RequestQuote method in the business assembly.

Listing 4-5. Delegation in the RequestQuote Web Method

```
[WebMethod()]
// XML and SOAP attributes not shown
public Quote RequestQuote(string Symbol)
{
    StockTraderBusiness b = new StockTraderBusiness();
    Quote q = b.RequestQuote(Symbol);
    return q;
}
```

The code is extremely simple because the Web service and the business assembly share the same type definitions and implement the same interface. The communication between the parties is seamless because they share a common vocabulary.

Figure 4-4 shows the Solution Explorer window for the project so far, with the References nodes expanded so that you can see how the assembly references are configured in each of the three projects: StockTraderTypes, StockTraderBusiness, and StockTraderContracts.

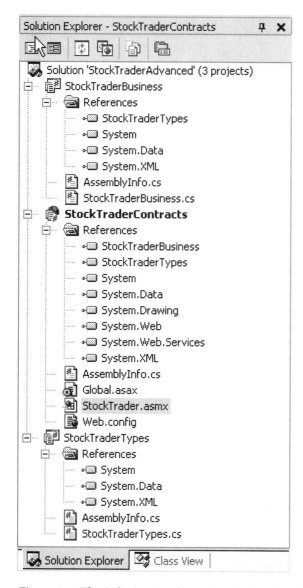

Figure 4-4. The Solution Explorer view for the StockTraderAdvanced solution

Create the Web Service Client (Step 6)

In this example, you are going to see how to build a tightly coupled Web service client that references the same definition assembly as the Web service itself. But as I clarified earlier, it is often advisable to implement a loosely coupled Web service client, whereby the client generates its own proxy file based on the Web service WSDL document and its associated XSD schemas. In fact, service-oriented architecture promotes loose coupling between Web services and consumers.

As I stated earlier, my purpose in building a tightly coupled Web service client is to show you an alternate approach to building clients. In some cases, you will want to build a tightly coupled Web service client in order to prevent any miscommunication or misunderstanding between the Web service and its client as to what methods and types are supported. Certainly, type definitions can change, and so tight coupling can add an additional burden to the developer of the client. However, WSDL definitions can also change just as easily, and there is no clear way for a Web service to communicate interface changes to its clients.

Ultimately, I advocate the design approach of loose coupling between a Web service and its clients. However, I believe that the Web service itself should reference a type definition assembly, and should delegate all of its business logic to a dedicated business assembly. So, the material in this chapter provides everything you need to understand and implement my design approach. You can, however, feel free to choose between a traditional loosely coupled client versus a more specialized tightly coupled client. We will look at both approaches next.

Build a Loosely Coupled Web Service Client

Add a new console application named StockTraderConsole to the Visual Studio .NET solution, and then do one of the following:

- Generate the proxy class manually with the wsdl.exe command-line utility applied to the Web service WSDL document, or

- Use the Add Reference wizard in Visual Studio .NET to automatically generate the proxy class in the client project.

Once you have generated the proxy class, you simply reference it directly from the client code, as shown in Listing 4-6.

Listing 4-6. Web Service Consumer Code

```
// Create an instance of the Web service proxy
StockTraderProxy serviceProxy = new StockTraderProxy();

// Retrieve the Web Service URI from app.config
serviceProxy.Url = ConfigurationSettings.AppSettings["remoteHost"];
```

```
// Call the Web service to request a quote
Quote q = serviceProxy.RequestQuote("MSFT");

// Display the Quote results in the form
Console.WriteLn("\t:Company:\t " + q.Company);
Console.WriteLn("\t:Symbol:\t " + q.Symbol);
Console.WriteLn("\t:Last:\t " + q.Last.ToString());
Console.WriteLn("\t:Prev Close:\t " + q.Previous_Close.ToString());
```

For more information on building loosely coupled clients, please refer to Chapter 3.

Build a Tightly Coupled Web Service Client

Auto-generated proxy class files are completely self-contained and essentially provide the client with a separate local copy of the interface and type definitions that the Web service supports. If the Web service interface changes, then the client will not automatically pick up on these changes unless they clear the existing Web reference and regenerate the proxy class. You can manage this risk by modifying the auto-generated proxy class to conform to the standard interface and type definitions that are contained in the StockTraderTypes assembly.

Add a new console application project named StockTraderConsole to the Visual Studio .NET solution file and copy over the proxy class file from the previous chapter's StockTrader Web service. Alternatively, you can auto-generate the proxy class from within the StockTraderConsole project as follows:

Step 1: Use the Add Web Reference Wizard to auto-generate the proxy class for the StockTraderContracts Web service at `http://localhost/ StockTraderContracts/StockTrader.asmx`.

Step 2: The auto-generated proxy class file is called Reference.cs and is stored in the solution under the Web References\[Reference Name]\ Reference.map subproject folder. (If you do not see this file, you can use the Project ➤ Show All Files menu option to expand all files.)

Step 3: Open the Reference.cs file and copy the entire code listing over to a new C# class file called StockConsoleProxy.cs.

Rename the proxy class file to StockConsoleProxy, and then do the following:

Step 1: Add a reference from the StockTraderConsole project to the StockTraderTypes assembly.

Step 2: In the StockConsoleProxy class, import the StockTraderTypes namespace, and add the IStockTrader interface to the StockConsoleProxy interface list immediately following SoapHttpClientProtocol.

Step 3: Comment out all of the type definitions in the StockConsoleProxy class. These include Quote, Trade, Trades, TradeType, and TradeStatus. They are now redundant because the definition assembly contains the same type definitions.

The pseudo-code for the proxy class now reads as shown in Listing 4-7 (modifications from the previous, or auto-generated, proxy classes are shown in bold).

Listing 4-7. The Proxy Class for the StockTraderContracts Web Service, Modified to Reference the Type Definition Assembly StockTraderTypes

```
using System.Web.Services;
using System.Web.Services.Protocols;

using StockTraderTypes;

[System.Web.Services.WebServiceBindingAttribute(Name="StockTraderServiceSoap",
    Namespace="http://www.bluestonepartners.com/schemas/StockTrader")]
public class StockConsoleProxy : SoapHttpClientProtocol, ➡
    StockTraderTypes.IStockTrader
{

    // Pseudo-code only: implementations and attributes are not shown
    public Quote RequestQuote() {}
    public System.IAsyncResult BeginRequestQuote() {}
    public System.IAsyncResult EndRequestQuote() {}

    // Additional operations are not shown
    // These include PlaceTrade(), RequestTradeDetails(),
    // and RequestAllTradesSummary()

    // Type definitions are commented out of the proxy class
    // because they are redundant to the type definition assembly
    // These include Quote, Trade, Trades, TradeType and TradeStatus

}
```

These are trivial modifications because the proxy class already implements all of the IStockTrader interface members. The benefit of explicitly adding the

IStockTrader interface is to ensure that the proxy class remains constrained in the way it implements the StockTrader operations. You could modify the proxy class in many other ways, but as long as the StockTrader operations remain untouched (interface-wise at least), the client application will compile successfully.

Once the proxy class has been modified, the client code can now be implemented in the console application. The StockTraderTypes namespace must be imported into the client class file so that the client can make sense of the type definitions. No additional steps are required to use the definitions assembly. Listing 4-8 shows the client code listing for calling the RequestQuote operation.

Listing 4-8. Client Code Listing for Calling the RequestQuote Operation

```
using StockTraderTypes;

namespace StockTraderConsole2
{
class StockTraderConsole2
{

[STAThread]
static void Main(string[] args)
{
StockTraderConsole2 client = new StockTraderConsole2();
client.Run();
}

public void Run()
{
// Create an instance of the Web service proxy
StockConsoleProxy serviceProxy = new StockConsoleProxy();

// Configure the proxy
serviceProxy.Url = ConfigurationSettings.AppSettings["remoteHost"];

// Submit the request to the service
Console.WriteLine("Calling {0}", serviceProxy.Url);
string Symbol = "MSFT";
Quote q = serviceProxy.RequestQuote(Symbol);

// Display the response
Console.WriteLine("Web Service Response:");
Console.WriteLine("");
Console.WriteLine( "\tSymbol:\t\t" + q.Symbol );
Console.WriteLine( "\tCompany:\t" + q.Company );
```

```
Console.WriteLine( "\tLast Price:\t" + q.Last );
Console.WriteLine( "\tPrevious Close:\t" + q.Previous_Close );
}


}
}
```

Figure 4-5 displays a client console application that interfaces to the StockTraderContracts Web service using the modified proxy class. Please refer to the sample application (available from the Downloads section of the Apress Web site at http://www.apress.com) for full code listings.

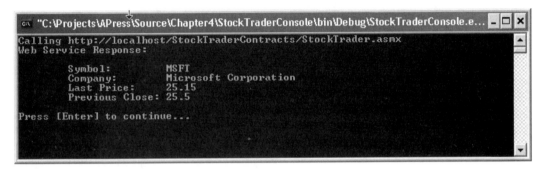

Figure 4-5. Client console application for the StockTraderContracts Web service

This concludes the overview of how to build a tightly coupled Web service client. Again, I would like to emphasize that this approach is not consistent with a pure SOA environment where the clients remain completely decoupled from the Web services they consume. However, it is always useful to consider alternative approaches and to realize new possibilities even if they never make it into a production environment.

Next, I will discuss a type of component that is unique to the service-oriented environment: the service agent.

Design and Build a Service Agent

Service agent components are essentially translator components that act as the intermediary between a business component and an external Web service. By *external*, I mean external to the domain where the business object is located. Service agents were discussed in some detail in Chapter 1, and are included in Figure 4-1 in this chapter. Briefly, the purpose of a service agent is to eliminate complexity in a business component by managing all interactions with an external service. If service agents did not exist, then the business component would need to implement proxy classes and all of the associated error handling logic for working with external services. Clearly, this adds an undesirable layer of code and complexity to the business component that is superfluous because the business client will never call this code directly.

For example, consider Company A, which has built a business component that processes stock trades and provides stock quotes. In order to provide this functionality, the business component uses an external Web service that is provided by a premier brokerage company, Company B. Company A uses its own custom data types, which are encapsulated in the StockTraderTypes assembly. Company B, however, defines its own data types that are equivalent but not the same as Company A's. For example, Company A uses a Quote data type that defines a property called Open, for the day's opening share price. Company B uses a Quote data type that defines an equivalent property called Open_Ext. Company A uses strings for all of its custom data type properties, whereas Company B uses a mix of strings, floats, and dates.

Given these differences, Company A's service agent will perform two important functions:

1. It will implement the infrastructure that is required to communicate with Company B's external service. It will be responsible for the maintenance work that will be required if the external service updates its interface.

2. It will translate the responses from the external service and will relay them back to Company A's business component using a mutually understood interface.

The benefits of a service agent are clear: The service agent eliminates complexity for Service A's business component because it encapsulates all of the implementation details for interacting with the Web service, and relays the requests back in the format that the business component wants. Figure 4-6 provides a schematic representation of this architecture.

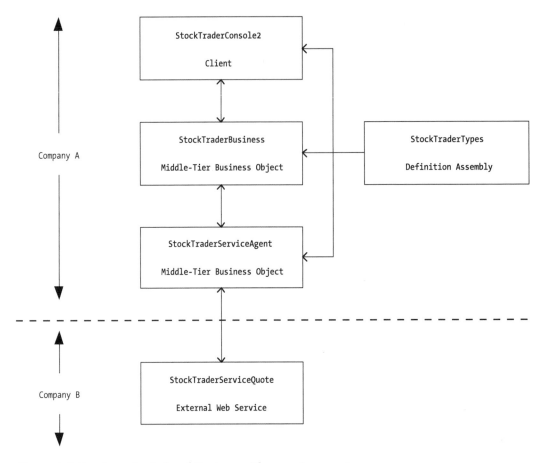

Figure 4-6. Service-oriented architecture with a service agent

Now let's look at how you implement this architecture in code.

Implement the StockTrader SOA Application Using a Service Agent

The StockTrader Web service has evolved in this chapter to where it delegates all requests to a business assembly (StockTraderBusiness). If a client contacts the Web service to request a stock quote, the Web service delegates the request to the business object's RequestQuote method. The Web service does not know or care how this method returns a stock quote, but it does expect to receive one every time it makes a request.

For the next evolution of the StockTrader Web service, your company signs a partnership agreement with another company that is a premier provider of stock quotes. You decide that going forward, the StockTraderBusiness assembly will delegate all stock quote requests to this external service. The StockTrader

Web service will continue to delegate requests to the business assembly, but the business assembly, in turn, will delegate the requests again, this time to an external Web service. You decide to build a service agent to minimize any change to the business assembly. Figure 4-7 shows the Solution Explorer for the solution that you are going to build, with selective References nodes expanded, so that you can see the relationships between the different components.

Figure 4-7. Solution Explorer for the StockTrader SOA application, including a service agent

The five components in this application are as follows:

1. **StockTraderConsole2:** The client application, providing a user interface

2. **StockTraderBusiness:** The middle-tier business component that handles processing for the client

3. **StockTraderServiceAgent:** The service agent used by the business component for communicating with external services

4. **StockTraderTypes:** The common type definition assembly, which is referenced by the three preceding components

5. **StockTraderServiceQuote:** The external Web service

If this gets confusing, you can consult either Figures 4-6 or 4-7, each including all five of these components. Let's look at how to build each component in turn, going from bottom to top, starting with the external StockTraderServiceQuote Web service.

The External Web Service (StockTraderServiceQuote)

StockTraderServiceQuote is a simple Web service that provides a single Web method for requesting stock quotes (RequestQuoteExt), and it returns its own equivalent to the StockTraderTypes.Quote type, which is named QuoteExt. The Quote and QuoteExt types are equivalent, but they differ from each other in three ways:

1. The QuoteExt type conforms to a different qualified namespace from the Quote type. Each type conforms to its own XSD schema file.

2. The QuoteExt type does not contain equivalents to the Quote type's Change and Percent_Change properties.

3. The QuoteExt type provides a timestamp property named DateTime_Ext, which is of type System.DateTime. The Quote type provides an equivalent timestamp property named DateTime that is of type String.

These are admittedly minor differences, but they illustrate the point: When you call an external service, it is unlikely that their type definitions will be equivalent to yours. You have to be prepared for some manual work to translate the differences.

In real life, of course, you would not have to create the external service yourself, but for the purposes of this demonstration you do.

The Service Agent (StockTraderServiceAgent)

The service agent is a companion assembly to the business assembly, and is installed in local (rather than remote) proximity. The service agent implements the same interface and type definitions as the business assembly by referencing the StockTraderTypes assembly (as shown in Figure 4-6). The service agent also includes a proxy class for the StockTraderServiceQuote external Web service.

Listing 4-9 shows the code listing for the service agent, including the complete listing for its RequestQuote method.

Listing 4-9. The StockTraderServiceAgent Code Listing

```
using System;
using StockTraderTypes;

namespace StockTraderServiceAgent
{
    public class StockTraderServiceAgent : StockTraderTypes.IStockTrader
    {
    public StockTraderServiceAgent(){}

    public Quote RequestQuote(string Symbol)
    {
        Quote q = null;

        // Request a Quote from the external service
        QuoteExt qe;
        StockQuoteService serviceProxy = new StockQuoteService();
        qe = serviceProxy.RequestQuoteExt("MSFT");

        // Create a local Quote object (from the StockTraderTypes namespace)
        q = new Quote();

        // Map the external QuoteExt object to the local Quote object
        // This requires some manual work because the types
        // do not map exactly to each other
        q.Symbol = Symbol;
        q.Company = qe.Company_Ext;
        q.DateTime = qe.DateTime_Ext.ToString("mm/dd/yyyy hh:mm:ss");
        q.High = qe.High_Ext;
        q.Low = qe.Low_Ext;
        q.Open = qe.Open_Ext;
        q.Last = qe.Last_Ext;
        q.Previous_Close = qe.Previous_Close_Ext;
```

```
            q.Change = (qe.Last_Ext - qe.Open_Ext);
            q.PercentChange = q.Change/q.Last;
            q.High_52_Week = qe.High_52_Week_Ext;
            q.Low_52_Week = qe.Low_52_Week_Ext;

            return q;
        }

        public Trade PlaceTrade(string Account, string Symbol, int Shares, ➥
            Double Price, TradeType tradeType)
        {
            // Implementation not shown
        }

        public Trades RequestAllTradesSummary(string Account)
        {
            // Implementation not shown
        }

        public Trade RequestTradeDetails(string Account, string TradeID)
        {
            // Implementation not shown
        }

    }
}
```

The code listing is very straightforward, and shows how the service agent delegates its RequestQuote method to the external service's RequestQuoteExt method. The service agent performs some manual translations to map between its native Quote type and the external QuoteExt type. Finally, the agent returns a native Quote object to the consuming application, which in this case is the business assembly.

The Business Assembly (StockTraderBusiness)

The business component sets references to both the service agent assembly and the definition assembly of custom types. Listing 4-10 shows how the business component calls the service agent.

Listing 4-10. The StockTrader Business Component Calling the Service Agent

```
using System;
using StockTraderTypes;
using StockTraderServiceAgent;

namespace StockTraderBusiness
{
    public class StockTraderBusiness : StockTraderTypes.IStockTrader
    {
        public StockTraderBusiness() {}

    public Quote RequestQuote(string Symbol)
    {

        // Create a new Quote object
        Quote q = new Quote();

        // Call the service agent
        StockTraderServiceAgent sa = new StockTraderServiceAgent();
        q = sa.RequestQuote(Symbol);

        return q;
    }

    }
}
```

As you would expect, the listing is very simple because the business assembly no longer has to provide its own implementation of the Quote request logic.

In summary, service agents are an elegant solution when you need to interface with one or more external services and wish to isolate the code that handles the communication. Service agents provide stability to a business assembly by bearing the responsibility of ensuring successful calls to external services, and returning results in a form that the business assembly natively understands. Service agents can also act as intermediaries between two or more Web services.

This concludes the discussion of how to build basic service-oriented Web services.

Summary

In this chapter, I expanded on the previous discussion of message-oriented Web services and showed you a six-step process for designing and building a service-oriented Web service from scratch. These steps are

Step 1: Create a dedicated type definition assembly.

Step 2: Create a dedicated business assembly.

Step 3: Create the Web service using the type definition assembly.

Step 4: Implement the business interface in the Web service.

Step 5: Delegate processing logic to the business assembly.

Step 6: Create a Web service client.

You saw how to build both tightly coupled clients and loosely coupled clients. In most SOA applications, you will want to build loosely coupled clients, but under some circumstances you may want a higher level of control over the type definitions. Tightly coupled clients reference the same type definition as the assembly, rather than generating their own using a proxy class.

Finally, I discussed the service agent component, which is a special feature of service-oriented applications. The service agent manages communication between a business assembly and an external Web service. It can also act as the intermediary between two or more Web services.

The goal of this chapter is to help you rethink your approach to Web services design so that you can start thinking in terms of service-oriented architecture.

CHAPTER 5

Web Services Enhancements 2.0

WEB SERVICES TECHNOLOGY has evolved rapidly since its debut a few years ago. Businesses were initially reluctant to fully adopt the technology because of a lack of industry-standard specifications to govern such important issues as message security and reliable delivery. Businesses will not send sensitive information across the wire if it is vulnerable to detection. And they will not implement large-scale distributed systems with this technology if the reliability of the messages cannot be guaranteed.

Web services technology was initially tailored toward point-to-point communication, based on the familiar HTTP Request/Response model in which a client request generates a timely server response. This model works well for Internet browsing, but it proves to be very limiting for distributed service applications. Web services that are involved in business processing cannot always generate a timely response. The business process may be long-running, or a required back-end system may be offline. There are times when a Web service cannot send a timely and complete response to a client request.

In addition, the point-to-point communication model proves to be overly limiting for executing complex distributed business processes. It is unlikely that one Web service has the ability to execute a business process 100 percent of the time. More likely it needs to interact with other systems and perhaps even with other Web services. Clearly, it is a problem if a Web service receives a request message, but then is unable to forward it on to other services for additional processing.

Industry leaders have been working together for several years to address the current limitations with Web services technology. Standards committees have formed to bring a sense of order to the wide variety of available technologies and versions. In Chapter 1, I discussed the WS-I Basic Profile, which outlines a set of Web-related technologies by version number and groups them together into a standard profile. You are considered to be in compliance with this standard if you are implementing the exact technology versions in this profile. In addition, nonprofit organizations such as OASIS are important forums where companies are actively cooperating in the development and advancement of new standards and specifications.

Companies, including Microsoft, IBM, BEA Systems, and VeriSign, are working on a set of specifications called the *Web Service Specifications* (WS-*) that are based on XML, SOAP, and WSDL extensibility models. Together, these specifications define a set of composable features to make Web services "secure, reliable, and transacted," as the standard tag line often reads. Composability refers to the fact that you can pick and choose the selected specifications that apply to your particular business scenario. None of the specifications are ever required, even the security specifications. Though as they become more widely accepted, it is likely that a subset of the specifications will be required in any robust, business-quality Web service.

The WS-Specifications are incredibly important to the future of Web services technology and to service-oriented architecture. Microsoft provides a set of tools for .NET called the *Web Services Enhancements* (WSE). WSE includes managed APIs for implementing selected WS-specifications in a composable manner. I say *selected* because the WS-Specifications continue to evolve, and it will take time for all of the current standards to be submitted, accepted, and then incorporated into Web Services Enhancements. New WS-Specifications continue to be released, so the future promises to hold many interesting and important developments in this evolving technology.

This chapter lays the groundwork for the second half of the book, where I will focus intensively on how to implement the WS-Specifications using Microsoft's Web Services Enhancements 2.0 for .NET. This chapter includes the following:

- Overview of the WS-Specifications

- Introduction to Web Services Enhancements 2.0

- Installing and configuring WSE 2.0, including the test certificates

- Using the WSE 2.0 utilities

This chapter is a must read in order to get the most out of the second half of the book. It will help you to understand the WS-Specifications, and how WSE fits into the context of service-oriented architecture. It will also get you started with installing and configuring Web Services Enhancements 2.0, including the test certificates, which are required for many of the code samples.

Overview of the WS-Specifications

The purpose of the WS-Specifications is to establish a set of standards for enterprise-level, service-oriented Web services. The focus of the specifications is on Web services in general, and on messages in particular, because messages are the essential aspects of a service-oriented architecture. Without messages, Web services cannot communicate. And without secure, reliable messages, businesses will never trust that they can send sensitive information between Web services. The integrity of the message is the key to gaining acceptance for Web services as a robust business solution.

Each of the WS-Specifications addresses a different business-critical issue. For example, WS-Security addresses how to implement digital signing and encryption technology in Web services. WS-Reliable Messaging addresses how to ensure that messages are always delivered, even if one part of the system is temporarily unavailable. Each specification is recorded directly in the header of the applicable SOAP message, using a dedicated XML schema. Some specifications, such as WS-Security, also modify the body of the SOAP message for encryption.

Listing 5-1 shows one example of a SOAP message that implements multiple specifications, including WS-Addressing, WS-Security, and WS-Reliable Messaging. Notice that the message header is divided into distinct parts, and that the individual specification schemas do not overlap. This is known as *composability* because the individual specifications may be added or removed from the message header as needed.

Listing 5-1. SOAP Message Illustrating Web Service Composability

```
<s:Envelope xmlns:S="http://www.w3.org/2002/12/soap-envelope"
     xmlns:wsa=http://schemas.xmlsoap.org/ws/2003/03/addressing
         xmlns:wsse=http://schemas.xmlsoap.org/ws/2003/03/security
         xmlns:wrm="http://schemas.xmlsoap.org/ws/2003/03/reliablemessaging">

<s:Header>

<!--WS-Addressing -->
<wsa:From>
     <wsa:Address>http://www.bluestonepartners.com/Buyer</wsa:Address>
</wsa:From>
<wsa:ReplyTo>
     <wsa:Address>http://www.bluestonepartners.com/Broker</wsa:Address>
</wsa:ReplyTo>
<wsa:To>http://www.bluestonerealty.com/Seller</wsa:To>
<wsa:Action>http://www.bluestonerealty.com/MakeOffer</wsa:Action>

<!--WS-Security -->
<wsse:Security>
     <wsse:BinarySecurityToken ValueType="wsse:X509v3"
         EncodingType="wsse:Base64Binary">
             JKH8dH7SJa8.......SKJa87DJsAK3
     </wsse:BinarySecurityToken>
</wsse:Security>
```

```
<!—WS-ReliableMessaging -->
<wrm:Sequence>
    <wsu:Identifier>http://www.bluestonerealty.com/mls123</wsu:Identifier>
    <wrm:MessageNumber>32<wrm:MessageNumber>
</wrm:Sequence>

</s:Header>

<s:body xmlns:po=
      "http://www.bluestonerealty.com/PurchaseHouse">
    <po:PurchaseHouse>
    ...
    </po:PurchaseHouse>

</s:body>

</s:Envelope>
```

As you can see, each of the specifications is encapsulated within the SOAP header, and each supports distinctive element tags so that no specification information can conflict. Web service composability is essential for allowing developers to choose which specifications are important for their Web services. In addition, this feature keeps message payloads smaller in size by not including element tags for unused specifications.

Introducing the WS-Specifications

Instead of simply listing out the various WS-Specifications, it is more useful to present them in the context of the framework's goals. There are different perspectives on what the full set of goals are because the specifications are always evolving and are being drawn together by diverse coalitions of companies and organizations. But in my mind, there are six primary goals for the WS-Specifications, as discussed next.

Interoperability

Web services must be able to communicate even if they are built and operated on different platforms. Web service messages must use standard protocols and specifications that are broadly accepted, such as the WS-I Basic Profile, which includes XML, SOAP, and WSDL. Interoperability is the key to widespread acceptance of Web services for handling critical business processes.

Composability

This is a design principle that is fundamental to the WS-Specifications. The term *composability* alludes to the fact that many of the WS-Specifications are independent of each other and that a given Web service may not need to implement them all. For example, one Web service may require security but not reliable messaging. Another Web service may require transactions, but not policy. Composability allows a developer to implement only those specifications that are required. The WS-Specifications support this because they are implemented as discrete sections within the SOAP message header (see Listing 5-1 for an example).

Security

Protocol-level security mechanisms such as HTTPS are currently in wide use, but they are designed for point-to-point security, rather than message-oriented security, which is much more dynamic. The WS-Security specification is a message-oriented security solution that supports the dynamic nature of messages. With WS-Security, the security information is stored directly in the message header, so it stays with the message, even if the message gets routed to more than one endpoint. Messages must carry their security information with them so they can remain dynamic. The WS-Trust and WS-Secure Conversation specifications enable you to create a secure token service that procures security tokens for the duration of a specific conversation between a client and a Web service.

Description and Discovery

Web services may be accessed from different clients across different domains. Web services must therefore be capable of publishing their metadata so that potential clients know how to call them. The WSDL document publishes supported types, operations, and port information. The WS-Policy specification documents and enforces usage requirements and preferences for a Web service. For example, WS-Policy will enforce that incoming SOAP requests must be signed and encrypted with digital certificates only, rather than any type of security token. The UDDI specification aims to provide a mechanism for clients to look up Web service metadata in a centralized directory.

Messaging and Delivery

The biggest vulnerability for a message besides security is the risk that it may never reach its intended destination. Or worse, that not only does the message fail to reach the destination, but the sender is also unaware that it never arrived.

You cannot correct a problem if you do not know it occurred. The WS-Reliable Messaging specification establishes a framework that is designed to keep all parties informed of where messages are and whether they arrived. This is critical in an architecture where a message may get routed between multiple endpoints. Failure at one endpoint should not bring down the entire workflow that the message is a part of.

Transactions

Transaction processing is a way of orchestrating multiple related business operations so that they succeed or fail together, and thereby preserve the integrity of the overall workflow. Transaction management is an extremely difficult challenge in a service-oriented architecture. Web services are inherently disconnected, stateless components that do not by nature participate in broadly distributed transactions. The WS-Coordination, WS-Atomic Transaction, and WS-Business Activity specifications are designed to address the challenge of implementing transactions across distributed Web services.

The WS-Specifications Covered in This Book

The WS-Specifications will allow developers to build Web services that are interoperable, reliable, secure, and transacted. Ultimately, the overarching goal is for Web services technology to make it into the business mainstream, and to be considered as good a business solution as more established technologies.

This book does not cover all of the available WS-Specifications for two reasons: First, it is impractical because some of the specifications are too new or too poorly established to be useful to most people. Second, it is problematic because WSE implements only a few of the available WS-Specifications, albeit many of the most important ones.

With these points in mind, here is a list of the WS-Specifications I will be covering in this book:

- WS-Security

- WS-Policy

- WS-Policy Assertions

- WS-Policy Attachments

- WS-Security Policy

- WS-Trust

- WS-Secure Conversation

- WS-Addressing

- WS-Reliable Messaging

Perhaps the most glaring omission from the current WSE 2.0 is the absence of the transaction-related family of specifications, including WS-Coordination and WS-Atomic Transaction. But many other important specifications are present, most notably WS-Security, WS-Policy, and the WS-Addressing specifications. Omissions in WSE do not equate to insufficiency because it continues to evolve along with the WS-Specifications themselves. WSE 2.0 will always lag behind to some degree because it takes time to package the specifications into developer-friendly APIs. Microsoft is working on a related initiative called *Indigo*, which will provide integrated support for message-oriented technology directly in the operating system, including greatly expanded infrastructure support. Many of the tasks that we must write complex code for today will become simpler in Indigo. You can read more about Indigo in Chapter 10.

The Appendix lists a number of useful references for learning more about the WS-Specifications. Surprisingly, the original WS-Specification documents are highly readable and very informative. They do not, of course, cover any vendor-specific developer toolkit, such as WSE. But they provide clear definitions and explanations of a specification, along with examples and references on how the specification is encoded within a SOAP message.

> **TIP** *You can find links to the original WS-Specification documents at*
> `http://www-106.ibm.com/developerworks/views/webservices/standards.jsp`.

One last thing to keep in mind is that just because a specification is absent from WSE does not mean that you cannot implement it yourself using custom code. The .NET Framework gives you support classes for working with XML, SOAP, and Web services, namely most of the core Web services technologies. In a sense, WSE provides you convenience, which is something you would rather have, but something that you can also live without if you have to. Developers already have a natural instinct to be self-motivated and to build custom solutions when nothing else is readily available. I am not advocating that you find your own way to implement something that should be standard. In the absence of a canned solution, you still have the tools to build a credible alternative solution yourself. However, be prepared for considerable complexity!

In general, this book will remain focused on implementing solutions using the WSE support classes. But at times, I will show you ways to make up for deficiencies in WSE so that you can remain true to the spirit of the specification while using additional support technologies. As a .NET developer, you will find that the current version of WSE, along with a measure of creative thinking, will bring a heightened maturity to your Web services development efforts. WSE enables you to implement many of the features that a robust, business-oriented solution should include.

Welcome to the dynamic, evolving world of service-oriented architecture with Web Services Enhancements!

Introducing Web Services Enhancements 2.0

Web Services Enhancements (WSE) generally refers to both a software development toolkit and an add-on processing infrastructure for implementing the WS-Specifications in .NET projects. From an infrastructure perspective, WSE is basically a processing engine for applying the WS-Specifications to SOAP messages. As you have seen, WS-Specifications are stamped across different parts of a SOAP message. All of the WS-Specifications append to the SOAP message header, while some of them also modify the SOAP message body directly (such as the WS-Security specifications). WSE automatically modifies SOAP messages to implement the WS-Specifications. It also provides the infrastructure for processing these SOAP messages. In this sense, it is similar to the ASP.NET Web services infrastructure, which provides SOAP and communications infrastructure support for the Web services you create using a friendlier API. Overall, the goal of WSE is to save developers from having to write custom code to implement basic required Web service infrastructure (such as security and policy).

WSE 2.0 is an SDK package for Microsoft .NET developers that includes the following:

The Microsoft.Web.Services2 assembly: Provides an API and includes several support classes, such as SOAP extensions and custom handlers.

Documentation and help files: These show you how to use and configure the WSE API and utilities.

QuickStart samples: These show you how to code with WSE.

Configuration Editor: A utility that provides a GUI interface for configuring WSE in your .NET projects.

X509 Certificate Tool: A utility that helps you work with X.509 digital certificates.

Policy Wizard: A utility that provides a GUI for generating XML policy expression files (located inside the Configuration Editor).

How the WSE Processing Infrastructure Works

WSE installs a set of filters that intercept and process inbound and outbound SOAP request messages, as shown in Figure 5-1. The WSE filters work together inside a processing pipeline that also integrates with the ASP.NET processing pipeline. When a client application generates a SOAP request that includes WS enhancements, it specifies these in code using the API provided by WSE. When the message is sent out, it goes through a set of WSE filters that translate the code into SOAP extensions that are then applied directly to the SOAP message.

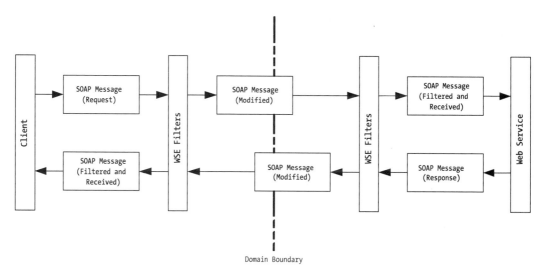

Figure 5-1. WSE processing of SOAP messages

The WSE filters are dedicated to specific WS-Specifications, or to groups of related specifications, including

- Security (including WS-Security)

- Policy (including WS-Policy and WS-Policy Attachments)

- Messaging (including WS-Addressing)

WSE is an extension to the existing ASP.NET framework, and is dedicated to modifying and processing SOAP messages. WSE must be configured to work with a project. Even if it is installed on your machine, it will not automatically apply to your projects unless they are configured to use it. When you use WSE in a project, you register one of its assembly types as a SOAP extension class.

When you want to use WSE in a project, you must add a reference to the Microsoft.Web.Services2 project. You must also register the Web services configuration class in the project's web.config file, as shown in Listing 5-2.

Listing 5-2. The WSE Configuration Class

```
<configuration>
  <configSections>
    <section name="microsoft.web.services2"
        type="Microsoft.Web.Services2.Configuration.WebServicesConfiguration,
        Microsoft.Web.Services2, Version=2.0.0.0, Culture=neutral,
        PublicKeyToken=31bf3856ad364e35" />
  </configSections>
</configuration>
```

If the project is an ASP.NET Web service or application, then you must also register the WSE SOAP extension class in the web.config file, as shown in Listing 5-3.

Listing 5-3. The WSE SOAP Extension Type

```
<system.web>
    <webServices>
        <soapExtensionTypes>
            <add type="Microsoft.Web.Services2.WebServicesExtension,
                Microsoft.Web.Services2, Version=2.0.0.0, Culture=neutral,
                PublicKeyToken=31bf3856ad364e35" priority="1" group="0" />
        </soapExtensionTypes>
    </webServices>
  </system.web>
```

This step instructs WSE to process the project's SOAP messages through its filters. By default, WSE automatically applies all of its filters to SOAP messages. However, you can optimize the process by turning off selected filters. For example, if you do not implement routing and referral, then you can turn off the related filters. This simply means that WSE will stop looking for these related elements when it processes incoming and outbound SOAP messages.

> **NOTE**   *WSE 2.0 ships with a utility called the Configuration Editor, which will automatically generate Listings 5-2 and 5-3 for you. These listings are the same in every project, so you should not have to manually enter them. The Configuration Editor is reviewed later in this chapter.*

How WSE Works with ASP.NET

WSE provides an API for applying WS-Specifications to SOAP messages. The key player in the WSE class framework is the SoapContext class, which directly records the Web specification options and then later makes them available to the WSE filters for processing. The SoapContext class applies to both request and response messages, and provides you with a programmatic window to examine the contents of a SOAP message, including its envelope, header, and body contents. Listing 5-4 shows you one example of using the SoapContext class to examine the security elements in a SOAP message.

Listing 5-4. Examining Message Security Elements Using the SoapContext Class

```
using Microsoft.Web.Services2;
using Microsoft.Web.Services2.Security;
using Microsoft.Web.Services2.Security.Tokens;

SoapContext requestContext = RequestSoapContext.Current;

foreach (ISecurityElement objElem in requestContext.Security.Elements)
{
if (objElem is MessageSignature)
{
MessageSignature clientSignature = (MessageSignature)objElem;

if (clientSignature.SignatureToken is X509SecurityToken)
{
// Add code to process the X509SecurityToken
}
else if (clientSignature.SignatureToken is UsernameToken)
{
// Add code to process the UsernameToken
}
}
}
```

Table 5-1 provides a summary of important SoapContext class properties. Many of these properties provide access to specialized classes with their own nested API. For example, the Security property provides access to the SoapHeader class called Security, which provides support members for examining existing security information and for appending new security information to the SOAP message header.

Table 5-1. The SoapContext Class Properties

Property	Description
Addressing	Provides access to the collection of WS-Addressing elements assigned to the SOAP message via the AddressingHeaders class.
Attachments	Provides the collection of DIME attachments assigned to the SOAP message via the DimeAttachmentCollection class.
Envelope	Provides direct access to the SOAP envelope via the SoapEnvelope class. This class provides several additional classes and properties that are useful for retrieving the contents of the SOAP envelope and body, via classes and properties, or directly as XML.
ExtendedSecurity	Indicates a collection of additional Security objects providing security information for other recipients besides the ultimate recipient of the SOAP message. These are used when routing the message across multiple recipients.
IsInbound	Indicates whether the SOAP message is incoming (true) or outbound (false).
Referrals	Provides the collection of referral elements assigned to the SOAP message via the ReferralsCollection class.
Security	Provides the security headers for the ultimate recipient of the SOAP message via the Security class.

As you look through the table, remember that the SoapContext class is always referenced in context, meaning that when you reference it in code, it will always be holding the contents of an active request or response message. By definition, there is no such thing as stand-alone or disconnected SoapContext. So it is useful to explore this class by setting a breakpoint in your code and examining the various member properties and their settings in the Immediate debug window. Also, the WSE 2.0 documentation contains a detailed class reference for the member classes. You can learn a lot about how WSE works by examining the various classes and properties and learning how they interact with each other.

The Microsoft.Web.Services2 assembly provides a large number of namespaces that cover several different WS-Specifications. These are summarized in Table 5-2, along with a brief description of which WS-Specifications they apply to. As you begin coding with the various WS-Specifications, you will need to import one or more of these namespaces into your Web services project.

Table 5-2. Namespaces in WSE 2.0 Microsoft.Web.Services2 Assembly

Namespace	Description
(Root)	Provides support classes for working with SOAP request and response messages, including the important SoapContext class.
.Addressing	Provides support for the WS-Addressing specification, which enables the SOAP message to contain its own addressing, destination, and routing information.
.Attachments	Provides support for the WS-Attachments specification, and provides general support classes for DIME attachments (which also have a dedicated namespace).
.Configuration	Provides support for processing the WSE configuration settings.
.Configuration.Install	Provides support functions to manage the installation of WSE.
.Diagnostics	Provides tracing support to log diagnostic information on a SOAP message before and after processing by the WSE filters.
.Dime	Provides classes for attaching and referencing attachments based on the DIME specification.
.Messaging	Provides support for WS-Messaging, which enables you to process SOAP messages for transport with the HTTP or TCP protocols. The classes support SOAP formatting and serialization.
.Messaging.Configuration	Provides support for working with configuration elements that relate to the WS-Messaging specification.
.Policy	Provides classes for processing policy expression files.
.Referral	Provides support for WS-Referral, which enables the routing of SOAP messages across multiple endpoints.
.Security	Provides support for WS-Security, including attaching security elements to SOAP messages and processing them.
.Security.Configuration	Provides support for working with configuration elements that relate to the WS-Security and WS-Secure Conversation specifications.
.Security.Cryptography	Provides support functions for processing cryptographic operations.
.Security.Policy	Provides support for the WS-Security Policy specification, which supports security-specific policy assertions.
.Security.Tokens	Indicates specialized classes for working with security tokens.
.Security.Tokens.Kerberos	Indicates specialized classes for working with security tokens that are associated with Kerberos tickets.

Continued

Table 5-2. Namespaces in WSE 2.0 Microsoft.Web.Services2 Assembly (continued)

Namespace	Description
.Security.X509	Indicates specialized classes for working with X.509 digital certificates.
.Security.Utility	Specifies generic classes for working with security-oriented properties, such as the creation and expiration timestamp information for a SOAP message.
.Security.Xml	Indicates specialized classes for working with XML signatures, which are an important support technology for digital signatures.
.Xml	Specifies general support classes for working with XML, particularly as it relates to the XML that is generated by the WS-Specifications. These classes are used in conjunction with other XML classes in the .NET Framework.

WSE provides programmatic hooks in the specifications that automatically generate the required SOAP elements for you, so you do not have to construct them manually. The WSE API is accessed differently by Web services versus Web service clients. Let's briefly look at the differences.

Web Service Access to the WSE API

Web services can access the SoapContext for either request or response SOAP messages using specialized classes called RequestSoapContext and ResponseSoapContext. These classes provide direct access to SOAP messages, and they support messages that are transported over different protocols, including the HTTP and TCP protocols. Each of the classes provides a static property called Current, which furnishes a reference to the SoapContext class.

For request messages, the SoapContext class is accessed using

```
SoapContext requestContext = RequestSoapContext.Current;
```

RequestSoapContext is a class provided by the WebServicesClientProtocol, and Current is a static property that returns the SoapContext class.

For response messages, the SoapContext class is accessed using

```
SoapContext responseContext = ResponseSoapContext.Current;
```

Once the client references the SoapContext for the request message, it can reference or assign WS-Specifications with the WSE API. For example, if the incoming request message requires digital signing with a certificate, then the

Web service can inspect the attached digital signatures using SoapContext (as shown in Listing 5-4 earlier). The Web service can also use SoapContext to modify outgoing response messages.

Unlike the service proxy class (described in the next section), the Web service itself does not need to derive from a specialized class in order to access the WSE functionality. However, you need to make sure the WSE support assemblies are correctly registered in the service's web.config file.

Web Service Client Access to the WSE API

A Web service client interacts with a Web service via a proxy class. WSE provides a new base class for this proxy class to inherit from

```
Microsoft.Web.Services.WebServicesClientProtocol
```

Without WSE installed, proxy class files inherit from

```
System.Web.Services.Protocols.SoapHttpClientProtocol
```

The WebServicesClientProtocol class provides access to the SoapContext class for both request and response messages, via the proxy class. Listing 5-5 shows an example of a Web client that is digitally signing a SOAP request message before sending it out to a service. The listing shows how you reference the SoapContext and then use it to assign the digital signature to the SOAP request message.

Listing 5-5. Digitally Signing a SOAP Request Message via the SoapContext

```
using Microsoft.Web.Services2;
using Microsoft.Web.Services2.Security;
using Microsoft.Web.Services2.Security.Tokens;

// Retrieve the SoapContext for the outgoing SOAP request message
StockTraderServiceWse serviceProxy = new StockTraderServiceWse();

// Retrieve the X509 certificate from the CurrentUserStore certificate store
X509SecurityToken token = GetSigningToken();

// Add signature element to a security section on the request to sign the request
serviceProxy.RequestSoapContext.Security.Tokens.Add( token );
serviceProxy.RequestSoapContext.Security.Elements.Add( ➥
    new MessageSignature( token ) );
```

This concludes the introduction to the WSE 2.0 API. The remaining chapters in the book are dedicated to showing you how to use the WSE API to implement the WS-Specifications in your own service-oriented applications.

Install and Configure WSE 2.0

WSE 2.0 is easy to install and to configure. During setup, the only thing to watch out for is to choose the correct setup type for what you need to do. Developers who are using Visual Studio .NET 2003 should select the Visual Studio Developer setup option, as shown in Figure 5-2. If you are running an earlier version of Visual Studio, then I strongly recommend that you upgrade your version before installing WSE 2.0. Otherwise, you will not be able to take advantage of a number of useful productivity tools and utilities, some of which integrate directly with Visual Studio .NET.

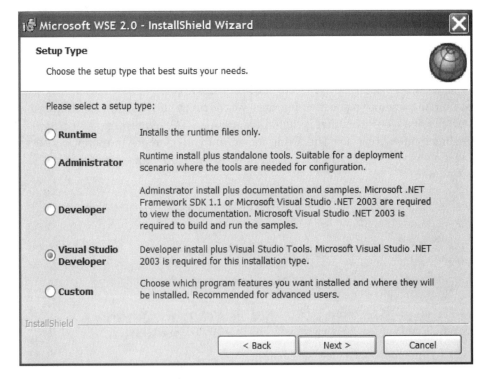

Figure 5-2. WSE 2.0 Setup Option screen

WSE 2.0 is a package of QuickStart sample applications and documentation that show you how to use the various classes in the WSE assembly. But the engine of WSE 2.0 is a single assembly called *Microsoft.Web.Services2.dll*, which is installed by default under C:\Program Files\Microsoft WSE\v2.0. In addition, this assembly gets automatically registered in the Global Assembly Cache (GAC).

In order to use the new assembly in your Web services projects, you will need to register it as a SOAP extension within either the machine.config or web.config configuration files. If you update the machine.config file, then the assembly will automatically be registered for all future Web services projects. Otherwise, you will need to update the web.config files for each new project individually.

Listing 5-6 shows the two additional elements that you must update in the web.config file in order for your project to use WSE. You may actually require additional entries, but these are specific to individual WS-Specifications such as WS-Security, and are only required as needed. Note that you must include each individual element on a single line. In Listing 5-6, elements such as <section> are broken out on multiple lines for clarity only. They must, however, be entered as single lines in the actual web.config file.

Listing 5-6. The web.config Updates for a WSE-Enabled Web Service Project

```
<?xml version="1.0" encoding="utf-8"?>
<configuration>

  <configSections>
    <section name="microsoft.web.services2"
        type="Microsoft.Web.Services2.Configuration.WebServicesConfiguration,
        Microsoft.Web.Services2, Version=2.0.0.0, Culture=neutral,
        PublicKeyToken=31bf3856ad364e35" />
  </configSections>

  <system.web>

    <!-- Other configuration settings -->

    <webServices>
      <soapExtensionTypes>
        <add type="Microsoft.Web.Services2.WebServicesExtension,
            Microsoft.Web.Services2, Version=2.0.0.0, Culture=neutral,
            PublicKeyToken=31bf3856ad364e35" priority="1" group="0" />
      </soapExtensionTypes>
    </webServices>

  </system.web>
</configuration>
```

Web service client projects do not need to register the SOAP extension, but they do need to register the WebServicesConfiguration class. In addition, the client's Web service proxy class must inherit from

```
Microsoft.Web.Services.WebServicesClientProtocol
```

Without WSE, the proxy class file inherits from

`System.Web.Services.Protocols.SoapHttpClientProtocol`

This change is required so that Web service requests get routed through the WSE filters, rather than through the standard HTTP-based SOAP filters.

> **NOTE** *If you want to update the machine.config file, simply copy the `<section>` element from Listing 5-1 into the machine.config file, under the `<configSections>` node.*

If you prefer not to type these entries manually (and I certainly do not!), then you can use the convenient Configuration Editor that ships with WSE 2.0. This tool provides a tabbed GUI interface in which you specify configuration settings for a project and then automatically apply the settings without having to write the code manually. The tool can be accessed directly from within your Visual Studio .NET project, as shown in Figure 5-3.

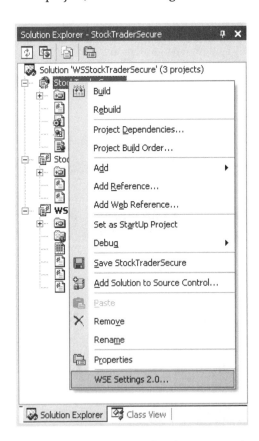

Figure 5-3. Menu access for the WSE 2.0 Configuration Editor

Figure 5-4 shows how you can use the editor to implement the basic settings I have covered so far. You can use the editor for all .NET project types. If you are using it for an ASP.NET Web application or service project, then the editor gives you an additional option to register the SOAP extension class. Otherwise, the second checkbox in the GUI interface is disabled. The editor settings shown in Figure 5-4 will generate the web.config settings that are shown in Listing 5-6. This is not bad for two simple checkbox clicks!

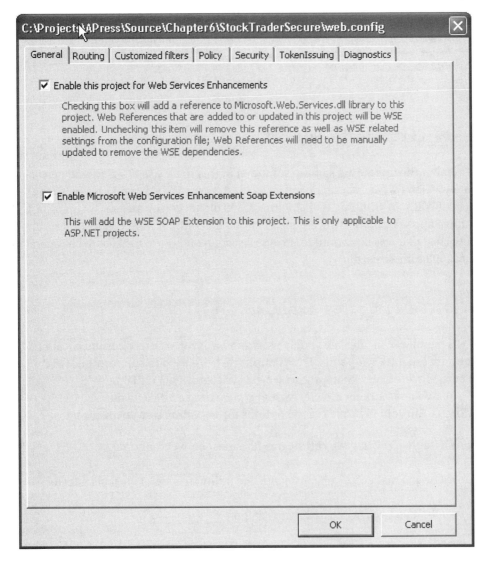

Figure 5-4. The WSE 2.0 Configuration Editor

When you create a new client application for your WSE-enabled Web service, you can generate the proxy class in two ways: Either you can generate it manually from the WSDL document, or you can generate it using Visual Studio .NET's Add Web Reference Wizard. If you use the wizard, then keep in mind that the generated proxy file will contain two separate proxy classes. One inherits from the WebServicesClientProtocol class, which is provided by the Microsoft.Web.Services2 assembly. The other class inherits from the traditional SoapHttpClientProtocol class, which is provided by the System.Web.Services assembly.

> **NOTE** *The Configuration Editor provides helpful configuration support for several of the WS-Specifications, as you can tell from the additional tabs in Figure 5-4. I will discuss the additional support that the Configuration Editor provides in the relevant chapters.*

X.509 Certificate Support

Several of the upcoming sample solutions in this book use X.509 digital certificates, which can be used to digitally sign and encrypt SOAP messages (with the help of WSE). In addition, WSE 2.0 uses X.509 digital certificates in its QuickStart sample applications. Certificate installation and configuration can be quite complex, so I felt it was important to provide a section on how to install and configure the X.509 sample certificates.

X.509 Certificates Explained

X.509 digital certificates are widely used as a basis for securing communications between separate endpoints. For example, they are used to support the HTTP Secure Sockets Layer (SSL) protocol, otherwise known as HTTPS.

You will be working directly with the X.509 test certificates that ship with WSE 2.0. You actually have several options for obtaining test certificates:

- Use the WSE 2.0 test certificates (the most convenient option).

- Use the makecert.exe command-line utility to generate test certificates.

- Obtain a test certificate from VeriSign.

Digital certificates are used for *asymmetric encryption*, also known as *public-key encryption*. The certificate is used to generate a public-private key pair, whereby the private key is known only to one party, while the public key may be distributed to anyone.

In a service-oriented application that includes a client and a Web service, it is the client that typically procures the certificate and the public-private key pair. This is the model that the sample applications use, so it is important to understand how it works. In an SOA application, certificates and keys are used as follows:

- The client uses the certificate to digitally sign an outgoing SOAP request message (to the Web service).

- The Web service uses the public key to encrypt the outgoing SOAP response message (to the client).

- The client uses the private key to decrypt the incoming SOAP response message (from the Web service).

Chapter 6 provides detailed explanations of how encryption and digital signing work under the hood, but for now this is all you need to know, because it helps you to understand where the certificates and keys need to be registered.

Installing the X.509 Test Certificates

Web servers such as Internet Information Server (IIS) provide good support tools for installing digital certificates that will be used to support HTTPS. In addition, Windows operating systems provide a Microsoft Management Console (MMC) snap-in called the Certificate Manager for working with certificates.

The sample applications in this book use the X.509 test certificate to support public-key encryption and to support digital signing; therefore, not only do you need the certificate itself, but you also need a public-private key pair that has been generated from the certificate. Luckily, WSE 2.0 ships with these keys already generated, so you are saved one more manual step.

NOTE *WSE 2.0 test certificates should not be used in production applications.*

The digital certificate and the keys need to be stored in a location called the *certificate store*, which you can access using the Certificate Manager snap-in. For testing purposes, most of us use the same machine to run the Web service and the client applications. This requires you to update two certificate stores:

- **The Local Computer certificate store:** Used by the Web service, this location should store the public key.

- **The Current User certificate store:** Used by the client, this location should store the certificate and the private key.

Here are the installation steps for installing the certificates:

Step 1: Open a new MMC console by typing **mmc** in the Run dialog window.

Step 2: Select File ➤ Add/Remove Snap-In. Click the Add button and then select Certificates from the available list. You will be prompted to select the type of account that will manage the certificates. Select My User Account and click Finish.

Step 3: Repeat Step 2, but this time when you are prompted for an account, select Computer Account and click Finish. Click OK to close out the dialog box for adding certificate stores. You should now be looking at an MMC console view that displays the Current User and Local Computer certificate stores, as shown in Figure 5-5. (Note, Figure 5-5 displays an imported client private key, which you will not yet have, but which you will add in Step 4.)

Step 4: Expand the Personal folder of the Current User certificate store and then right-click it to select the All Tasks ➤ Import menu option. Import the sample personal information exchange file titled Client Private.pfx. The sample certificates and private keys are installed with WSE 2.0, and their default location is C:\Program Files\Microsoft WSE\ v2.0\Samples\Sample Test Certificates\. Client Private.pfx is the private key that the Web service client will use to encrypt requests to the Web service. Note that you will be prompted to enter a password for the private key during the import. For the WSE 2.0 test certificates, you can locate this password in a file called readme.htm, which is located in the same folder as the test certificates.

Step 5: Right-click again the Personal folder of the Current User certificate store and select the All Tasks ➤ Import menu option. Import the sample test certificate titled Server Public.cer. This is the public key that the client uses to digitally sign requests for the Web service.

Step 6: Expand the Personal folder of the Local Computer certificate store and import the sample test certificate titled Server Public.cer. This is the public key that the Web service uses to decrypt the client's request.

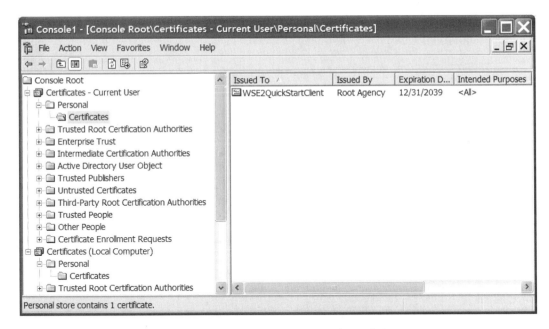

Figure 5-5. MMC Console displaying the Current User and Local Computer certificate stores

This completes the installation of the certificates. But in order to use them from within ASP.NET, you will need to adjust permission levels for the ASP.NET worker process.

Set ASP.NET Permissions to Use the X.509 Certificates

WSE 2.0 ships with a useful utility called the *X509 Certificate Tool*. You can use this tool for several purposes:

- Browse installed certificates in the Current User and Local Computer certificate stores.

- Set permissions on the keys in the MachineKeys folder, which provides access to Local Computer certificates.

- Retrieve the base64 key identifier for installed certificate keys.

Figure 5-6 shows you the X509 Certificate Tool with a selected certificate, which in this case is the private key certificate for the Local Computer user.

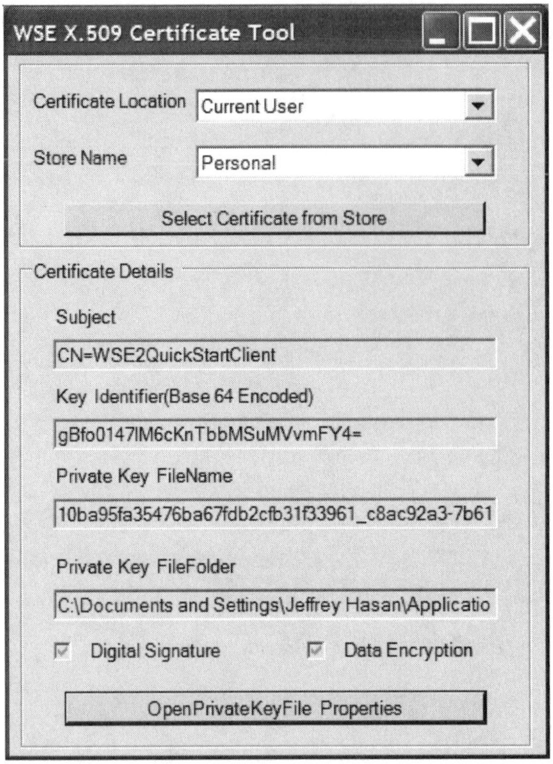

Figure 5-6. The WSE X509 Certificate Tool

The ASP.NET worker process needs Full Control access to the folder that stores the Local Computer certificates. Click the lower button labeled Open Private Key File Properties to open property pages for the folder. Switch to the Security tab to display the list of users who have access to the folder. Add the account that is assigned to the ASP.NET worker process, and give it Full Control permissions. By default, the worker process runs under a machine account called ASP.NET. Figure 5-7 shows you what the Security tab looks like once you have added the ASP.NET worker process account.

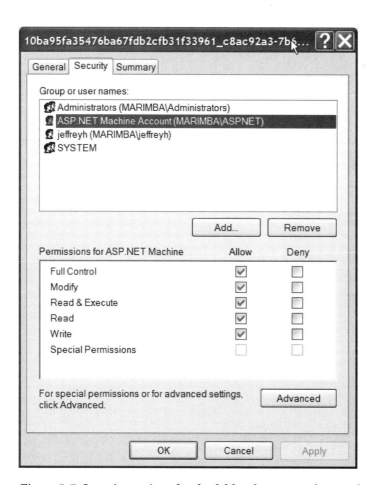

Figure 5-7. Security settings for the folder that stores the Local Computer certificates and keys

The X509 Certificate Tool provides the base64-encoded key identifier for the certificate. You will need this identifier in the code listings in order to retrieve the correct certificate. Listing 5-7 shows you how to retrieve a certificate from the certificate store using its key identifier.

Listing 5-7. Retrieving a Certificate from the Local Computer Certificate Store Using Its Key Identifier

```
using Microsoft.Web.Services2.Security.X509;

private X509SecurityToken GetSigningToken()
{
// NOTE: If you use the WSE 2.0 sample certificates then
// you should not need to change these IDs
string ClientBase64KeyId = "gBfo0147lM6cKnTbbMSuMVvmFY4=";

X509SecurityToken token = null;

// Open the CurrentUser Certificate Store
X509CertificateStore store;
store = X509CertificateStore.CurrentUserStore( X509CertificateStore.MyStore );
if ( store.OpenRead() )
{
X509CertificateCollection certs = store.FindCertificateByKeyIdentifier(  ➥
    Convert.FromBase64String( ClientBase64KeyId ) );

if (certs.Count > 0)
{
// Get the first certificate in the collection
token = new X509SecurityToken( ((X509Certificate) certs[0]) );
}
}
return token;
}
```

Certificates require some effort to install and to configure, but it is well worth it. Certificates are easy to use once they are installed, and you get a high level of security from asymmetric encryption compared to other methods. Asymmetric encryption does have the drawback of being more processor-intensive than other methods, so it can suffer in performance compared to other methods. But there are workarounds to this. For example, you can implement WS-Secure Conversation, which optimizes the performance of encrypted communications between a Web service and client. WS-Secure Conversation is covered in detail in Chapter 8. Finally, you will learn a lot more about using certificates in your solutions by reading Chapter 6, which focuses on the WS-Security specification.

Final Thoughts on WSE

WSE is an evolving product that implements only a subset of the available ratified WS-Specifications. Microsoft has done a good job of implementing the more popular WS-Specifications, including security and policy. But the WSE product cannot keep pace with the rapid pace of change of the WS-Specifications. Existing specifications continue to change, and new ones continue to be released. Even within a given specification, WSE will probably only cover a subset of what is available. This is in fact why Microsoft develops WSE on a separate release schedule from the .NET Framework.

> **NOTE** *WSE is a rapidly evolving product and is one of the fastest SOA SDKs to hit the market.*

For example, WSE implements the WS-Policy family of specifications (including WS-Policy Attachments and WS-Security Policy). Policy is expressed through so-called policy assertions, and WSE dutifully implements a set of standard assertions. But the list is limited, and so it provides support for you to create custom assertions when a canned one is not available. This is typical of how WSE will always try to be useful for you. If it cannot provide something out of the box, then it at least tries to give you tools so you can build it yourself.

Summary

This chapter introduced you to the Web services specifications, or WS-Specifications, which provide a framework for building secure, reliable, service-oriented Web services. The WS-Specifications provide the following benefits when they are implemented in Web services:

- Interoperability

- Composability

- Security

- Description and discovery

- Messaging and delivery

- Transactions

Microsoft Web Services Enhancements 2.0 is a software developer kit for implementing the WS-Specifications in .NET applications. It includes the Microsoft.Web.Services2 assembly, configuration tools, QuickStart application samples, and documentation. WSE is an excellent productivity tool that implements many of the important WS-Specifications. The current version of WSE does have gaps, most notably in its support for transactions. Developers will need to build some aspects of the WS-Specifications manually for now.

This chapter lays the groundwork for the rest of the book, which explores several of the WS-Specifications in detail.

CHAPTER 6

Secure Web Services with WS-Security

COMPANIES HAVE NOT widely adopted Web services technology to this point because the technology has lacked a security specification that can ensure the integrity of transmitted messages and data. The WS-Security specification is a joint effort by Microsoft, IBM, and VeriSign to address this most important issue.

What do we actually mean when we talk about "security"? In broad terms, we are talking about authentication and authorization:

Authentication is the process of validating a user's identity based on credentials, or tokens. The token may be a username-password combination, or it may be based on an X.509 certificate. This certificate is a signed public key that has been issued by a certificate authority to vouch for the identity and integrity of a user.

Authorization is the process of allowing access to selected resources based on a user's authenticated identity. For example, you can restrict access to a Web service's methods by specific users.

Together, authentication and authorization provide for a security model by allowing you to identify users and then to give them selective access to resources.

Currently, it is possible to secure SOAP communications over HTTP using the certificate-based Secure Sockets Layer (SSL) protocol. SSL provides encryption and digital signing of both SOAP messages and standard HTTP requests and responses. But SSL has two major limitations that make it unsuitable for securing Web services communications within a service-oriented application. First, SSL is designed for point-to-point communication. However, service-oriented Web services may exchange SOAP messages between two or more endpoints, and so they require a security solution that supports hops across multiple endpoints and multiple domain boundaries. Second, the SSL protocol is built on the HTTP protocol. Web services technology is transport neutral and supports message exchange across different protocols, including TCP and SMTP, in addition to HTTP. The SSL protocol is simply too limiting for Web services technology.

The WS-Security specification is designed to overcome these limitations, and to provide an extensible security implementation that will evolve as Web services technology becomes more sophisticated.

The WS-Security Specification

The prime currency in service-oriented architecture (SOA) applications are SOAP messages because they are the means by which requests are made and responses are received from Web service methods. The WS-Security specification provides a way for you to protect the integrity and confidentiality of messages and to implement authentication and authorization models in your Web services. The WS-Security specification enables you to implement the following protections in your Web service calls:

Authentication: Security credentials, or tokens, may be exchanged between a client and a Web service to validate the identity of the caller. The tokens are added directly to the header of the SOAP message.

Digital signing: This is the process of signing a SOAP message with a signature that is based on a security token (such as a username-password combination or an X.509 certificate). Digital signing creates a cryptographic signature attached to the message that uniquely identifies the sender. The receiver can check this signature to verify the identity of the sender and the integrity of the message. A SOAP exception is raised on the receiving end if the contents of a SOAP message have been tampered with. Digital signing is especially important in an SOA architecture that includes routing, in which a single SOAP message may be routed through multiple SOAP endpoints and across multiple servers. Message integrity is essential in any Web service-based architecture, but especially so in an SOA architecture.

Encryption: This is the process of hashing a SOAP message to ensure its confidentiality. A number of available encryption algorithms are available. In addition, you can encrypt a SOAP message based on an X.509 certificate.

The WS-Security specification is platform independent and transport neutral, as are all of the other WS specifications. Security information is generated by the client and stored within the envelope of the SOAP request message. The Web service in turn will deserialize this information, verify its validity, and then process the requested operation. In the event that the message security does not pass verification, the Web service will return a SOAP fault back to the client.

Listings 6-1 and 6-2 compare two SOAP request messages for the same Web service method. The Web service is StockTrader.asmx, and the requested method is RequestQuote, which accepts a single stock ticker symbol as an input parameter. Listing 6-1 is an unsecured Web method call, while Listing 6-2 is secured and implements digital signing (based on an X.509 certificate). The listings are greatly simplified for clarity and for length, and were originally generated using the SOAP Toolkit Trace Utility.

Listing 6-1. An Unsecured SOAP Request Message (Simplified for Clarity)

```
<?xml version="1.0" encoding="utf-8" ?>
<soap:Envelope xmlns:soap="http://schemas.xmlsoap.org/soap/envelope/"
    xmlns:wsa="http://schemas.xmlsoap.org/ws/2003/03/addressing"
    xmlns:wsu="http://docs.oasis-open.org/wss/2004/01/
    oasis-200401-wss-wssecurity-utility-1.0.xsd">
<soap:Header>
    <wsa:Action wsu:Id=GUID>
        http://www.bluestonepartners.com/schemas/StockTrader/RequestQuote
    </wsa:Action>
    <wsa:From wsu:Id=GUID>
    <wsa:Address>
        http://schemas.xmlsoap.org/ws/2003/03/addressing/role/anonymous
    </wsa:Address>
    </wsa:From>
    <wsa:MessageID> Message ID and UUID </wsa:MessageID>
    <wsa:To wsu:Id=GUID>
        http://localhost:8080/StockTraderSecure/StockTrader.asmx
    </wsa:To>
    <wsu:Timestamp>
        Contains Message Creation/Expiration TimeStamps
    </wsu:Timestamp>
</soap:Header>
<soap:Body>
    <Symbol xmlns="http://www.bluestonepartners.com/schemas/StockTrader/">
        MSFT
    </Symbol>
</soap:Body>
</soap:Envelope>
```

Listing 6-2. A Digitally Signed SOAP Request Message with Highlighted Differences from an Unsigned SOAP Message (and Simplified for Clarity)

```
<?xml version="1.0" encoding="utf-8" ?>
<soap:Envelope xmlns:soap="http://schemas.xmlsoap.org/soap/envelope/
    xmlns:wsa="http://schemas.xmlsoap.org/ws/2003/03/addressing"
    xmlns:wsu="http://docs.oasis-open.org/wss/2004/01/
    oasis-200401-wss-wssecurity-utility-1.0.xsd"
```

```
                xmlns: wsse="http://docs.oasis-open.org/wss/2004/01/
                oasis-200401-wss-wssecurity-secext-1.0.xsd">
        <soap:Header>
            <wsa:Action wsu:Id=GUID>
                http://www.bluestonepartners.com/schemas/StockTrader/RequestQuote
            </wsa:Action>
            <wsa:From wsu:Id=GUID>
                <wsa:Address>
                  http://schemas.xmlsoap.org/ws/2003/03/addressing/role/anonymous
                </wsa:Address>
            </wsa:From>
            <wsa:MessageID> Message ID and UUID </wsa:MessageID>
            <wsa:To wsu:Id=GUID>
                http://localhost:8080/StockTraderSecure/StockTrader.asmx
            </wsa:To>
            <wsu:Timestamp>
                Contains Message Creation/Expiration TimeStamps
            </wsu:Timestamp>
            <wsse:Security soap:mustUnderstand="1">
            <wsse:BinarySecurityToken>
                Parameters for the X.509 certificate-based token including the hash value
            </wsse:BinarySecurityToken>
            <Signature xmlns="http://www.w3.org/2000/09/xmldsig#">
                <SignedInfo> Encoding parameters for the Digital Signature </SignedInfo>
                <SignatureValue> The Signature hash value </SignatureValue>
            </Signature>
            </wsse:Security>
        </soap:Header>
        <soap:Body wsu:Id=GUID>
            <Symbol xmlns="http://www.bluestonepartners.com/schemas/StockTrader/">
                MSFT
            </Symbol>
        </soap:Body>
    </soap:Envelope>
```

The main difference between Listings 6-1 and 6-2 is the addition of WS-Security tags in the secured request message. Also, in Listing 6-2 the <soap:Body> tag is assigned a GUID-based ID, so that it can be referred to from within the <wsse: Security> section. Listing 6-2 is a clear example of Web service composability, whereby additional specifications may be added or subtracted to a SOAP message as needed.

Web Services Enhancements (WSE) provides the API for implementing WS-Security in .NET-based Web services and client applications. The API allows you to write code to format secured SOAP request messages in the client and to process secured messages within a Web service.

Implement WS-Security Using WSE 2.0

The focus of this chapter is to show you how to write the code to implement WS-Security in Web services and their client applications. I will show you four examples:

1. Digitally sign a SOAP request message with a username and password token.

2. Digitally sign a SOAP request message with an X.509 certificate.

3. Encrypt a SOAP request message with an X.509 certificate.

4. Encrypt a SOAP response message with an X.509 certificate, based on a digitally signed SOAP request message.

The code examples in this chapter use a modified project based on the StockTrader Web service that was presented in Chapters 3 and 4. You will get the most out of the following discussion if you have first reviewed these chapters.

Digitally Sign SOAP Messages

A digital signature is essentially a cryptographic hash that is added to a SOAP message, and is based on a security token. Digital signatures may currently be generated based on the following tokens:

A username-password combination, referred to by the WSE as a *UsernameToken*

A digital certificate, such as an X.509 certificate

A Kerberos token, which is a Microsoft proprietary format that can only be issued and verified by Windows XP with Service Pack 1, or by Windows Server 2003

A custom binary token, based on an algorithm of your choosing

The mechanism for programmatically adding a digital signature to a SOAP request message is the same regardless of what kind of token you base the signature on (although the code for generating or retrieving the actual security token will vary). This approach makes it easy for you to change the token type in the future with minimum impact on the current code base. The code for verifying a signed SOAP message on the receiver will vary depending on the security token that the signature is based on.

A note on terminology: The sender and the receiver are equivalent to the client and the Web service. The terms *sender* and *receiver* are misleading because the client and the Web service take on both roles in a classic request-response communication. The client acts as a sender when it issues a request message to the service, but it acts as a receiver when it receives a response message back from the service. So for purposes of clarity, I will need to refer to *client* and *service*, where the client is understood to initiate the first message.

How Digital Signing Works with UsernameToken Security Tokens

For signatures based on UsernameToken security tokens, the service must have access to the same username and password information as the client in order to verify it. This approach is potentially less secure than using certificates because it relies on a shared secret that is known to both client and service. In addition, cryptographic hashes based on simple UsernameToken security tokens may not be as robust as those based on more complex X.509 certificates.

The digital signing process with UsernameToken security tokens works as follows:

1. The client and service establish shared secret information, such as username and password credentials. Both the client and service must take responsibility to store these credentials in a secure location.

2. The client generates a UsernameToken security token based on the username and password information.

3. The client creates a digital signature based on the UsernameToken and adds it to the outgoing SOAP request message.

4. The service receives the message and checks the security token type.

5. Once the service determines that a UsernameToken was used, it uses a token manager to extract the username and password information that was used to sign the message.

6. The service then compares the extracted credentials against its stored credentials. If the credentials do not match, then a SOAP exception is raised.

Digital signatures with UsernameToken security tokens are easy to create and can be processed very quickly on the receiving end. However, they are potentially vulnerable to compromise if the shared secret that they are based on gets discovered.

How Digital Signing Works with X.509 Certificates

Digitally signing messages with X.509 certificates is a more complicated process than with UsernameToken security tokens; however, you benefit from a more secure solution. The X.509 certificate is used to generate a pair of related keys, called the *private and public keys*. The private key is known only to the client, and is used for the following purposes:

- Digitally sign an outgoing SOAP request message.

- Decrypt an incoming SOAP response message.

The public key is made available to authorized services, which use it for the following purposes:

- Verify an incoming signed SOAP request message.

- Encrypt an outgoing SOAP response message.

The digital signing process with X.509 certificates works as follows:

1. The client obtains an X.509 certificate and generates a private-public key pair. The service receives a copy of the public key. (This process assumes that the service trusts the client's public key.) In addition, the client and service must agree on a standard hash algorithm.

2. The client applies a hash algorithm to the message, which creates a so-called message digest. (The client may use any hash algorithm that it wants; however, the digital signing process will only work if the service knows what hash algorithm the client is using.)

3. The client then encrypts the message digest with its private key, which creates the digital signature.

4. The client attaches the digital signature to the SOAP request message. (Programmatically, the WSE performs steps 3 and 4 together.)

5. The client sends the SOAP request message out to the service.

6. The service receives the SOAP message and checks the security token type.

7. Once the service determines that an X.509 certificate was used, it decrypts the message signature using the public key. This process allows the services to retrieve the original message hash. If the decryption process fails, then the service assumes that the client is not the original sender of the message, or the message has been tampered with, and a SOAP exception is raised.

8. The service then generates its own message digest using the same algorithm that the client used.

9. The service compares its generated message digest against the one that has been obtained from the client. If the two message digests match, then the signature has passed verification. If it does not, then the service assumes that the message has been tampered with, and a SOAP exception is raised.

Digital signatures can have real consequences on message delivery if they are not applied correctly, or if the verification process fails, because either of these issues will prevent the service from processing the incoming SOAP request message. In addition, certificates will expire, so verification will fail if the certificate is not current. The X509SecurityToken and X509SecurityCertificate classes both provide a Boolean IsCurrent property that verifies whether a given certificate is still valid.

If you use an X.509 certificate for your digital signature, then you must be prepared for the relatively high administrative burden of ensuring that the client and the service have proper access to the necessary certificate and key information.

NOTE *You cannot assume that a certificate-based security token automatically supports digital signing and encryption. The .NET BinarySecurityToken class provides Boolean properties that tell you whether the currently loaded token supports digital signing and encryption. (See Listing 6-10 in the section "Modify the Web Service Client" later in this chapter.)*

Getting Started with the Sample Solution

The sample solution that is presented here looks at two ways of signing SOAP messages: using UsernameToken security tokens and using X.509 certificates.

Figure 6-1 shows the Solution Explorer window for the Visual Studio .NET solution that I will use in this chapter. It is based on the StockTrader application that was presented in Chapters 3 and 4, and includes the following:

A Web service called StockTraderSecure, which provides methods for requesting stock quotes and executing trades.

A client console application called WSStockTraderClient, which invokes the StockTrader Web service via a proxy class.

A reference assembly called StockTraderTypes, which provides code definitions for the custom types that are used by the StockTrader Web service. (The source project is included in this chapter's solution for clarity. However, future chapter projects will simply reference the compiled StockTraderTypes assembly instead.) The type definitions are contained in a separate assembly in order to be accessible to any application that wants to interact with the StockTrader Web service. (Recall that these custom types are based on the StockTrader XSD schema, which is presented in Chapter 3.)

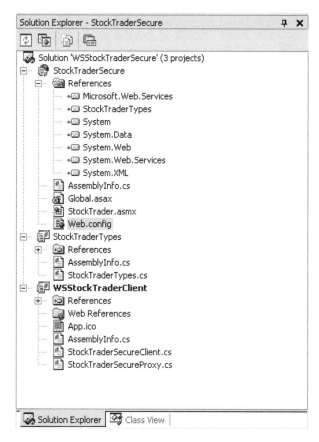

Figure 6-1. The WSStockTraderSecure .NET solution, containing three projects

The StockTraderSecure Web service is a copy of the StockTrader Web service presented in Chapter 3, with additional code for processing SOAP request messages that have been digitally signed and encrypted. To get started with building the solution, you need to perform the following steps:

Step 1: Install and configure WSE (refer to Chapter 5 for detailed instructions).

Step 2: Install and configure the X.509 test certificates (refer to Chapter 5 for detailed instructions).

Step 3: Create a new Visual Studio .NET Solution called WSStockTraderSecure.sln.

Step 4: Add a new Web services project to the solution called StockTraderSecure.csproj.

Step 5: Copy the existing files StockTrader.asmx and StockTrader.asmx.cs from the StockTraderContracts project in Chapter 4 over to the new StockTraderSecure project. Add these files to the new project using the menu option File ➤ Add Existing Item.

Step 6: Add the StockTraderTypes reference assembly or project to the solution. Again, you can obtain this reference project from the Chapter 4 sample files. Alternatively, you can just copy the StockTraderTypes.dll compiled assembly over to the \bin directory of the StockTraderSecure Web service project. Use the Project ➤ Add Reference menu option to set a reference to the StockTraderTypes assembly or project from the StockTraderSecure Web service project.

Step 7: Enable the Web service project for WSE 2.0, either manually or using the WSE Configuration Editor.

WSE 2.0 is enabled by adding the appropriate entries in the web.config files of the Web service and client projects. In addition, you the client must use a Web service proxy class that inherits from WebServicesClientProtocol instead of SoapHttpClientProtocol.

There are two ways to enable WSE 2.0 in a project: You can either update the project files manually, or you can use the WSE 2.0 Configuration Editor that is installed with WSE, which you can access directly from within Visual Studio .NET.

Initially, I would recommend that you update the files manually, so that you understand exactly how WSE is enabled. Later, once you are comfortable with the configuration settings, I recommend that you rely on the convenience of the WSE 2.0 Configuration Editor.

The required web.config settings for the StockTraderSecure Web service project are shown in Listing 6-3. The <security> element contains a <securityTokenManager> subelement that registers a custom manager class for processing security tokens.

It also contains a subelement called <x509> with attributes that allow this project to use unverified test root certificates. Without this setting, your Web service calls will generate a SOAP exception alerting you that your certificate is not valid. The <x509> element also contains an important attribute called storeLocation, which specifies the location of the certificate that is used to validate or decrypt incoming requests.

> **NOTE** *Please refer to Chapter 5 for detailed discussions on how to configure WSE and how to work with certificate stores.*

Listing 6-3. The web.config Settings for the StockTraderSecure Web Service Project

```
<configuration>
    <configSections>
    <section name="microsoft.web.services2"
        type="Microsoft.Web.Services2.Configuration.WebServicesConfiguration,
        Microsoft.Web.Services2, Version=2.0.0.0, Culture=neutral,
        PublicKeyToken=31bf3856ad364e35" />
    </configSections>
    <system.web>
      <webServices>
        <soapExtensionTypes>
          <add type="Microsoft.Web.Services2.WebServicesExtension,
              Microsoft.Web.Services2, Version=2.0.0.0, Culture=neutral,
              PublicKeyToken=31bf3856ad364e35" priority="1" group="0" />
        </soapExtensionTypes>
      </webServices>
    </system.web>
    <microsoft.web.services2>
      <security>
        <securityTokenManager type="StockTrader.CustomUsernameTokenManager,
          StockTraderSecure" xmlns:wsse="http://docs.oasis-open.org/wss/2004/01/
          oasis-200401-wss-wssecurity-secext-1.0.xsd" qname="wsse:UsernameToken" />
        <x509 storeLocation="LocalMachine" allowTestRoot="true"
          allowRevocationUrlRetrieval="false" verifyTrust="false" />
      </security>
    </microsoft.web.services2>
  </configuration>
```

Create the Web Service Client

So far the WSStockTraderSecure solution only contains a Web service, and I have not yet shown you how to modify the Web service code to handle digitally signed SOAP messages. First you will write a Web service client that generates signed SOAP request messages. The steps are as follows:

Step 1: Add a new Console Application project to the solution called WSStockTraderClient.csproj.

Step 2: Rename the default C# class file to StockTraderSecureClient.cs.

Step 3: Add a reference from the project to the assembly Microsoft.Web.Services2.dll.

Step 4: Add a Web service proxy file to the console project. There are two ways to do this, outlined in Steps 4A and 4B.

Step 4A: Add a Web reference to the StockTraderSecure Web service from the Console application project using the Project ➤ Add Web Reference menu option. This will auto-generate a proxy class file called Reference.cs, under the Web References\[Reference Name]\Reference.map subproject folder. (If you do not see this file, you can use the Project ➤ Show All Files menu option to expand all files.) Next, open the Reference.cs file and copy the entire code listing over to a new C# class file called StockTraderSecureProxy.cs.

Step 4B: Alternatively, you can copy the StockTrader Web service proxy class file over from the Chapter 3 sample project. You will need to set the namespace for the proxy class to WSStockTraderClient, in order to match the namespace for the rest of the project files. If you do not, then the console project will be unable to use the proxy class, and will therefore be unable to communicate with the StockTraderSecure Web service.

Step 5: Set a reference to the StockTraderTypes assembly or project. This step is not required if you generated the proxy class file using Step 4A because the Add Web Reference Wizard automatically adds the StockTrader custom types to the proxy class file. However, if you followed Step 4B, then you must manually add this reference because this proxy class file does not contain definitions for the StockTrader custom types.

> **TIP** *The Add Web Reference Wizard is a convenient tool, but you should always copy the auto-generated proxy class code to a separate class file. This is because existing Web references are easily overwritten by updating the Web reference. You will then lose any customizations that you have made to the proxy class file.*

As a quick aside, be careful when using the Add Web Reference Wizard. Although it is a convenient tool, it creates auto-generated code that may require editing. Chapters 3 and 4 highlighted the importance of breaking out custom type definitions into a separate single reference assembly. This ensures that multiple dependent projects use the same custom type definitions. The Add Web Reference Wizard will automatically generate type definitions in the proxy class code, which potentially creates a second, unwanted copy of the custom type definitions. Clearly, this issue also depends on the approach that you are taking in interacting with a Web service. If you are a casual, recreational, or temporary user of a particular Web service, then you can happily rely on an auto-generated proxy class. It would be unnecessary overhead in this case to customize your own proxy class. However, a corporate user of a Web service that is part of a business process workflow will want more control over the proxy class. This type of user works in a shared environment and must communicate using standard types. This user will likely need to use a reference assembly for the custom types.

Listing 6-4 shows the basic, unsigned code listing for the Web service client.

Listing 6-4. Unsigned Code Listing for the Web Service Client

```
// Set a reference to the proxy class
StockTraderServiceWse serviceProxy = new StockTraderServiceWse();

// Call the Web service RequestQuote() method
Console.WriteLine("Calling {0}", serviceProxy.Url);
Quote strQuote = serviceProxy.RequestQuote("MSFT");

// Results
Console.WriteLine("Web Service call successful. Result:");
Console.WriteLine( "Symbol: " + strQuote.Symbol );
Console.WriteLine( "Price:   " + strQuote.Last );
Console.WriteLine( "Change: " + strQuote.PercentChange + "%");
```

Recall that there are several ways to create a security token for signing SOAP request messages. Listing 6-5 shows you how to create a token based on a username and password combination. Listing 6-6 shows you how to create a token based on an X.509 certificate.

Listing 6-5. Creating a Security Token Based on a Username-Password Combination

```
using Microsoft.Web.Services2.Security;
using Microsoft.Web.Services2.Security.Tokens;

UsernameToken token;
```

```
string username      = "myUsername"; // Hardcoded username
byte[] passwordBytes = System.Text.Encoding.UTF8.GetBytes( username );
Array.Reverse( passwordBytes );

string passwordEquivalent = Convert.ToBase64String( passwordBytes );
token = new UsernameToken( username, passwordEquivalent, ➥
    PasswordOption.SendHashed );

// Add the token and digital signature to the SOAP request message
serviceProxy.RequestSoapContext.Security.Tokens.Add( token );
serviceProxy.RequestSoapContext.Security.Elements.Add( ➥
    new MessageSignature( token ) );

// Execute the Web service request
// (Refer to Listing 6-4. Code not shown here.)
```

Listing 6-6. Creating a Security Token Based on an X.509 Certificate

```
using Microsoft.Web.Services2.Security;
using Microsoft.Web.Services2.Security.Tokens;
using Microsoft.Web.Services2.Security.X509;

X509CertificateStore store;
X509SecurityToken token;

// Open the CurrentUser Certificate Store
store = X509CertificateStore.CurrentUserStore( X509CertificateStore.MyStore );

// Retrieve the X.509 certificate from the CurrentUserStore certificate store
string ClientBase64KeyId = "gBfo0147lM6cKnTbbMSuMVvmFY4=";
X509CertificateCollection certs = store.FindCertificateByKeyIdentifier( ➥
    Convert.FromBase64String( ClientBase64KeyId ) );

if (certs.Count > 0)
{
    // Get the first certificate in the collection
    token = new X509SecurityToken( ((X509Certificate) certs[0]) );
}

// Add the token and digital signature to the SOAP request message
serviceProxy.RequestSoapContext.Security.Tokens.Add( token );
serviceProxy.RequestSoapContext.Security.Elements.Add( ➥
    new MessageSignature( token ) );

// Execute the Web service request
// (Refer to Listing 6-4. Code not shown here.)
```

The code listings for creating token-based signatures are self-explanatory. The code for generating the tokens differs between listings, but the code for assigning the token and signature is the same since the UsernameToken and X509CertificateToken classes both derive from the same SecurityToken base class. Listings 6-5 and 6-6 actually accomplish two goals: Not only do they add a token-based digital signature to the SOAP request message, but they also add the token itself to the message, which serves to identify the sender of the message.

Modify the Web Service to Process Signed SOAP Messages

The Web service must be modified to iterate through the collection of signatures and tokens that are assigned to a SOAP request message. It is in fact possible to add multiple tokens and signatures to a single message, although the code listings shown here do not do this. The Web service should process the signed SOAP message as follows:

1. Loop through the collection of signatures attached to the SOAP message.

2. For each signature in the collection, determine what type of token it is based on.

3. For username tokens, implement a custom token manager to validate the token.

Listing 6-7 shows you how to loop through the collection of signatures and tokens attached to a SOAP request message. Note that this code listing is implemented directly inside the RequestQuote Web method so that a SOAP fault may be raised directly from the method should the user fail to be authenticated or authorized to access the method.

Listing 6-7. Loop Through the Collection of Signatures and Tokens Attached to a SOAP Request Message

```
using System.Web;
using System.Web.Services;

using System.Web.Services.Protocols;
using System.Web.Services.Description;
using System.Xml.Serialization;

using Microsoft.Web.Services2;
using Microsoft.Web.Services2.Security;
using Microsoft.Web.Services2.Security.Tokens;
using System.Security.Permissions;
using StockTraderTypes;
```

```
[WebService()]
public class StockTraderService : System.Web.Services.WebService, IStockTrader
{
  [WebMethod()]
  public override Quote RequestQuote(string Symbol)
  {

    // Initialize the custom token manager, in case it is needed
    CustomUsernameTokenManager objMgr = new CustomUsernameTokenManager();

    // Verify the signature on the Web service request to this method
    bool SignatureIsValid = false;
    SoapContext requestContext = RequestSoapContext.Current;

      foreach (ISecurityElement objElem in requestContext.Security.Elements)
      {
        if (objElem is MessageSignature)
        {
          MessageSignature clientSignature = (MessageSignature)objElem;

          if (clientSignature.SigningToken is X509SecurityToken)
          {
            SignatureIsValid = true;
          }
          else if (clientSignature.SigningToken is UsernameToken)
          {
            SignatureIsValid = true;
            objMgr.VerifyToken( clientSignature.SigningToken );
          }
        }
      }

    // Proceed with request if signature is valid
    Quote q = new Quote();
    if (SignatureIsValid) {}
      // Implementation code for RequestQuote()
    }
    return q;
}
```

Listing 6-8 shows you how to implement a custom token manager, which only applies when you are using a UsernameToken (as opposed to a certificate token, or custom binary token). The purpose of the manager is to return a password, which the WSE engine will use to compare against the password that generated the token. If the passwords do not match, then a SOAP fault will be raised. The manager gives you a place to write custom code for validating the authenticated user's password. You could, for example, extract the username from the token and then perform a database lookup to retrieve the user's password. You can then return this password, and WSE will automatically compare it against the token password.

Listing 6-8. A Custom Token Manager

```
[SecurityPermissionAttribute(SecurityAction.Demand,
 Flags=SecurityPermissionFlag.UnmanagedCode)]
public class CustomUsernameTokenManager : UsernameTokenManager
{
  protected override string AuthenticateToken( UsernameToken token )
  {
    // Step 1: Retrieve the username from the token
    byte[] username = System.Text.Encoding.UTF8.GetBytes( token.Username );

    // Step 2: Retrieve the user's password from a separate source,
    // e.g., database table
    // Code goes here

    // Step 3: Return the retrieved password
    // WSE will automatically compare it against the password
    // that created the token
    return Convert.ToBase64String( password );
  }
}
```

The custom token manager must be registered in the Web service web.config file as follows:

```
<microsoft.web.services2>
  <security>
    <securityTokenManager type="StockTrader.CustomUsernameTokenManager,
      StockTraderSecure" xmlns: wsse="http://docs.oasis-open.org/wss/2004/01/
      oasis-200401-wss-wssecurity-secext-1.0.xsd" qname="wsse:UsernameToken" />
    <x509 allowTestRoot="true" allowRevocationUrlRetrieval="false"
        verifyTrust="false"
      storeLocation="CurrentUser"/>
  </security>
</microsoft.web.services2>
```

The manager's token authentication feature is accessed using the VerifyToken method, which you can see being called in Listing 6-7. If the token password and the password that the manager returns do not match, then the VerifyToken method raises a SOAP fault with the following exception message:

```
The security token could not be authenticated or authorized.
```

However, if the Web service call is successful, then the console will display the requested stock quote:

```
Calling http://localhost/ StockTrader Secure/StockTrader.asmx
Web service call successful. Result:
Symbol: MSFT
Price: 25.15
Change: -0.0137%
Press [Enter] key to continue...
```

Encrypt SOAP Messages with an X.509 Certificate

Security tokens and digital signing allow you to identify a service requestor and to determine whether a request message has been tampered with, but they do nothing to protect the contents of a SOAP message from network sniffers. Encryption technology enables you to generate a cryptographic hash of the SOAP message for transport and to decrypt the message contents at the receiving end.

There are two kinds of encryption:

Symmetric encryption: Also known as *private-key encryption* or *shared-secret encryption*, this method generates a cryptographic hash using a key that is known to both the sender and the receiver. Symmetric encryption is the least secure encryption method because both sender and receiver must share the same key, and so the encryption is only effective if the key remains secret.

Asymmetric encryption: Also known as *public-key encryption*, this method generates a cryptographic hash based on a public key, which can only be decrypted using a corresponding secret private key. The sender of a secure message is given a public key by the receiver. The sender uses the public key to encrypt the message prior to delivering it to the receiver. In turn, the receiver decrypts the message hash with the corresponding private key. Asymmetric encryption is the most secure method, and there are a number of related encryption methodologies to choose from, including SHA1 and Triple-DES.

Interestingly enough, when a SOAP message is encrypted, only the body of the message gets hashed. If your SOAP message includes custom SOAP header values, then you must encrypt them separately. In this section, you will see how to encrypt the body of a SOAP message using asymmetric encryption.

Getting Started

For asymmetric encryption, you must set things up as follows:

Step 1: Generate a private-public key pair based on a digital certificate.

Step 2: Install the public key in the client's local certificate store.

Step 3: Install the private key in the server's local certificate store.

Step 4: Implement code in the Web service client to generate an encrypted SOAP request message.

You have a number of options for obtaining test certificates:

- Use the WSE 2.0 test certificates.

- Use the makecert.exe command-line utility to generate test certificates.

- Obtain a test certificate from VeriSign.

The WSE 2.0 sample projects ship with test certificates and keys, which you will use here because they are convenient. Alternatively, you can obtain a test certificate from VeriSign at `http://www.verisign.com`, although you will have to provide information about yourself or your company, as well as the specific server name that you are generating the test certificate for. Finally, you have the option of using the makecert.exe command-line utility, which will generate self-signed certificates that you can use in your test projects. This utility is located under the Microsoft Visual Studio .NET 2003 program files directory, typically under \SDK\v1.1\bin\. You will want to add this path to your computer's environment variables in order to call the utility from within any subdirectory.

Whichever certificate option you choose, you will need to obtain a private key and a public key, and register them in certificate stores for the client and the server, respectively. Even if you are developing on the same machine, the private and public keys will typically reside in separate certificate stores. Chapter 5 provides a detailed description on how to install test certificates, so please refer there for a more detailed discussion. But briefly, and assuming you are using the sample certificates that ship with WSE 2.0, here are the installation steps that you need to take:

Step 1: Open the MMC console and add the Certificates snap-in for both Current User and Local Computer.

Step 2: Open the Personal folder of the Current User certificate store and import the sample test certificate titled Server Public.cer. This is the public key that the Web service client will use to encrypt requests to the Web service.

Step 3: Open the Personal folder of the Local Computer certificate store and import the personal information exchange file titled Client Private.pfx. This is the private key that the Web service uses to decrypt the client's request.

Once the certificates are installed you are ready to modify the Web service client to generate encrypted SOAP request messages.

> **WARNING** *Certificates can be tricky to work with. It is not uncommon to receive cryptographic errors or permission errors when you attempt to generate encrypted requests. Always verify that you have installed the certificates correctly. Chapter 5 provides detailed information on how to install the sample certificates that ship with WSE 2.0. Unfortunately, certificate issues may also be caused by the way your local computer has its operating system and folder permissions configured. Your best source for troubleshooting information is the WSE 2.0 documentation, newsgroups, developer Web sites, your peers, and, of course, this book!*

Modify the Web Service Client

The client code for generating encrypted SOAP request messages is very similar to the code for digitally signing messages. The client retrieves the applicable X.509 certificate-based private key from its personal certificate store and then uses this key to generate a hash of the SOAP message. Listing 6-9 shows you the required code.

Listing 6-9. Encrypt a SOAP Request Message Using an X.509 Certificate

```
public void EncryptRequestUsingX509Certificate()
{
    // Retrieve the X.509 certificate from the CurrentUserStore certificate store
    X509SecurityToken token;
    string ClientBase64KeyId = "gBfo01471M6cKnTbbMSuMVvmFY4=";
```

```
// Open the CurrentUser Certificate Store
X509CertificateStore store;
store = X509CertificateStore.CurrentUserStore( X509CertificateStore.MyStore );

// Find the certificate based on the server's base64 key identifier
X509CertificateCollection certs = store.FindCertificateByKeyIdentifier( ➥
    Convert.FromBase64String( ClientBase64KeyId ) );

if (certs.Count > 0)
{
    // Get the first certificate in the collection
    token = new X509SecurityToken( ((X509Certificate) certs[0]) );
}

if (token == null) throw new ➥
    ApplicationException("Unable to obtain security key.");

StockTraderServiceWse serviceProxy = new StockTraderServiceWse();

// Add the certificate key to encrypt the request
serviceProxy.RequestSoapContext.Security.Elements.Add( ➥
    new EncryptedData( token ) );

// Call the Web service RequestQuote() method
Console.WriteLine("Calling {0}", serviceProxy.Url);
WSStockTraderClient.StockTraderEncrypted.Quote strQuote = ➥
    serviceProxy.RequestQuote("MSFT");

// Results
Console.WriteLine("Web Service call successful. Result:");
Console.WriteLine( " " );
Console.WriteLine( "Symbol: " + strQuote.Symbol );
Console.WriteLine( "Price:  " + strQuote.Last );
Console.WriteLine( "Change: " + strQuote.PercentChange + "%");
}
```

Certificate-based keys must be retrieved from the certificate store using their base64 key identifier. WSE ships with a useful utility called the WSE X509 Certificate Tool, which allows you to browse certificates for the Current User and Local Computer certificate stores, and to retrieve base64 key identifier information. Figure 6-2 shows the tool displaying the client private key certificate that is used in the preceding example. Please refer to Chapter 5 for more information on certificate installation and the WSE X509 Certificate Tool.

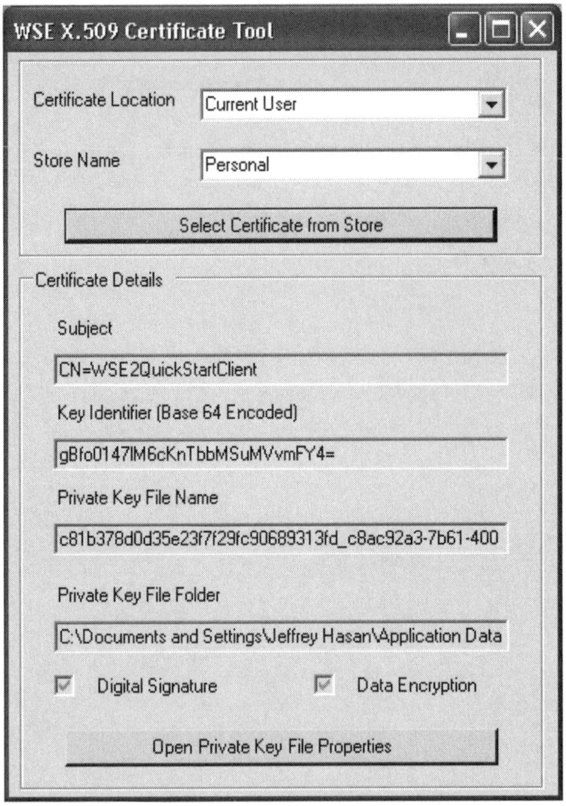

Figure 6-2. The WSE X509 Certificate Tool

Listing 6-10 shows you what the X509SecurityToken class looks like in the Visual Studio .NET Debug window once it has been retrieved from the certificate store. This listing can be seen by running Listing 6-9 in debug mode, and then setting a breakpoint on the retrieved security token. Notice the properties that indicate the certificate supports both digital signatures and data encryption. You cannot assume that every certificate will support these features (although most likely they will). It is a good idea to check these property values in code prior to attaching the certificate to the SOAP message.

Listing 6-10. The X509SecurityToken Class As Shown in the Visual Studio .NET Debug Window

```
?token
    {Microsoft.Web.Services2.Security.X509SecurityToken}
    Microsoft.Web.Services2.Security.BinarySecurityToken:
        {Microsoft.Web.Services2.Security.X509SecurityToken}
    _certificate: {Microsoft.Web.Services2.Security.X509.X509Certificate}
    AuthenticationKey: {Microsoft.Web.Services2.Security.AuthenticationKey}
```

```
Certificate: {Microsoft.Web.Services2.Security.X509.X509Certificate}
DecryptionKey: {Microsoft.Web.Services2.Security.AsymmetricDecryptionKey}
EncryptionKey: {Microsoft.Web.Services2.Security.AsymmetricEncryptionKey}
IsCurrent: true
RawData: {Length=456}
SignatureKey: {Microsoft.Web.Services2.Security.SignatureKey}
SupportsDataEncryption: true
SupportsDigitalSignature: true
ValueType: {System.Xml.XmlQualifiedName}
WsseX509v3: {Microsoft.Web.Services2.Xml.QualifiedName}
```

Modify the Web Service to Process Encrypted SOAP Messages

For asymmetric encryption, the Web service does not require additional code
for processing encrypted SOAP request messages. You must just ensure that the
public key for decryption is installed in the Local Computer certificate store on
the same server where the Web service is installed. If the public key is not installed
correctly, then the client application will receive a SOAP fault indicating a problem on the receiving end.

However, from a policy standpoint, you may still want to put code in place in
the Web method to verify that the request message is in fact encrypted. Listing 6-11
shows the policy-oriented code listing for verifying that an incoming request
message is encrypted.

Listing 6-11. Code to Verify That an Incoming Request Message Is Encrypted

```
bool EncryptionIsValid = false;
SoapContext requestContext = RequestSoapContext.Current;
foreach (ISecurityElement objElem in requestContext.Security.Elements)
{
    if (objElem is EncryptedData)
    {
        // Encrypted Data exists in the Element collections.
        // Now check if it is the body that was encrypted.
        EncryptedData encData = objElem as EncryptedData;
        if (encData.TargetElement.LocalName == "Body")
        {
            EncryptionIsValid = true;
        }
    }
}
```

Listing 6-11 can be inserted within Listing 6-7, directly after the code block
that analyzes the digital signature. As you will see in Chapter 7, you can omit all

of the verification code entirely once you create a policy framework file for the Web service.

Encrypt a SOAP Response Message with an X.509 Certificate, Based on a Digitally Signed SOAP Request Message

All of the examples so far have focused on the SOAP request message that is sent from a client to a Web service. But this is only half the story because we have not focused on the SOAP response message. It is unrealistic to expect that you would send an encrypted SOAP request message and then expect an unsecured SOAP response message in return. If anything, you are probably more interested in having an encrypted SOAP response message because the Web service response is almost certain to contain sensitive information.

In this section, I will present a new version of the WSStockTraderSecure solution that implements the following:

1. The client sends a digitally signed request message to the Web service, using an X.509 certificate.

2. In return, the Web service provides an encrypted response, using the same X.509 certificate that was used to sign the request message.

For clarity, I have created a new Visual Studio .NET solution called WSStockTraderSecure2, which is identical in structure to the original WSStockTraderSecure solution. However, the code has been modified in both the client and the Web service to implement the new security requirements.

Listing 6-12 shows the code for digitally signing the SOAP request message that is generated by the client.

Listing 6-12. Digitally Sign a SOAP Request Message Using an X.509 Certificate

```
public void SignRequestUsingX509Certificate()
{
    // Retrieve the X.509 certificate from the CurrentUserStore certificate store
    X509SecurityToken token = null;
    string ClientBase64KeyId = "gBfoo1471M6cKnTbbMSuMVvmFY4=";

    // Open the CurrentUser Certificate Store
    X509CertificateStore store;
    store = X509CertificateStore.CurrentUserStore( X509CertificateStore.MyStore );
    X509CertificateCollection certs = store.FindCertificateByKeyIdentifier( ➥
        Convert.FromBase64String( ClientBase64KeyId ) );
```

```
if (certs.Count > 0)
{
    // Get the first certificate in the collection
    token = new X509SecurityToken( ((X509Certificate) certs[0]) );
}

if (token == null) throw new ➥
    ApplicationException("Unable to obtain security token.");

StockTraderServiceWse serviceProxy = new StockTraderServiceWse();

// Add the signature element to a security section on the request
// to sign the request
serviceProxy.RequestSoapContext.Security.Tokens.Add( token );
serviceProxy.RequestSoapContext.Security.Elements.Add( ➥
    new MessageSignature( token ) );

// Call the Web service RequestQuote() method
Console.WriteLine("Calling {0}", serviceProxy.Url);
Quote strQuote = serviceProxy.RequestQuote("MSFT");

// Results
Console.WriteLine("Web Service call successful. Result:");
Console.WriteLine( " " );
Console.WriteLine( "Symbol: " + strQuote.Symbol );
Console.WriteLine( "Price:  " + strQuote.Last );
Console.WriteLine( "Change: " + strQuote.PercentChange + "%");
}
```

Notice that the X.509 certificate-based private key is retrieved from the Current User certificate store. Once the SOAP request message is received by the Web service, the following steps need to happen:

1. The Web service must retrieve the public key for the certificate from its LocalMachine certificate store.

2. The Web service method must verify the digitally signed message.

3. The Web service must then decrypt the SOAP message body and process the requested operation.

4. Finally, the Web service must encrypt the response and send it back to the client.

Clearly, this is a lot of additional overhead for the Web service to handle, compared to delivering an unsecured response. But keep in mind that encryption-based security generally creates less overhead compared to other types of binary tokens, such as UsernameToken security tokens, because less code is required on the client and Web service combined. And if your Web service implements a WS-Policy framework, then you will need to write even less code. (WS-Policy is the subject of Chapter 7.)

Listing 6-13 shows the code that is required to accomplish Steps 1 through 4 listed previously.

Listing 6-13. Encrypt a SOAP Response Message Based on the Certificate Used to Digitally Sign the Incoming SOAP Request Message

```
using System.Web.Services.Protocols;
using System.Web.Services.Description;
using System.Xml.Serialization;

using Microsoft.Web.Services2;
using Microsoft.Web.Services2.Security;
using Microsoft.Web.Services2.Security.Tokens;
using Microsoft.Web.Services2.Security.X509;

using System.Security.Permissions;
using StockTraderTypes;

[WebMethod()]
public Quote RequestQuote(string Symbol)
{
    SoapContext requestContext = RequestSoapContext.Current;
    SoapContext responseContext = ResponseSoapContext.Current;

    // Get the signing certificate
    X509SecurityToken token = GetEncryptionToken(requestContext);

    if( token != null )
    {
        // Encrypt the response with the key in the request.
        responseContext.Security.Elements.Add( new EncryptedData( token ) );
    }
    else
    {
        throw new ApplicationException("Unable to retrieve the ➥
            encrypting certificate." );
    }
```

```
    // Step 2: Create a new Quote object, but only populate if signature is valid
    Quote q = new Quote();
    // Generate the quote (code not shown)
    }
    return q; // Return a Quote object
}

private X509SecurityToken GetEncryptionToken(SoapContext requestContext)
{
    X509SecurityToken x509token = null;

    // Look for a digital signature, which contains the token that the Web Service
    // will use for encrypting the response
    if ( requestContext.Security.Tokens.Count > 0 )
    {
        //
        // Check for a Signature that signed the soap Body and uses an x509 token.
        //
        foreach ( ISecurityElement element in requestContext.Security.Elements )
        {
            MessageSignature signature = element as MessageSignature;

            // The signature we seek signed the soap Body
            if ( signature != null && (signature.SignatureOptions & ➥
                SignatureOptions.IncludeSoapBody) != 0 )
            {
                x509token = signature.SigningToken as X509SecurityToken;

                if ( x509token != null )
                {
                    // Return the certificate for encrypting the response
                    // if it is capable of encryption
                    X509Certificate cert = x509token.Certificate;
                    if ( !cert.SupportsDataEncryption )
                    {
                        // return x509token;
                        // Reset x509token to null, so it does not get used
                        x509token = null;
                    }
                }
            }
        }
    }
    return x509token;
}
```

This code listing not surprisingly shares many similarities to several of the previous listings. The biggest difference is within the GetEncryptionToken Web method, which loops through the available digital signatures and then extracts the certificate-based security token that was used to sign the request. This is just another means of retrieving the public key that is needed for encrypting the SOAP response message. Alternatively, you could have written code that retrieves the public key directly from the Web service's Local Computer certificate store.

The Web service code for encrypting the SOAP response message is no different from the code you have already seen in the client for encrypting SOAP request messages. Programmatically, the Web service method appends the certificate-based security token to the security elements collection, and then continues processing the requested operation. The WSE infrastructure then processes the encryption of the resulting SOAP response message. Once the client receives the response, it will have no trouble decrypting it as long as it still has access to the original certificate. And it is likely that the client will since it originally used this same certificate to encrypt the request message.

Final Thoughts on Security Authentication and Encryption

Encryption technology is a complicated field that presents a wide variety of options for end users. You can choose between symmetric and asymmetric encryption, and between a wide variety of acceptable encryption algorithms. Microsoft Windows Server 2003 provides built-in capabilities for certificate generation, and allows you to set up your own personal Certificate Authority. This can be a useful and more affordable option than paying for an expensive certificate from an established Certificate Authority such as VeriSign, Inc. Of course, a certificate is only as trustworthy as the company that issues it, or as trustworthy as the company that it is generated for. As long as your clients trust you as a company, there is no reason you cannot act as a Certificate Authority.

This capability to act as a Certificate Authority (CA) can be especially useful if you implement WS-Secure Conversation, which allows for a dynamic approach in setting up a trusted relationship between services and clients. Two or more services and clients basically agree to establish a trusted relationship with each other using a security token that is provided by an acceptable party. This party acts as the CA. By generating security tokens for the communication, this party is effectively vouching that all of the involved services and clients are trustworthy with respect to each other.

Microsoft has published an excellent whitepaper on WS-Security that provides a detailed discussion of both WS-Security and WS-Secure Conversation, along with a number of excellent architecture diagrams. Please refer to the "WS-Security 2.0 Drilldown" article in the references list in the Appendix.

One important thing to take away from this chapter's discussion is that you must specifically secure SOAP messages in both directions: request and response. Even if you secure the request message that is sent from the client to the Web service, the Web service response will be unsecured, unsigned, and unencrypted unless you specifically implement these measures in the SOAP response messages. It can be quite startling to realize that the most highly secured request message may result in a completely unsecured response message if the Web service provider has not taken equivalent steps.

This chapter has shown you how to implement several types of security measures in SOAP messages. However, I did not address two key related points:

- How does a client know the level of security that a Web service requires?

- How does a Web service provide selective access to its methods and resources, based on the authorization level for the authenticated user?

In the absence of the Web service telling you what its security policy is, you will be forced to play a guessing game of trying out different kinds of security and hoping they work. Clearly, the Web service needs to inform its clients as to what level of security it requires in SOAP request messages. This responsibility is governed by the WS-Policy and WS-Policy Assertions specifications, which are the subject of the next chapter. Regarding authorization, it is clear that a Web service needs to be able to provide selective access to its resources based on a client's privilege level. The service cannot simply allow any authenticated user full access to its resources. Just because certain users are authenticated does not mean that they are fully authorized to use all of the available resources. Security policy and authorization are related topics because both have to do with restricting access to a Web service to only those clients that meet strict usage requirements. Chapter 7 provides detailed discussions on both of these important topics.

For more information on security and encryption in general, and on WS-Security in particular, consult the list of excellent references in Appendix A.

TIP *You can find the WS-Security specification at* http://www-106.ibm.com/
developerworks/webservices/library/ws-secure/.

Prevent Replay Attacks Using Timestamps, Digital Signatures, and Message Correlation

I will close out this chapter with a look at a different kind of security issue called *replay attacks*. These are a type of denial-of-service (DoS) attack that is specific to Web services. A replay attack occurs when a client makes multiple Web service calls to the same service without waiting for a response from one or more previous requests. If enough of these calls are made, then it is possible to overwhelm the Web service's hosting server, and to then cause the service to become unresponsive or to go offline. Replay attacks are at best a nuisance, and at worst can cause critical system breakdowns.

The WS-Security specification mentions replay attacks and briefly describes a strategy for dealing with them. The key to preventing a replay attack is for a Web service to monitor the status of incoming messages and to verify their uniqueness. The Web service needs to verify that an incoming SOAP request message is unique, and has not already been sent, before the service starts processing the message.

> **NOTE** *You can eliminate replay attacks by unauthorized clients by using an encrypted communication channel such as Secure Sockets Layer. However, SSL provides no protection if the authorized client decides to conduct a replay attack. Other protective measures are required. The strategies that are outlined in this section assume that you want to prevent replay attacks by verifying request messages for uniqueness, and by verifying that the request messages have not been tampered with.*

Standard Web service calls are stateless, and SOAP messages are inherently stateless, one-way communications. SOAP messages must therefore include extra information that tracks their uniqueness, and thereby helps the service to verify whether a request message has already been received. There are three main ways to track this information and to enable message verification and protection against replay attacks:

- Message timestamps (including Created and Expires)

- UsernameToken nonce values

- Message correlation (including sequence numbers)

Let's consider each of these in turn, and see how they can be used to secure SOAP messages, and Web services, against replay attacks.

Use Timestamps for Message Verification

Message timestamps are added to an outgoing SOAP request message by the sender, either automatically or manually, depending on how the client is configured. The WSE output filters contain a specific filter called TimestampOutputFilter, which automatically applies timestamp information to outgoing SOAP messages. This filter is enabled in the pipeline by default, and you should never remove it because timestamps help in detecting unauthorized SOAP message requests, as described later. Listing 6-14 shows how the service can then retrieve the timestamp information programmatically from the message's SoapContext class.

Listing 6-14. Retrieving Timestamp Information from a SOAP Request Message

```
using Microsoft.Web.Services2.Security;
using Microsoft.Web.Services2.Security.Tokens;

// Retrieve the request message SOAP context
SoapContext requestContext = RequestSoapContext.Current;

// Retrieve Timestamp information
System.DateTime dtCreateDate = requestContext.Security.Timestamp.Created;
System.DateTime dtExpirationDate = requestContext.Security.Timestamp.Expires;
long dtTimeToLive = requestContext.Security.Timestamp.TtlInSeconds;// in seconds
string TimestampID = requestContext.Security.Timestamp.Id;
```

The client may choose to set an expiration date and time on the request message, which means that the message is only valid for a specific number of seconds after it is issued. This ensures that if the SOAP message is intercepted and re-sent by an unauthorized sender, then it will only be useful to them for a limited amount of time. And of course, if the message expiration is set short enough, then there will not be time for an unauthorized party to intercept and reroute the message. Message timestamps and expiration are a useful first defense for preventing the unauthorized use of legitimate SOAP messages. As added protection, the client may digitally sign both the message body and the timestamp directly. This allows the receiving service to detect a scenario wherein the timestamp itself was tampered with and altered by an unauthorized user.

In this chapter, I did not discuss how to digitally sign SOAP message headers. I only explained how to sign the SOAP message body. Or so you may have thought, because it turns out that WSE actually incorporates selected SOAP message headers into the digital signature (in addition to the SOAP message body), and the Created and Expires timestamp information is included. In fact, if you study the WS-Security encoding in a SOAP request message, you will see a listing of all signed message elements. This information is stored within the <wsse:Security><Signature><SignedInfo> node. So the good news is that you do not have to do any manual work to either timestamp a message or digitally sign this information. WSE takes care of it for you, as long as the TimestampOutputFilter is enabled, and as long as you add a digital signature to the SOAP request message.

> **NOTE** *SOAP message interception and tampering is a serious security issue that will become more widely understood (and worried about!) once Web services become more commonly deployed and used by companies. If a thief steals your credit card, then they have access to a legitimate source of credit even though they themselves are an unauthorized user. SOAP message interception potentially creates the same security compromise scenario.*

Once the service receives the request message, it can cache the SoapContext while it processes the message. Subsequent incoming request messages can then be compared against the cached SoapContext objects and rejected if the service detects that the request has already been received. Recall that the SoapContext is a WSE-specific class representation of a SOAP message, and is a member of the Microsoft.Web.Services2 namespace. You can use the SoapContext class to programmatically access the properties of a SOAP message, including its headers and body. By now you should be getting very familiar with the SoapContext class. In this chapter, for example, I also showed you how to use the SoapContext class to set and retrieve security tokens assigned to a message.

There are no specific rules as to what kind of information you should use to correlate SoapContext information between messages. Basically, any unique identifying information makes for a good candidate, as long as it cannot be spoofed by an unauthorized third party. So you will want to choose a piece of information that can be digitally signed in the request message. Good candidates include addressing headers and security token IDs. In Chapter 9, I will discuss the WS-Addressing specification, which allows you to add addressing headers to a SOAP message, including sender origin and reply to address information. In addition to addressing headers, you can correlate messages using specific contents of the SOAP message body, or any other header information that is uniquely set by the client. If the message uses a security token, then the token itself can be used to uniquely identify a message.

Use UsernameToken Nonce Values for Message Verification

If you find yourself struggling to extract a unique piece of information from a message (using the SoapContext class), and the message includes a UsernameToken security token, then you can use a nonce-based token ID as a unique identifier. A *nonce* is simply a random cryptographic string that can be assigned as the ID value for the UsernameToken security token. When the service receives a request message, it can extract the nonce value from the security token and cache the value for the duration of the request message. These ID values are part of the message signature and cannot be spoofed. And because they are nonce values, it is highly unlikely that two request messages will coincidentally share the same ID values. However, this could happen if you choose to rely on the auto-generated ID value for the security token.

Again, the burden remains on the service to cache information on incoming request messages. But if you need to take this approach, then a nonce value is the simplest way to do so.

Listing 6-15 shows how the client can assign a nonce value to a UsernameToken security token.

Listing 6-15. Assigning a Nonce Value to a UsernameToken Security Token

```
using Microsoft.Web.Services2.Security;
using Microsoft.Web.Services2.Security.Tokens;

SecurityToken token = new UsernameToken(username, passwordEquivalent, ➡
    PasswordOption.SendHashed);

// Assign a random nonce value to the security token
Nonce objNonce = new Nonce(34);
token.Id = objNonce.Value;
```

You may be wondering why nonce values apply specifically to the UsernameToken security token. This is because other security tokens are more sophisticated and do not require the additional guarantee of uniqueness that a nonce value provides. A UsernameToken security token is, after all, simply a hashed username-password combination, and there is nothing inherently unique about this combination. Usernames and passwords can be duplicated between users much more easily than cryptographic values can, especially if a malicious client is intentionally using another client's credentials.

If you use an alternate security token such as an X.509 certificate, then you are automatically afforded some protection because the client and the service are using credentials that are not easily discovered. However, as I pointed out with SSL, this does not provide protection against replay attacks. You cannot assume that authorized clients will by their nature avoid carrying out a replay attack. For example, consider a client that auto-generates Web service calls in batch mode. If this client were to experience a system error or breakdown in business logic, then it is conceivable that the client might generate duplicate request messages to the service. This is why you must tackle replay attacks at the message and service level. You cannot protect against replay attacks under the umbrella of a trusted relationship between client and service.

Use Message Correlation and Sequence Numbers for Message Verification

The key to preventing replay attacks is for the Web service to verify the uniqueness of incoming request messages. The WS-Addressing specification describes a GUID-based message ID that is one of several addressing headers that can be assigned to a SOAP message. WSE provides support for the WS-Addressing specification in general, and for addressing headers specifically. Once again, the burden is on the Web service to store message correlation information and to determine whether an incoming message has already been received. As with other kinds of identifiers, the message ID does not in and of itself prevent replay attacks, but it provides another simple, unique identifier for an incoming SOAP message.

> **NOTE** *Refer to Chapter 9 for more information on the WS-Addressing specification.*

Another type of message identifier is the sequence number, which stamps a message with the sequential role that it plays in a business process. Sequence numbers are part of the WS-Reliable Messaging specification, and are designed to enable business orchestration, which refers to a business process or workflow that spans multiple components. In service-oriented architectures, sequenced messages are exchanged between multiple Web services, and the collective outcome represents the completion of the business workflow.

Sequence numbers provide an additional advantage for preventing replay attacks because a message that contains a duplicate sequence number is automatically suspect. Sequence numbers alone do not ensure uniqueness, but they will in conjunction with a message ID.

Summary

This chapter has shown you how to use WS-Security to implement several types of security measures in SOAP messages, including the following:

1. Message authentication using security tokens based on username-password combinations and X.509 certificates.

2. Digital signatures on SOAP messages to detect message tampering.

3. Encryption of SOAP messages (using asymmetric encryption) to protect the contents of a SOAP message from network sniffers.

This chapter focused on the digital signing and encryption of SOAP messages in two directions: request and response. One-way signing and encryption (from the client to the service) is easier to implement, but this may create a significant security exposure. I also provided a discussion on the role of Certificate Authorities in certificate-based trusted relationships between clients and services, and I highlighted again the distinction between authenticated users versus authorized users. Security measures such as digital signatures and encryption enable services to authenticate clients. However, authenticated clients are not necessarily authorized to access the full capabilities of a given Web service. The topic of authorization is discussed in the next chapter.

Finally, I closed with a discussion of replay attacks, which are a form of denial-of-service (DoS) attack. The risk of replay attacks can be minimized if the Web service correlates incoming request messages and verifies their uniqueness prior to processing them.

CHAPTER 7

Use Policy Frameworks to Enforce Web Service Requirements with WS-Policy

SERVICE-ORIENTED WEB SERVICES enforce specific usage requirements that clients must meet in order to use the service. Web services cannot simply respond to any request that comes in. Instead, they must be selective and can only process incoming requests that conform to their stated requirements. For example, a Web service may require that all incoming service requests be digitally signed and encrypted. Furthermore, a Web service may specifically require that the digital signature be based on an X.509 certificate, rather than another type of security token. Clients that send nonconforming service requests to the Web service, such as unsigned, unencrypted requests, will receive a SOAP fault as their response message.

Sometimes policies need to be enforced, but do not need to be this restrictive. For example, a Web service may require digital signatures, but will accept signatures based on any type of security token. Web services need to inform their potential clients as to what requirements they enforce in order to provide a service. Without this information, potential clients can only guess at what requirements are enforced. Clearly, this would be an inefficient approach that just will not work in a service-oriented production environment.

The WS-Policy specification provides the means to implement and enforce a standard policy framework for Web services. The WS-Policy specification itself is more of a generic model that outlines general syntax for documenting a policy framework. There are many kinds of potential policies that a Web service may need to communicate and enforce, including security requirements and quality of service of requirements. Each of these specific policy needs is governed by a more specific WS specification that works with the more general WS-Policy specification. For example, security policy is governed by the specialized WS-Security Policy specification.

Web Services Enhancements (WSE) 2.0 provides support for configuring and implementing policy frameworks. WSE provides the infrastructure to automatically enforce a policy framework without requiring any additional lines of code. As long as the policy framework is documented correctly, the infrastructure will automatically support it. This is a tremendous productivity benefit for developers.

Policy frameworks are a welcome addition to Web services technology because they formalize operating requirements within a service-oriented architecture. This level of formality brings with it the maturity that Web services technology needs in order to gain wider acceptance and use within the business community and across industries that are very sensitive to the exchange of information.

Overview of the Policy Framework Specifications

Policy frameworks are governed by a cooperative set of related specifications starting with WS-Policy, which provides a generic model for documenting Web service policy. WS-Policy provides an extensible XML-based grammar and a schema for defining the structure of policy framework documents. The actual requirements themselves are referred to as *policy assertions*, and are governed by another specification called WS-Policy Assertions. The container document holds a *policy expression* that is composed of one or more individual policy assertions. So, the WS-Policy specification governs the policy expression, while the WS-Policy Assertions specification governs the policy assertions.

Policy assertions may be of a specialized nature and may therefore require dedicated specifications. For example, security policy is documented with the specialized WS-Security Policy specification. Every WS-Specification provides its own associated XML schema, and WS-Security Policy is no exception. It provides specialized tags that distinguish a security-oriented policy assertion from a more general policy assertion.

Policy expressions do not exist in a vacuum; they must always apply to so-called *policy subjects*, which are the targets that policy expressions apply to. A policy subject can include different aspects of a Web service, including specific endpoints or more general messages. The most straightforward example of a policy expression is one that applies to the body of all incoming SOAP messages for all Web service operations, for example, a policy stating that all incoming messages must be digitally signed and encrypted. The default policy subject is the entire Web service, namely, all of its operations and their associated SOAP messages. Table 7-1 provides a glossary of the most important terms that apply to the WS-Policy family of specifications.

Table 7-1. Glossary of Terms That Apply to the WS-Policy Specifications

Term	Definition
Policy framework	A set of requirements, preferences, and capabilities that apply to a Web service, mainly focused on security, including digital signing and encryption.
Policy expression	An XML document that contains one or more policy assertions, as well as support elements that make up the well-formed, qualified document.
Policy assertion	An individual requirement, preference, or capability. One or more assertions make up a policy expression.
Policy subject	The target of a policy expression. This includes either an entire Web service or a specific endpoint within the Web service.
Policy attachment	The means by which a policy expression is associated with one or more policy subjects.

The WS-Policy Attachments specification allows you to associate policy expressions with different kinds of policy subjects, including XML messages and specific Web service endpoints. The WS-Policy Attachments specification integrates with WSDL documents, meaning that you can apply this specification's XML attributes to selected elements within the WSDL document. These include the <portType> and <binding> elements, which give you a fine level of control over the policy expression for specific Web service operations (or endpoints, to be more accurate). Refer to Chapter 2 if you need a refresher on what these elements are. The material in Chapter 2 is essential to understanding Web services architecture in general, and is especially helpful in understanding how to apply the WS-Policy family of specifications.

Figure 7-1 provides an overview of how the various policy specifications work together to implement a policy framework.

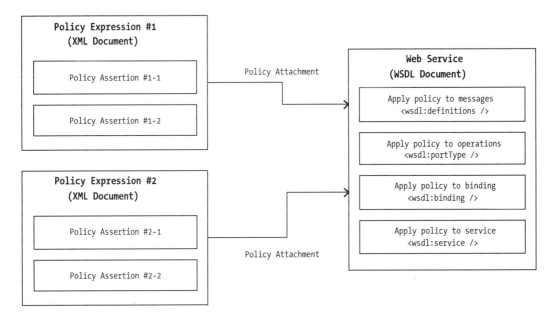

Figure 7-1. An implemented policy framework

The policy expressions are contained within XML documents that are installed with the Web service. Optionally, you can use the WS-Policy Attachments specification to associate policies with specific aspects of the Web service. You do not have to take this additional step; policies apply to all Web service operations and messages by default.

Now let's look at how to implement policy frameworks for Web services.

Overview of Policy Frameworks

The WS-Policy family of specifications defines a set of XML schemas that allow you to store policy information directly in a SOAP message. In fact, each of the WS-Specifications provides its own XML schemas, each with a unique set of qualified XML elements for storing custom information in the SOAP message header. In many cases the WSE class framework shields you from the underlying XML elements because the classes automatically generate the tags for you. Unfortunately, with WS-Policy, you do not have this luxury.

The purpose of WS-Policy, quite simply, is to provide a declarative model for Web service requirements, rather than a programmatic model. The sample solutions in Chapter 6 are a perfect example. Recall that these samples show you how to add digital signatures and encryption to SOAP request and response messages. This creates a programmatic burden in the receiving Web services because you have to write code to verify that the security info has been properly administered.

With WS-Policy, all of this verification code goes away, and instead the Web service references an XML-based policy framework file that contains the applicable security requirements. For example, a Web service may establish a policy that incoming service requests must be encrypted with public key encryption based on an X.509 certificate only. This policy information may be verified programmatically in code (as I did in the Chapter 6 sample solutions), or you can create a declarative policy framework file that stores this same information using XML markup. The WSE infrastructure in turn uses the policy framework file to verify an incoming SOAP request at runtime. If the SOAP message fails verification, then a SOAP exception is raised, just as with programmatic verification.

Policy framework files are actually very versatile, and they can be written to trigger verification on specific elements within a SOAP message. Policy frameworks may also be applied on both incoming and outgoing messages. A request policy applies to incoming messages, whereas a response policy applies to outgoing messages. There is no difference in the construction of a request versus a response policy. You need only specify which direction the policy applies to. I will show you how to build policy framework files in detail later in the chapter.

By default, policy frameworks apply to the entire Web service. However, you may choose to narrow the policy subject to a specific endpoint, including a specific Web method (or operation, which is the more accurate term in this context).

Policy frameworks save you a lot of time because you no longer have to write any verification code. In addition, a policy framework serves as a clear document of the requirements, preferences, and capabilities of a Web service.

There are four main steps for creating a policy framework file:

Step 1: Create the policy framework shell. This is an XML configuration file that is accessible to the applicable Web service project.

Step 2: Implement a set of applicable policy assertions. You have a limited choice of built-in policy assertions to choose from. If none of these apply to a specific policy requirement that you have, then you can create a custom policy assertion to describe the custom requirement.

Step 3: Map the policy expression file to the applicable SOAP endpoints (by default, the entire Web service).

Step 4: Configure the policy framework in the applicable Web service project. This step ensures that the Web service is aware of the policy framework and that the WSE infrastructure applies the policy automatically at runtime.

WSE 2.0 provides great support for the WS-Security Policy specification, which governs a set of policy assertions that are specifically geared toward security. Table 7-2 summarizes the most important built-in WS-Security Policy assertions that are currently available in WSE 2.0.

Table 7-2. Built-in WS-Security Policy Assertions in WSE 2.0

Policy Assertion	Description
Integrity	Specifies a signature format, including the security token type and the applicable hash algorithm. The Integrity assertion contains one or more SecurityToken assertions.
Confidentiality	Specifies an encryption format, including the hash algorithm, the security token type, and the SOAP elements that must be encrypted.
SecurityToken	Specifies a security token type; included within the Integrity and Confidentiality policy assertions.
MessageAge	Specifies the time period within which messages are considered current and may be processed. Outside of this time period, messages are considered to be expired, and will not be processed.

In addition, WSE 2.0 provides built-in support for the MessagePredicate policy assertion, which allows you to define custom business validation rules using XPath expressions. The SOAP message must conform to these rules in order to pass the policy check. The term MessagePredicate sounds confusing until you consider its meaning. Namely, it has to do with predicates for a message, otherwise known as the (policy) prerequisites for a message. The MessagePredicate policy assertion operates on the SOAP envelope, and it provides a flexible way to validate one or more parts of the SOAP message.

There are certain common predicates for messages. For example, a Web service could implement a policy stating that all incoming SOAP request messages must include specific addressing headers, such as To, From, Message ID, and Action. This is a fairly common prerequisite, and so it would be an unnecessary burden to have to write custom XPath expressions for this straightforward message predicate. To keep things simpler, WSE 2.0 supports alternate dialects, including one based on message parts, which simply requires you to list those message parts in the policy file that must be present within the SOAP envelope. Without these elements, a SOAP message cannot be considered in compliance with the Web service policy.

If you find that the built-in policy assertions do not fit what you need, then WSE 2.0 provides support for building custom policy assertions. WSE allows you to build a custom handler class for policy assertion logic that integrates into the WSE pipeline. This topic is beyond the scope of this chapter, but please refer to the Appendix for reference articles that provide detailed information on how to build custom policy assertions.

Listing 7-1 provides one example of a policy framework, in which the Web service requires that the body of an incoming SOAP request message must be digitally signed with a UsernameToken security token. The listing includes a MessagePredicate policy assertion that is restricted to the message body in this listing. However, it could also be used to require the message to include specific addressing headers, for example, using wsp:Header(wsa:To), wsp:Header(wsa:Action), wsp:Header(wsa:MessageID), and wsp:Header(wsa:From).

Listing 7-1. A Sample Policy Framework

```xml
<?xml version="1.0" encoding="utf-8"?>
<policyDocument xmlns="http://schemas.microsoft.com/wse/2003/06/Policy">
  <mappings xmlns:wse="http://schemas.microsoft.com/wse/2003/06/Policy">
    <endpoint uri="http://localhost/StockTraderSecurePolicy/StockTrader.asmx">
      <defaultOperation>
        <request policy="#Encrypt-X.509" />
        <response policy="" />
        <fault policy="" />
      </defaultOperation>
    </endpoint>
  </mappings>
  <policies xmlns:wsu="http://docs.oasis-open.org/wss/2004/01/
    oasis-200401-wss-wssecurity-utility-1.0.xsd"
    xmlns:wsp="http://schemas.xmlsoap.org/ws/2002/12/policy"
    xmlns:wssp="http://schemas.xmlsoap.org/ws/2002/12/secext"
    xmlns:wse="http://schemas.microsoft.com/wse/2003/06/Policy"
    xmlns:wsse="http://docs.oasis-open.org/wss/2004/01/
    oasis-200401-wss-wssecurity-secext-1.0.xsd"
    xmlns:wsa="http://schemas.xmlsoap.org/ws/2004/03/addressing">
    <!-- This policy ensures that the message is encrypted
      with an x.509 Certificate -->
    <wsp:Policy wsu:Id="Encrypt-X.509">
      <!-- The MessagePredicate indicates where to apply the policy -->
      <wsp:MessagePredicate wsp:Usage="wsp:Required"
        Dialect="http://schemas.xmlsoap.org/2002/12/wsse#part">
          wsp:Body()
      </wsp:MessagePredicate>
      <!--The Confidentiality assertion is used to ensure that
        the SOAP Body is encrypted.-->
      <wssp:Confidentiality wsp:Usage="wsp:Required">
        <wssp:KeyInfo>
        <!--The SecurityToken element within the KeyInfo element describes which
            token type must be used for Encryption.-->
        <wssp:SecurityToken>
          <wssp:TokenType>http://docs.oasis-open.org/wss/2004/01/
            oasis-200401-wss-x509-token-profile-1.0#X509v3</wssp:TokenType>
        </wssp:SecurityToken>
        </wssp:KeyInfo>
```

```
    <wssp:MessageParts Dialect="http://schemas.xmlsoap.org/2002/12/wsse#part">
      wsp:Body()</wssp:MessageParts>
    </wssp:Confidentiality>
  </wsp:Policy>
 </policies>
</policyDocument>
```

Listing 7-1 defines a policy framework called #Encrypt-X.509 that is a default policy, meaning that it applies to the entire Web service. The <wssp:TokenType> element specifies the required security token, while the <wssp:MessageParts> element specifies that the digital signature must apply to the body of the SOAP message. (Alternatively, you could extend the applicable message parts to include header elements.)

WSE 2.0 supports other built-in policy assertions outside of WS-Security Policy; however, the assertions presented in Table 7-2 are the most important ones from the standpoint of usefulness. Other policy assertions govern requirements for text encoding and language; however, most of the time you can simply rely on the default settings for these requirements. The exception is the MessagePredicate policy assertion, which enforces the required set of elements that a SOAP message must contain. Listing 7-1 includes this policy assertion, and it requires that the incoming SOAP message contain a body tag along with several WS-Addressing–related elements. Clearly, this is a SOAP message that may get routed across multiple services before returning to the client.

Listing 7-1 illustrates examples of namespaces associated with the WS-Policy, WS-Policy Assertions, and WS-Security Policy specifications. By default, the policy expression applies to the entire Web service, meaning that every SOAP message is validated in the same way, regardless of what Web service operation it is intended for. If you need to map the policy expression to a specific set of Web service endpoints, then you will also need to include the namespace for the WS-Policy Attachments specification. Listing 7-2 shows an example of how WS-Policy Attachments and WS-Addressing work together to associate a policy expression with a specific Web service endpoint.

Listing 7-2. XML Markup for the WS-Policy Attachment Specification

```
<wsp:PolicyAttachment>
    <wsp:AppliesTo>
        <wsa:EndpointReference
            xmlns:st="http://www.bluestonepartners.com/schemas/StockTrader">
            <wsa:Address>http://www.bluestonepartners.com/stocktrader</wsa:Address>
            <wsa:PortType>st:BasicUserPortType</wsa:PortType>
            <wsa:ServiceName>st:StockTrader</wsa:ServiceName>
        </wsa:EndpointReference>
```

```
        </wsp:AppliesTo>
        <wsp:PolicyReference URI="http://www. bluestonepartners.com/policy.xml" />
        <wsse:Security>
            <ds:Signature> ...
            </ds:Signature>
        </wsse:Security>
</wsp:PolicyAttachment>
```

Listing 7-2 states that the policy expression applies to the collection of operations under the BasicUserPortType. Recall that the <portType> element in a WSDL document groups a collection of related operations and may be a subset of the total number of available operations that the Web service supports. In this example, the referenced <portType> refers to the subset of operations that are accessible by basic users only.

You can be forgiven if your head is spinning by now because policy frameworks encompass a wide range of specifications and corresponding XML namespaces, and it is hard to get your mind around everything at once. The good news is that the typical policy expression is a relatively simple XML file you can reuse across multiple Web services. The bad news is that WSE 2.0 makes you code the file by hand (although it does provide a limited GUI tool that helps you create basic policy expression files).

Remember, policy files ultimately save you work because you avoid having to write the policy verification code manually. Let's jump straight into some sample code and XML to show you how to implement your own policy framework files with WSE 2.0.

Implement a Policy Framework

In this section, you will see the structure of a basic policy expression file, including the minimum required elements that it must support. I will then show you an actual policy expression file and how it affects the code listing in the associated Web service. I will compare this code listing against a similar sample solution that does not include a policy file, and which must implement verification manually.

Required Elements in a Policy Expression File

A basic policy expression file defines a set of policy assertions and the endpoints that they map to. Policies may be created for both the sender and receiver, but typically the policy information will be stored at the receiver, that is, at the Web service. The receiver can maintain two policy files: one for the incoming request message and one for the outgoing response message at the service.

Listing 7-3 shows the minimum required XML elements for a policy expression file. This is the basic file structure that you will fill in to create the actual policy framework file.

Listing 7-3. Minimum Required XML Elements for a Policy Expression File

```
<policyDocument>
    <mappings>
        <endpoint
                <defaultOperation>
                        <request policy="[ID]" />
                        <response policy="[ID]" />
                        <fault policy="[ID]" />
                </defaultOperation>
        </endpoint>
    </mappings>
    <policies>
        <policy/>
    </policies>
</policyDocument>
```

Listing 7-3 does not actually do anything because no policy assertions have been defined. There are four steps for creating a basic policy framework file. Let's consider an example of a policy that requires all incoming SOAP request messages to be encrypted with an incoming X.509 certificate.

Step 1: Create the Basic XML File

Policy expression files are bounded with the <policyDocument> element. Within this element are two main elements: <policies> and <mappings>. The <policies> element contains the collection of policy assertions that will apply. Each policy assertion is stored in a <policy> element. A <policies> element may contain one or more <policy> elements.

Step 2: Add a Policy Assertion

As you saw earlier in Table 7-2 and Listing 7-1, WSE 2.0 provides built-in support for five standard policy assertions: Integrity, Confidentiality, SecurityToken, MessageAge, and MessagePredicate. These policy assertions are composable, and each must be stored within separate <policy> elements. In turn, the <policy> elements are added within the <policies> element. This design enables you to specify more than one applicable policy assertion to the Web service.

The XML for these standard policy assertions is tightly defined in the WS-Policy and WS-Security Policy specifications, so you can use established, qualified XML to define your assertions. There is more flexibility with the MessagePredicate policy assertion because it supports multiple dialects, including custom XPath statements and a fixed message parts dialect.

Policy assertions should be assigned with an identifier so that they can be referenced from other areas within the policy framework file. Listing 7-4 provides an example of a standard policy assertion for requiring that a message provide an expiration timestamp.

Listing 7-4. A Standard Policy Assertion

```xml
<?xml version="1.0" encoding="utf-8" ?>
<policyDocument xmlns="http://microsoft.com/wse/2003/06/PolicyDocument">
  <mappings>
    <endpoint>
        <defaultOperation />
    </endpoint>
  </mappings>
  <policies xmlns="http://schemas.microsoft.com/wse/2/PolicyDocument"
      xmlns:wsu="http://docs.oasis-open.org/wss/2004/01/
      oasis-200401-wss-wssecurity-utility-1.0.xsd"
      xmlns:wsse="http://docs.oasis-open.org/wss/2004/01/
      oasis-200401-wss-wssecurity-secext-1.0.xsd"
      xmlns:wsp="http://schemas.xmlsoap.org/ws/2002/12/policy">
    <wsp:Policy wsu:Id="#policy-123">
      <wsse:MessageAge wsp:Usage="wsp:Required" Age="4" />
    </wsp:Policy>
  </policies>
</PolicyDocumentpolicyDocument>
```

The WSE 2.0 online documentation provides clear examples of how to write the XML for standard policy assertions such as the one shown in Listing 7-4. WSE 2.0 does not provide much support for auto-generating WS-Policy–related XML markup. WSE's Configuration Editor provides minimal auto-generation support for policy framework files. WSE also ships with a simple security settings wizard, but you can use any XML editor that you are comfortable with. Your main asset in generating your own policy framework files will be to copy the XML from existing files, and customizing it to suit your needs.

What WSE 2.0 lacks in WS-Policy XML support, it more than makes up for in what it does with the files. When properly configured, the policy framework files save you from writing custom code for common tasks, such as authenticating security credentials.

Step 3: Map the Policy to the Web Service

The <mappings> element contains one or more <endpoint> elements that bind the policy to specific Web service endpoints. The simplest mapping is one in which the policy applies to the entire Web service. In this case, you simply specify the URI for the Web service, as shown in Listing 7-5.

Listing 7-5. A Default Policy Mapping

```
<mappings>
  <endpoint="http://www.bluestonepartners.com/stocktrader.asmx">
    <defaultOperation>
        <request policy="#policy-123" />
        <response policy=" " />
        <fault policy=" " />
    </defaultOperation> policy="#policy-7u8hs-j87sh"/>
  </endpoint>
</mappings>
<policies>
    <policy Id="#policy-123" />
</policies>
```

Notice that the policy ID shown in Listing 7-5 corresponds to the policy assertion that is shown in Listing 7-4. This policy framework file specifies a request policy only. However, you could easily extend this file to specify additional policy requirements. For example, let's say that policy ID #policy-123 specifies encryption. The policy itself does not care if it applies to request or response messages. You set this association using the <request> and <response> nodes within <defaultOperation>. If you want to specify encryption on both request and response messages, then you simply assign the same policy ID #policy-123 to both the <request> and <response> nodes.

If you use a default policy mapping, then the client must also implement the WS-Addressing specification. Specifically, the URI in the policy framework file's <endpoint> element and attribute must match the URI in the <wsa:To> addressing header element. If it does not, then the SOAP message will not be considered in compliance with the policy.

Step 4: Configure the Policy

The policy framework file should be stored as an XML file within the Web service project. For example, you could save Listing 7-4 as policyCache.xml, and store it in the root of the StockTrader Web service project.

Next, you need to configure the policy framework file in the Web service web.config file so that it knows to use it. Assuming that you have configured the project to use WSE 2.0, you will already have a new <section> entry for the Microsoft.Web.Services2 assembly within the <configuration><configSections> element.

Scroll down within the file and locate the <microsoft.web.services2> element. Add a <policy> element and a <cache> element to specify the name of the policy framework file, as shown in Listing 7-6.

Listing 7-6. Configuring a Policy Framework File

```
<microsoft.web.services2>
    <security>
        <x509 allowTestRoot="true" allowRevocationUrlRetrieval="false"
            verifyTrust="false" storeLocation="LocalMachine" />
    </security>
    <policy>
        <cache name="policyCache.xml" />
    </policy>
    <diagnostics />
</microsoft.web.services2>
```

The <policy> element itself is very straightforward. Listing 7-6 also includes a <security> element that shows you how to configure the test root certificate that ships with WSE 2.0.

Policy Discovery

WSE 2.0 does not support the automatic discovery or retrieval of policy files. Currently, the publisher of the policy must take responsibility to deliver the policy file manually to all prospective clients. There are three ways to do this. One way is for the publisher to post the policy framework file on a Web site or FTP site for prospective clients to download. The second way is for the publisher to simply e-mail the policy framework file to prospective clients. Either way, once the client receives the policy framework file, it can be registered with the client application. This ensures that the WSE pipeline will catch policy violations at the client before the request message even goes out to the Web service.

The third way is for the publisher to simply inform prospective clients of its policy requirements without sending a policy framework file. The disadvantage of this approach is that it puts the burden on the client developer to manually verify that it is in compliance with the Web service policy. For example, if the Web service requires encrypted request messages, and the client does not send one, then the client will receive an error back from the Web service directly. If on the other hand the client implements its own copy of the policy framework file, then the issue will be caught at the client rather than rejected by the Web service. This gives the client more control in heading off potential policy violations early.

If this all seems confusing, just keep in mind that the client is dependent on the service to set policy. At some level it really does not matter how the client gets informed of the service policy, or how it verifies policy compliance, just as long as the policy requirements get implemented. For example, if the service requires incoming requests to be digitally signed, then the client simply needs to know this and then implement this. Otherwise, the client's requests will get rejected by the service.

Ultimately, you should use policy files to the degree that they will save you from having to manually write verification code for SOAP messages.

In closing the discussion on the discovery of policy framework files, I should note another major shortcoming related to the lack of automatic discovery. Policy framework files do not currently have an easy way to integrate with WSDL documents. Up until now, we have come to expect that WSDL documents contain all of the information that is required for a client to bind to a Web service. While this is still largely true, there are exceptions, especially with the newer and evolving specifications such as WS-Policy. It is highly likely that policy information will be incorporated into the next version of the WSDL specification, although as of now it is unclear exactly where it will fit. I am bringing this point up because you will either come across it in your own research or, as I did, you will start to realize this shortcoming once you start working with policy framework files. The WS-Policy specification has firm traction and fills an important niche, so it is only a matter of time before it is integrated with the WSDL specification.

Generate a Policy Expression File

The XML markup for policy files is difficult to code by hand, so you will want to consider using the Configuration Editor tool that ships with WSE 2.0. In this section, you will learn to create and implement policy expression files, and will see how policy violations are raised back to the client.

Figure 7-2 shows a simple solution called WSTestPolicy.sln that demonstrates how to implement policy files. The standard StockTrader application that we have been using throughout the book contains a lot of extraneous code that will blur the picture as you work through the policy code. So I have created a stripped down sample solution that is structured along the same lines as the other StockTrader applications.

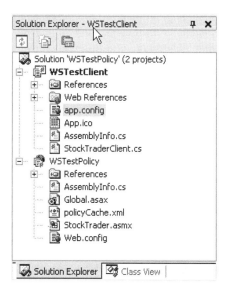

Figure 7-2. The Visual Studio .NET WSTestPolicy solution

The StockTrader.asmx Web service file contains two shell Web methods that return status strings. The code listing is shown in Listing 7-7.

Listing 7-7. The WSTestPolicy StockTrader Web Service

```
[WebMethod]
public string RequestQuote()
{
  return "RequestQuote() service call was successful";
}

[WebMethod]
public string PlaceTrade()
{
  return "PlaceTrade() service call was successful";
}
```

The Web service implements a policy framework file for request operations called policyCache.xml. You can generate this file automatically using the WSE Security Setting Tool, which is accessed from the Configuration Editor's Policy tab, as shown in Figure 7-3.

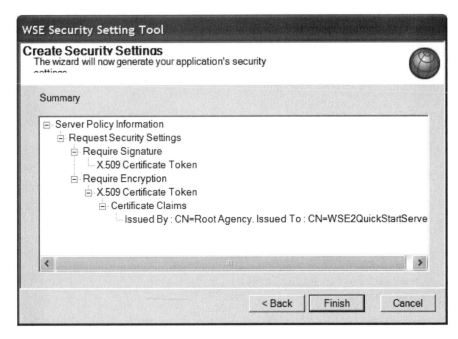

Figure 7-3. The WSE Security Setting Tool, used for generating a policy expression

This policy expression states that the Web service will only accept request messages that have been encrypted with an X.509 certificate. Listing 7-8 shows what the resulting configuration file looks like, and Listing 7-9 shows you how you attach the policy file to the Web service using a configuration setting in the web.config file. This policy expression is a default policy, meaning that it applies to every operation and portType that the Web service supports.

Listing 7-8. The policyCache.xml Policy Expression File

```
<?xml version="1.0" encoding="utf-8"?>
<policyDocument xmlns="http://schemas.microsoft.com/wse/2003/06/Policy">
  <mappings xmlns:wse="http://schemas.microsoft.com/wse/2003/06/Policy">
    <endpoint uri="http://localhost/StockTraderSecurePolicy/StockTrader.asmx">
      <defaultOperation>
        <request policy="#Encrypt-X.509" />
        <response policy="" />
        <fault policy="" />
      </defaultOperation>
    </endpoint>
  </mappings>
<policies xmlns:wsu=" http://docs.oasis-open.org/wss/2004/01/
    oasis-200401-wss-wssecurity-utility-1.0.xsd">
```

```
<wsp:Policy wsu:Id="#Encrypt-X.509"
    xmlns:wsp="http://schemas.xmlsoap.org/ws/2002/12/policy">
  <wssp:Confidentiality wsp:Usage="wsp:Required">
    <wssp:KeyInfo>
      <wssp: SecurityToken>
        <wssp:TokenType>http://docs.oasis-open.org/wss/2004/01/
          oasis-200401-wss-x509-token-profile-1.0#X509v3</wssp:TokenType>
      </wssp:SecurityToken>
    </wssp:KeyInfo>
    <wssp:MessageParts Dialect="http://schemas.xmlsoap.org/2002/12/wsse#part">
        wsp:Body()</wssp:MessageParts>
  </wssp:Confidentiality>
</wsp:Policy>
</policies>
</policyDocument>
```

Listing 7-9. The web.config Settings to Attach the Policy Expression File to the Web Service

```
<configuration>
  <microsoft.web.services2>
    <diagnostics />
    <policy>
            <cache name="c:\projects\WSTestPolicy\policyCache.xml" />
    </policy>
    <security>
      <x509 allowTestRoot="true" allowRevocationUrlRetrieval="false"
          verifyTrust="false" />
    </security>
  </microsoft.web.services2>
</configuration>
```

The wonderful thing about policy files is that you do not need to write any code in the Web service to verify that an incoming request is valid. You can still write code that processes the request messages manually, if you have a special processing function that you need to apply. However, be aware that the policy verification intercepts the request first. If the incoming message does not pass verification, then it will not be allowed through and it will not run through any custom functions. Instead, the client that issued the request will receive a SOAP exception along the lines of Listing 7-10.

Listing 7-10. A SOAP Exception Raised When a Request Message Does Not Pass Policy Verification

```
SOAP-Fault code: http://schemas.xmlsoap.org/soap/envelope/:
    Client System.Web.Services.Protocols.SoapHeaderException:
    Microsoft.Web.Services2.Policy.PolicyVerificationException:
    The message does not conform to the policy it was mapped to.
    at Microsoft.Web.Services2.Policy.SimplePolicyVerifier.Verify(
        SoapEnvelope message) at
    Microsoft.Web.Services2.Policy.PolicyVerificationInputFilter.
        ProcessMessage(SoapEnvelope envelope)
    at Microsoft.Web.Services2.Pipeline.ProcessInputMessage(
        SoapEnvelope envelope) at
    Microsoft.Web.Services2.WebServicesExtension.
        BeforeDeserializeServer(SoapServerMessage message) at
    System.Web.Services2.Protocols.SoapHttpClientProtocol.
        ReadResponse(SoapClientMessage message, WebResponse response,
            Stream responseStream, Boolean asyncCall) at
    System.Web.Services.Protocols.SoapHttpClientProtocol.
        Invoke(String methodName, Object[] parameters)
    at WSTestClient.StockTraderWse.RequestQuote()
```

For redundancy, you can add an identical policy expression file to the Web client to ensure that the WSE pipeline catches policy violations at the client before their request even goes out to the Web service.

The Configuration Editor provides limited support for implementing the WS-Policy family of specifications, but it does cover the most common policy requirements. You can always edit the policy file to modify it to your specifications. For example, you can modify one of the policy assertions to be Optional rather than Required, as shown here:

```
<wssp:Confidentiality wsp:Usage="wsp:Required"
    xmlns:wssp="http://schemas.xmlsoap.org/ws/2002/12/secext" />
<wssp:Confidentiality wsp:Usage="wsp:Optional"
    xmlns:wssp="http://schemas.xmlsoap.org/ws/2002/12/secext" />
```

Overview of Role-Based Authorization

The discussions on security and policy so far have been greatly skewed toward authentication, but I have said very little about authorization. When I talk about securing a Web service, I really mean two things:

- Authenticating the sender of an incoming request, and

- Authorizing that sender to receive a processed response.

In a business environment it is very likely that users will need to be classed into different groups, divided between administrative-level users, who can access all Web service operations; and less privileged users, who can only access a subset of the available Web service operations. Web services need the ability to selectively grant access to an operation based on a user's authorization level.

Authorization, like authentication, is a technology based on security tokens. Once a user has been authenticated, the Web service has two options. One option is that it can automatically grant the user access to the requested operation. This is the most common implemented option because it is the easiest, and requires no additional verification. Alternatively, the Web service can perform an additional authorization check before granting access to the requested operation. So authorization can only take place once authentication has been successfully completed.

The design pattern for authorization is very straightforward. The steps are as follows:

1. The client digitally signs a SOAP request with a security token based on either a UsernameToken or a Kerberos ticket. This is necessary in order for the client's username information to be assigned to the message. (Alternatively, you can add the username separately to the message header, but this creates additional development work.)

2. The client sends the SOAP request to the Web service.

3. The service receives the SOAP request and then extracts the available security tokens.

4. The service verifies the security token. For example, it can run the security token information through a custom token manager that extracts the username and password information, and then compares it against a separate information store. If verification fails, then the service raises a SOAP exception back to the client.

5. If verification passes, then the service performs an authorization check on the user to determine their privilege level. This can be done in two ways: The service checks the user's Windows group information directly, using the security token's Principal object (described in the next section); or the service implements a custom authorization process. For example, it can maintain its own list of group information for all authenticated users. It can then determine the user's privilege level based on its own information store.

6. Once the authorization check is complete, the service may deny access if the user's privilege level is insufficient for the requested operation. Otherwise, the service proceeds to process the requested operation.

There are several variations you can implement for the individual steps in this design pattern. We will look at two approaches that should cover most basic authorization requirements.

> **NOTE** *Authorization checks must be done directly in the requested Web method. You can abstract the code out to a centralized security authorization class, but you will still need to make some kind of authorization call from within the Web method.*

Authorization Roles and the Principal Object (Based on Shared Windows Groups)

WSE 2.0 authorization is focused around an object called the Principal object that is accessible from the security token object as long as it is based on a UsernameToken, or on a Kerberos ticket. WSE 2.0 automatically populates the Principal object with the Windows security information for the user who created the security token as long as the Web application uses Windows authentication. This information is carried across the wire with the security token and can be accessed from the receiving Web service.

The Principal object provides a useful Boolean property called IsInRole, which allows you to check the group membership for the current user. (Note that the Principal object is not limited to working with Windows groups only. It can also work with custom membership lists, as discussed in the next section.) Let's say that the Web service caters to two groups of users: premium users and basic users. Premium users can access all Web service operations, whereas basic users can access only a few of the available operations. If the client creates two corresponding Windows groups on their machine, then the Web service could in theory extract the group membership information and then authorize access accordingly. Alternatively, the client and service can exchange a Kerberos ticket, which provides an equivalent level of information.

> **NOTE** *Kerberos security is available only on newer Windows operating systems, including Windows XP with Service Pack 1 and Windows Server 2003. Kerberos is not available on Windows 2000. I will not discuss Kerberos in this book, but please consult the Appendix for references on this technology.*

Listing 7-11 shows how you can access the Principal object from the security token object. The code listing is for a Web method called PlaceTrade that restricts access to members of the Premium group only. This listing shows how the Web method authorizes the incoming digitally signed SOAP request message.

Listing 7-11. Authorize a SOAP Message Using the Principal Object

```
[WebMethod()]
public Trade PlaceTrade(string Account, string Symbol, int Shares, ➥
    System.Double Price, TradeType tradeType)
{
    // Execute the trade only if the user is in the "Premium" role

    // Initialize the custom token manager, in case it is needed
    CustomUsernameTokenManager objMgr = new CustomUsernameTokenManager();

    // Verify the signature on the Web service request to this method
    bool SignatureIsValid = true;
    bool blnIsAuthorized = false;

    // Code to verify that the request has been digitally signed
    SoapContext requestContext = RequestSoapContext.Current;

    foreach (ISecurityElement objElem in requestContext.Security.Elements)
    {
        if (objElem is MessageSignature)
        {
            MessageSignature clientSignature = (MessageSignature)objElem;

            if (clientSignature.SecurityToken is UsernameToken)
            {
                SignatureIsValid = true;
                objMgr.VerifyToken( clientSignature.SecurityToken );

                // Additional Code for Role-Based analysis

                // Step 1: Retrieve the username from the authenticated token
                UsernameToken token = (UsernameToken)clientSignature.SecurityToken;
                string username = token.Username;

                // Step 2: WORKAROUND CODE ONLY
                // NOTE: You must be running Windows authentication in order
                // for the Principal object to be automatically populated

                // The following 4-line code-listing is a workaround, for testing
                // purposes only, which manually creates the Principal object
                string role = "Premium";
                ArrayList roles = new ArrayList();
                roles.Add(string.Format("{0}\\Premium", Dns.GetHostName()));
                token.Principal = new GenericPrincipal( ➥
                    new GenericIdentity(role), ➥
                    roles.ToArray(typeof(string)) as string[] );
```

```
                      // Step 3: Give the user authorization rights to this method
                      // if they are in the correct role

                      // You can run either of these steps:
                      // Step 3A: Check the Principal object to determine if the user
                      // is a member of the Premium role
                      if (token.Principal.IsInRole(string.Format("{0}\\Premium",
                          System.Net.Dns.GetHostName())))) blnIsAuthorized = true;

                      // Step 3B: Perform a database lookup to determine the user's role
                      // Simulate result return as 'premium' user
                      string role = "premium"; // hardcode database result
                      if (role == "premium") blnIsAuthorized = true;

                  }
              }
          }

      Trade t = new Trade();

      if (blnIsAuthorized)
      {
          t.TradeID = System.Guid.NewGuid().ToString();
          t.OrderDateTime = "11/17/2003 18:30:00";
          t.Symbol = Symbol;
          t.Shares = Shares;
          t.Price = Price;
          t.tradeType = tradeType;
          t.tradeStatus = TradeStatus.Ordered; // Initialize Trade status to Ordered

          // Implement code here to persist trade details to the database by
          // account number and trade ID
          // <-- Code goes here -->
      }
      return t; // Return the Trade object
  }
```

This lengthy code listing pulls together many elements that should be familiar to you by now. Please note that Step 2 is a workaround only, designed to simulate the automatic addition of the Principal object to the security token's Principal property. If you are running Windows authentication, then the Principal property will automatically be assigned.

Very few actual lines of code are devoted to authorization directly (only Step 3, not counting the workaround in Step 2). Most of the work comes from extracting the security token from the SOAP request message. Of course, this entire authorization process hinges on the assumption that the Web service and the client have a common understanding of roles, and that the Web method knows the set of roles that it can provide access for. (This is accomplished if the client and server are on the same domain, or if they exchange a Kerberos ticket.) The biggest challenge with implementing authorization is the administrative legwork that is required to make the authorization process work. Clearly, this type of authorization is not possible for situations in which the client and service are anonymous to one another.

Other security token types do not support the Principal object, but this is not a problem because you can always add multiple security tokens to a single SOAP message. For example, you can encrypt a message using an X.509 certificate, while also digitally signing it using a UsernameToken. This is easily accomplished by adding the two security tokens to the message, so that they are both available.

Policy-Based Authorization Using Shared Windows Groups

Policy files can simplify authorization implementations even further. WSE 2.0 supports elements called <claims> and <role>, which are assigned to a <SecurityToken> element in order to specify the Windows groups that are authorized to access the Web service. Listing 7-12 illustrates a policy file for a Web service that provides two available operations: RequestQuote and PlaceTrade. Basic users are only authorized to call RequestQuote, whereas Premium users are authorized to call both RequestQuote and PlaceTrade.

Listing 7-12. Policy File for Role-Based Authorization to Web Service Operations

```xml
<?xml version="1.0" encoding="utf-8"?>
<policyDocument xmlns="http://schemas.microsoft.com/wse/2003/06/Policy">
    <mappings xmlns:wse="http://schemas.microsoft.com/wse/2003/06/Policy">
        <endpoint uri="http://www.bluestonepartners.com/StockTrader.asmx">
            <operation
                requestAction="http://www.bluestonepartners.com/
                StockTrader.asmx/PlaceTrade">
                <request policy="#policy-premium" />
                <response policy="" />
                <fault policy="" />
            </operation>
            <defaultOperation>
                <request policy="#policy-basic" />
                <response policy="" />
                <fault policy="" />
            </defaultOperation>
        </endpoint>
```

```
        </mappings>
        <policies xmlns:wsu="http://docs.oasis-open.org/wss/2004/01/
            oasis-200401-wss-wssecurity-utility-1.0.xsd">
    <wsp:Policy wsu:Id="policy-basic"
        xmlns:wsp="http://schemas.xmlsoap.org/ws/2002/12/policy"
        xmlns:wsa="http://schemas.xmlsoap.org/ws/2004/03/addressing" >
        <wssp:Integrity wsp:Usage="wsp:Required"
            xmlns:wssp="http://schemas.xmlsoap.org/ws/2002/12/secext">
            <wssp:TokenInfo>
                <SecurityToken xmlns="http://schemas.xmlsoap.org/ws/2002/12/secext">
                    <wssp:TokenType>http://docs.oasis-open.org/wss/2004/01/
                        oasis-200401-wss-username-token-profile-1.0#UsernameToken
                        </wssp:TokenType>
                    <wssp:Claims>
                        <wse:Role
                          xmlns:wse="http://schemas.microsoft.com/wse/2003/06/Policy"
                            value="Basic" />
                    </wssp:Claims>
                </SecurityToken>
            </wssp:TokenInfo>
        </wssp:Integrity>
        </wsp:Policy>
    <wsp:Policy wsu:Id="policy-premium"
    xmlns:wsp="http://schemas.xmlsoap.org/ws/2002/12/policy"
    xmlns:wsa="http://schemas.xmlsoap.org/ws/2004/03/addressing" >
        <wssp:Integrity wsp:Usage="wsp:Required"
    xmlns:wssp="http://schemas.xmlsoap.org/ws/2002/12/secext">
            <wssp:TokenInfo>
                <SecurityToken xmlns="http://schemas.xmlsoap.org/ws/2002/12/secext">
                    <wssp:TokenType>http://docs.oasis-open.org/wss/2004/01/
                        oasis-200401-wss-username-token-profile-1.0#UsernameToken
                        </wssp:TokenType>
                    <wssp:Claims>
                        <wse:Role
                          xmlns:wse="http://schemas.microsoft.com/wse/2003/06/Policy"
                            value="Premium" />
                    </wssp:Claims>
                </SecurityToken>
            </wssp:TokenInfo>
        </wssp:Integrity>
        </wsp:Policy>
        </policies>
</policyDocument>
```

Note that I have omitted the <MessagePredicate> elements from this policy file in order to keep the code listing shorter. The <MessagePredicate> element should be included because it specifies which SOAP message elements are required to be included and signed within the request message. Without this, no checks are done on specific elements, only on the message as a whole.

Once this policy framework is implemented in the Web service, the client simply calls an operation and signs the request with a UsernameToken, where the username can be associated to a shared Windows group on the server (as specified in the <wse:Role> element). Once this has all been verified, the service allows the client access to the requested operation, and then proceeds to generate a response.

Authorization Roles Not Based on Shared Windows Groups

In reality, of course, it may be impractical for a Web service to keep its role membership information in synchronization with the Windows group membership information of its clients. It will be possible if the Web service is hosted on the same domain as its clients. However, if the clients are scattered across multiple domains, then this will quickly become an administrative headache for multiple different groups of clients. In addition, WSE 2.0 authorization based on the Principal object is closely tied to Microsoft Windows domain-level security, and so it may be unsuitable for Web services that interact with clients that are running non-Windows operating systems.

There is an alternative for implementing role-based authorization without relying on Windows groups. This approach relies on the Web service being able to maintain its own list of registered users and their associated predefined custom roles. You will need to implement a custom token manager that processes security tokens and then generates role assignments on the fly. The custom username token manager is centralized and is automatically processed as soon as the Web service receives a SOAP message, so it is a convenient location for doing custom processing prior to handling the actual request. Listing 7-13 provides one example of how you can implement a custom username token manager that handles authorization.

Listing 7-13. A Custom Username Token Manager with Authorization

```
using System.Net;
using System.Security;
using System.Security.Principal;
using System.Security.Permissions;

[SecurityPermissionAttribute(SecurityAction.Demand, ➥
    Flags=SecurityPermissionFlag.UnmanagedCode)]
public class CustomUsernameTokenManager : UsernameTokenManager
{
  protected override string AuthenticateToken( UsernameToken token )
  {

  // Custom authorization scheme
  ArrayList roles = new ArrayList();

  // Run a lookup on the token username, and extract role information
  // This step assumes that the token manager has access to
  // a database of registered users
  string role = RetrieveUserGroupInformation();

    switch(role)
    {
      case "premium":
        roles.Add(string.Format("{0}\\Premium", Dns.GetHostName()));
        token.Principal = new GenericPrincipal( new GenericIdentity(role), ➥
            roles.ToArray(typeof(string)) as string[] );
        break;
      default:
        roles.Add(string.Format("{0}\\Basic", Dns.GetHostName()));
        token.Principal = new GenericPrincipal( new GenericIdentity(role), ➥
            roles.ToArray(typeof(string)) as string[] );
        break;
  }
  return token.Password;

  }
}
```

In Listing 7-13, the token manager is able to perform a lookup on the authenticated users and extract their group assignments. Next, the token manager assigns the authenticated user's role information to the security token's Principal property using a customizable version of the Principal object, called GenericPrincipal. Notice that the token manager has done nothing one way or the other to provide or deny access to the user based on their role. Instead, the token manager is simply retrieving the role information in an accessible format so that the Web service can make a downstream assessment of the user's privilege level for their requested operation.

Finally, the execution thread begins processing the target Web method, in this case PlaceTrade, as shown in Listing 7-10. This Web method will execute conditionally based on the user's authorized role.

Summary

This chapter discussed two important topics: policy frameworks and security authorization. These topics are grouped together in this chapter because they are both advanced security implementations that you can appreciate only after you have understood the basic WS-Security specification. In addition, policy frameworks and security authorization both serve to restrict access to a Web service by enforcing specific usage requirements.

Policy frameworks are a declarative approach for documenting and processing the requirements, preferences, and capabilities of a Web service. The WSE infrastructure automatically processes Web service policies without requiring additional code. In fact, I demonstrated how policy files allow you to eliminate verification code that was required in the sample solutions for previous chapters.

Security authorization is the process of verifying a client's privilege level and determining whether to grant them access to a Web service operation that they have requested (by submitting a request SOAP message to the Web service). Authorization, like authentication, is based on security tokens. Users can only be authorized once they have been authenticated. WSE 2.0 provides good support for security roles that are based on Windows user and domain groups, or Kerberos tickets. You will need to implement a custom solution if you want to use a different type of role. I explained one approach for building a custom authorization manager based on custom roles.

In the next chapter, I will discuss the WS-Secure Conversation specification, which is an important relative of the WS-Security family of specifications.

CHAPTER 8

Establish Trusted Communication with WS-Secure Conversation

THE WS-SECURE CONVERSATION specification allows Web services and clients to establish a token-based, secure conversation for the duration of a session. It is analogous to the Secure Sockets Layer (SSL) protocol that provides on-demand, secure communications over the HTTP transport channel. Secure conversations are well suited to participants that do not inherently trust each other, either because they have no ongoing relationship, or, for example, because they have not established certificate-based public-private keys to secure their conversations. In Chapters 6 and 7, you saw how the WS-Security and WS-Policy family of specifications combine to provide a comprehensive approach to securing Web services. Together these specifications provide an assortment of security options, including digital signatures, encryption algorithms, and custom authorization schemes.

In previous chapters, I discussed these technologies in the context of protective security, meaning that they protect messages in transit and keep unwanted eyes from discovering sensitive information. This is certainly an important application of these technologies, and it needs no further explanation. But for the purpose of this chapter, I need to expand the context within which to view these technologies. They are no longer needed just for protective security; in a broader context, they are needed for establishing trusted communications.

In the discussions so far, we have made the big assumption that the client and Web service automatically trust each other. By this, I mean the assumption that they both have an equivalent confidence in the integrity of the security tokens they are using to sign, encrypt, and otherwise secure their communications. For example, if a client and a Web service agree to encrypt their messages using a digital X.509 certificate, then they must both trust the source of the certificate, and must be comfortable using the private and public keys that are generated from the certificate. In a sense, both the client and the Web service have come to a mutual agreement that they will offload the burden of proving trust to a third-party (trusted!) source, which issues a digital certificate to act as the tangible record of that trust.

Of course, the issue is more complex than this. When it comes to certificates, for many of us they are a necessary requirement for trusted communication. As a client, I may have all the trust in the world for a service provider, but I still need to use a digital certificate for the mechanics of signing and encrypting shared messages. I happen to be comfortable with digital certificates for most communication requirements because it represents certified trust. However, other client-service communications may be just as well off using a simpler UsernameToken security token, which is based on a simple username-password combination that gets hashed during transit. Luckily, the WSE implementation of the WS-Security specification is flexible, and you have a choice of security token types to use for conducting trusted communication.

The point is that your preferred security tokens and your preferred hashing and encryption algorithms are simply a means to a bigger goal of establishing trusted communication, otherwise known in the Web services world as *secure conversation*. There is no single correct choice of technologies that you should always use. Instead, you need to be using those technologies that are appropriate for establishing a trusted, secure conversation between a given client and Web service. The rules can change depending on who is doing the communicating.

This chapter focuses on how you establish session-oriented, trusted communications using the WS-Secure Conversation specification. The great thing about the WS-Specifications is that many of the concepts complement each other and build on each other. The understanding that you now have about WS-Security and WS-Policy will translate directly into the concepts behind WS-Secure Conversation. By the end of this chapter, you will have a good understanding of what constitutes secure conversation, and a broader appreciation for the usefulness of the WS-Security family of specifications.

Overview of Secure Conversation

The WS-Secure Conversation (and WS-Trust) specifications provide the means for a client and a service to establish an optimized secure communication channel for a limited duration of time. Secure conversation is based on security tokens that are procured by a service token provider. This process involves an initial amount of overhead, but once the channel is established, the client and service exchange a lightweight, signed security context token, which optimizes message delivery times compared with using regular security tokens. The security context token enables the same signing and encryption features that you are used to with regular security tokens.

Secure conversation is analogous to communications over the HTTPS protocol. HTTPS establishes a secure channel for the duration of a session, and ceases to be in effect once that session is over. The classic example is an eCommerce transaction, in which you browse a catalog over an unsecured channel, but then you establish a secure channel for the purpose of completing a sales transaction with the vendor. The communication needs to be secure because sensitive payment and order information is being exchanged, and so the client and the vendor need to establish a secured channel for as long as it takes to complete the transaction. For performance reasons, the client does not need or even want to establish a continuous secure session for every interaction with the vendor. HTTPS is useful for providing on-demand secure communication for exactly as long as it is needed.

> **NOTE** *HTTPS and WS-Secure Conversation differ in one important way: HTTPS is not typically used for client authentication, whereas secure conversation is.*

A secure conversation has the following characteristics:

- It is based on established security tokens, including UsernameTokens and X.509 certificates.

- It uses a dedicated service token provider to generate a signed service context token, which is a lightweight security proxy.

- It provides a secure communication channel for the duration of the session.

- It provides optimized performance for session-oriented communications with multiple round-trips (by using the security context token).

The difference between secure conversation and standard secure message exchange (with WS-Security and WS-Policy) is that a standard security policy framework establishes a fixed security policy that all service clients must adhere to. However, secure conversation has a more dynamic aspect. The client and service can initiate a secure channel as needed, rather than based on an established policy framework. Secure conversation uses security tokens that are issued for the purpose of a specific communication. The service itself can act as the provider of these security tokens. Alternatively, this responsibility can be offloaded to a third-party service token provider, which is a dedicated resource that acts as a trusted intermediary between clients and services, and the issuer of security tokens for their secure conversations. Figure 8-1 provides an architecture diagram for typical secure conversation solutions.

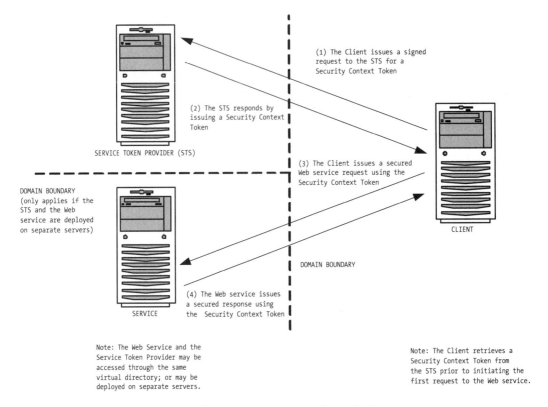

Figure 8-1. Architecture diagram for a secure conversation solution

A secure conversation is initiated by a client that requires an on-demand secure communication session with a Web service. The session may be required for the duration of one request, or for several back-and-forth requests and responses between the client and Web service.

The workflow for establishing and conducting a secure conversation is presented in Figure 8-1, and typically follows four steps:

Step 1: The client issues a signed request to the security token service provider for a security context token.

The client initiates the secure conversation by issuing a signed request to the security token service (STS) provider for a security context token. The client may sign the request with any standard security token, including UsernameToken and X.509 certificates. The sample solution will demonstrate using a UsernameToken security token.

Step 2: The security token service provider verifies the request and issues a security context token back to the client.

The STS provider verifies the integrity of the signed request. It then generates a security context token and delivers it to the client. In the sample solution the Web service itself also acts as the security token service. You can, however, deploy the STS as a separate service. The security context token is actually returned from the STS as a so-called request security token (RST). The client can then extract the security context token from the RST. WSE 2.0 provides all of the support classes that you need to handle these tasks in code.

Steps 3 and 4: The client and the Web service use the security context token for further communication.

The client and Web service use the security context token to secure back-and-forth request and response communications with each other. The security context token can be used like any standard security token. It inherits from the same base classes and its usage is no different from the security tokens you learned how to work with in Chapter 6. Security context tokens may be cached in a global cache for future retrieval, for example, when the client will be issuing multiple requests over a period of time. We will look at how to do this later in the chapter.

Programming-wise, Web Services Enhancements (WSE) 2.0 makes it very easy to implement a service token provider because the WSE infrastructure will automatically issue security context tokens. This feature is enabled by simply adding a configuration element to the service token provider's configuration file. The STS provider can be incorporated into the client's target Web service, or the STS provider can be implemented as a dedicated Web service. There is little difference in the code between a "hosted" service token provider (that resides in the client's target Web service) and a dedicated service token provider (that resides on a separate domain). There are some significant configuration and deployment differences between the two models, but code-wise they are very similar.

> **NOTE** *The feature you know as Secure Conversation uses several WS-Specifications, including WS-Trust, WS-Secure Conversation, and WS-Security. In addition, you can reduce code listings (and potential errors!) by implementing policy frameworks for the participating services and clients. This chapter does not focus on when particular WS-Specifications come into play. Instead, the focus is on understanding the concepts, and discussing practical code samples.*

How to Implement a Secure Conversation Solution

It is time to dust off the familiar StockTrader service-oriented application and retrofit it to participate in a secure conversation. I will discuss how to construct both the client and the Web service. In the solution, the Web service is both a service provider and a secure token service provider. This means that the Web service is responsible for supplying its clients with the security token for establishing a session-oriented secure conversation.

Figure 8-2 shows the Solution Explorer for a new sample solution called WSSecureConversation.sln, which you will see how to build in this section. It includes three projects, which represent the following four components:

1. **The Web service provider:** WSSecureConvService.csproj

2. **The Security Token Service provider:** WSSecureConvService.csproj

3. **The Web service client:** WSSecureConvClient.csproj

4. **Interface definition assembly:** StockTraderTypes.csproj

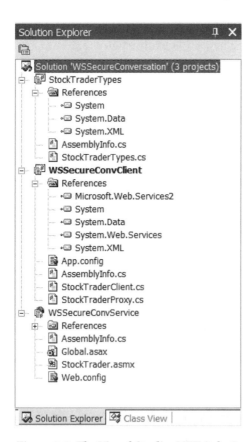

Figure 8-2. The Visual Studio .NET Solution Explorer for the WSSecureConversation solution

As noted earlier, the Web service hosts the security token service provider, so it is playing double duty in this project. All that the Web service actually does is to provide an endpoint for clients to access the STS HTTP handler.

The References nodes are expanded so you can see dependencies. However, the complexity is not in the project structure; rather, it lies in the nature of the communication pathways between the client and service. The sample solution follows the architecture that is presented in Figure 8-1. Before I present the solution, let's review the required implementation steps for both the Web service and the client who are participating in the secure conversation.

Before we look at how to build the sample solution, let's review the conceptual steps that are required to implement the Web service, the Security Token Service provider, and the client projects.

How to Implement the Web Service and the Security Token Service Provider

The implementation for the Web service requires the following four steps:

Step 1: Configure the Web service to use WSE 2.0.

Verify that the web.config file includes the standard WSE elements for the WebServicesConfiguration and WebServicesExtension classes. Remember to use the WSE 2.0 Configuration Settings Editor to avoid having to manually type these entries.

Step 2: Configure the security token service provider in the web.config file.

The WSE class framework provides a ready-to-use handler for implementing the STS provider. All you have to do is register it correctly in the web.config file, as outlined in more detail later in this chapter. The handler will automatically generate a security token for use in the secure conversation.

Step 3: Create a custom token manager.

This step is required in order to process the signature of the client request that initiates the secure conversation. If the client's signature cannot be verified, then the rest of the workflow cannot proceed. Recall that this signature will later be used to sign the security context token.

Step 4: Implement policy verification.

In the Web service itself, implement code to verify policy requirements programmatically, including digital signature and encryption requirements. Alternatively, you can create a policy framework file.

How to Implement the Client

The client application requires a fair amount of custom code, although it shares many similarities with what you have seen in previous chapters. The biggest difference from before is that the client now implements the workflow for initiating the request to the security token service provider. This code is in addition to any code that the client already implements for interfacing with the target Web service.

The implementation for the client requires the following six steps:

Step 1: Generate a security token for signing the upcoming service token request.

This security token has nothing to do with the security context token that you will ultimately use to secure the conversation between service and client. Instead, this security token is only used by the client to generate a signed request to receive a security context token from the STS provider. In turn, the STS provider will sign its response when it delivers a security context token back to the client. In this example, I will show you how to use a simple UsernameToken security token to sign the initial request and response for the security context token. Note that the request to the STS provider must be signed, otherwise the request will be rejected.

Step 2: Set a proxy reference to the security token service provider.

Clients communicate with standard Web services using a proxy class. In the same way, they also communicate with a Security Token Service provider using a proxy class, called SecurityContextTokenServiceClient, which is a member of the Microsoft.Web.Services2.Security namespace.

Step 3: Issue a signed request to the provider for a security context token.

The request for a security context token is issued by the client via a specialized proxy class called the SecurityContextTokenServiceClient class, which is initialized with a URI reference to the security token service provider. The specialized proxy class provides a method called IssueSecurityContextTokenAuthenticated for issuing the request and for receiving the response back from the STS provider. Note that this method may be called synchronously or asynchronously. However, you will usually call the method synchronously because no further communication is typically possible between the service and client if this method fails to return a valid security context token. So you may prefer to wait for a synchronous call to return, and to thereby hold off on executing additional code until you know that you can proceed.

Step 4: Retrieve the security context token from the provider.

The IssueSecurityContextTokenAuthenticated method will return a valid SecurityContextToken object if the call is successful. You are now ready to make secured Web service requests using this security context token.

Step 5: Add security elements to sign and encrypt upcoming Web service requests using the new security context token.

The security context token is no different from other security tokens that you worked with in Chapter 6, including the UsernameToken and X509SecurityToken classes. You add the security context token to the SOAP request message header, just as you would any other security token. If you need to make multiple service requests over an extended period of time, then you may wish to add the security context token to a global cache for future retrieval. You will also then need to store the token ID for future reference because it is possible that the global cache will contain other security tokens, and you will need a way to retrieve the correct token from the cache.

Step 6: Proceed to call the Web service methods as usual.

After all this work, nothing much changes. The Web service methods are called as usual, and the only difference is that the requests and responses are being secured with the security context token for the duration of the session.

Build a Secure Conversation Solution

I will now review the detailed steps for building the Web service and the client in a secure conversation solution. This section follows the outlines of the previous sections on how to implement the Web service and the client.

Build the Web Service and the Security Token Service Provider

The Web service and STS provider are contained within the project WSSecureConvService.csproj, and are built as described in the following sections.

Step 1: Configure the Web Service to Use WSE 2.0

This step will add registration information to the web.config file for the standard WebServicesConfiguration and WebServicesExtension classes. Use the WSE 2.0 Configuration Settings Editor, or else manually add the required configuration settings.

Step 2: Configure the Security Token Provider

The WSE 2.0 infrastructure will automatically issue security context tokens with the simple configuration entry shown in Listing 8-1.

Listing 8-1. Configure the Security Token Service Provider

```
<microsoft.web.services2>
    <tokenIssuer>
      <autoIssueSecurityContextToken enabled="true" />
      <serverToken>
        <KeyInfo xmlns="http://www.w3.org/2000/09/xmldsig#"
            xmlns:wsse="http://www.docs.oasis-open.org/wss/2004/01/
            oasis-200401-wss-wssecurity-secext-1.0.xsd">
        <wsse:SecurityTokenReference>
            <!-- The certificate is from the Local Machine store's
                Personal folder -->
            <wsse:KeyIdentifier ValueType="http://docs.oasis-open.org/wss/2004/01/
                oasis-200401-wss-x509-token-profile-1.0#X509SubjectKeyIdentifier">
                bBwPfItvKp3b6TNDq+14qs58VJQ=</wsse:KeyIdentifier>
        </wsse:SecurityTokenReference>
        </KeyInfo>
      </serverToken>
    </tokenIssuer>
</microsoft.web.services2>
```

The key element in Listing 8-1 is the <autoIssueSecurityContextToken> element, which instructs the WSE 2.0 infrastructure to automatically generate a security context token as long as the client has sent a properly formatted request. Listing 8-1 also includes a <serverToken> element that documents the security token that the STS provider will use to sign and encrypt its response to the client. WSE 2.0 does not appear to allow any security token other than an X.509 certificate. Note that the certificate must be stored in the Local Computer's Personal certificate store in order for the Web service to have access to it. If you have installed the Chapter 6 sample solutions, then you will already have the certificates and keys properly configured. If you have not done so, then please refer to Chapter 5 for information on how to configure the test certificates that are provided with WSE 2.0.

Of course, you can only use the <tokenIssuer> and <serverToken> elements if the Web service and the security token service are installed in the same virtual directory. If this is not the case, then your secure conversation architecture must be using a stand-alone security token service.

Step 3: Create a Custom Token Manager

The custom token manager verifies the digital signature on the original request from a client to the security token service provider. Recall that this request must be signed by the client, or it will be rejected by the STS provider. The custom token manager verifies UsernameToken signing tokens. It should be implemented as a separate class in the Web service, although you should provide it with the same namespace as the Web service .asmx file. Listing 8-2 shows the code listing for the custom token manager.

Listing 8-2. The Custom Token Manager

```
using System;
using System.Security.Permissions;
using Microsoft.Web.Services2.Security;
using Microsoft.Web.Services2.Security.Tokens;

namespace WSSecureConvService
{

  [SecurityPermissionAttribute(SecurityAction.Demand, ➥
      Flags=SecurityPermissionFlag.UnmanagedCode)]
  public class CustomUsernameTokenManager : UsernameTokenManager
  {

    protected override string AuthenticateToken( UsernameToken token )
    {
      // Retrieve the password from the token
      password = ( token.Password );

      // Optional: Validate the password with custom code
      // Add code here (e.g., perform database lookup)
```

```
        // Return the validated password
        return Convert.ToBase64String( password );
    }
  }
}
```

In addition, you must register the custom token manager in the web.config file, as shown in Listing 8-3. Look at the <securityTokenManager> element, and notice that the custom token manager class is registered using the namespace of the STS provider (WSSecureConvService).

Listing 8-3. Register the Custom Token Manager in the web.config File

```
<configuration>
    <security>
        <x509 allowTestRoot="true" allowRevocationUrlRetrieval="false"
            verifyTrust="false" />
    <securityTokenManager type="WSSecureConvService.CustomUsernameTokenManager,
            WSSecureConvService" xmlns:wsse="http://docs.oasis-open.org/wss/2004/01/
            oasis-200401-wss-wssecurity-secext-1.0.xsd" qname="wsse:UsernameToken" />
    </security>
</configuration>
```

As an alternative to a custom token manager, you can implement a policy file which states that incoming requests to the service token provider must be digitally signed. The WSE 2.0 infrastructure will automatically enforce the policy without requiring you to write custom code.

By this point you may have lost track of all the edits to the web.config file that are required in order to implement support for secure conversation. Listing 8-4 shows the full listing for the web.config file.

Listing 8-4. The web.config Configuration Settings for the Security Token Service Provider (Implemented in the WSSecureConvService Sample Solution)

```
<?xml version="1.0" encoding="utf-8"?>
<configuration>

    <configSections>
        <section name="microsoft.web.services2"
            type="Microsoft.Web.Services2.Configuration.WebServicesConfiguration,
            Microsoft.Web.Services2, Version=2.0.0.0, Culture=neutral,
            PublicKeyToken=31bf3856ad364e35" />
    </configSections>
```

```
    <system.web>
      <webServices>
        <soapExtensionTypes>
          <add type="Microsoft.Web.Services2.WebServicesExtension,
               Microsoft.Web.Services2, Version=2.0.0.0, Culture=neutral,
               PublicKeyToken=31bf3856ad364e35" priority="1" group="0" />
        </soapExtensionTypes>
      </webServices>
    </system.web>

    <microsoft.web.services2>

      <security>
        <x509 allowTestRoot="true" allowRevocationUrlRetrieval="false"
              verifyTrust="true" />
        <securityTokenManager
            type="WSSecureConvService.CustomUsernameTokenManager,
            WSSecureConvService" xmlns:wsse="http://docs.oasis-open.org/wss/2004/01/
            oasis-200401-wss-wssecurity-secext-1.0.xsd" qname="wsse:UsernameToken" />
      </security>

      <tokenIssuer>
        <autoIssueSecurityContextToken enabled="true" />
        <serverToken>
          <KeyInfo xmlns="http://www.w3.org/2000/09/xmldsig#"
              xmlns:wsse="http://docs.oasis-open.org/wss/2004/01/
              oasis-200401-wss-wssecurity-secext-1.0.xsd">
            <wsse:SecurityTokenReference>
              <!-- The certificate is from the Local Machine store's
                   Personal folder -->
              <wsse:KeyIdentifier ValueType="http://docs.oasis-open.org/wss/2004/01/
                  oasis-200401-wss-x509-token-profile-1.0#X509SubjectKeyIdentifier">
                  bBwPfItvKp3b6TNDq+14qs58VJQ=</wsse:KeyIdentifier>
            </wsse:SecurityTokenReference>
          </KeyInfo>
        </serverToken>
      </tokenIssuer>
    </microsoft.web.services2>

  </configuration>
```

> **NOTE** *If your custom token manager does not work correctly, verify that it is properly registered in web.config, with correct type and assembly information. This is the most common reason issues may occur with the manager.*

Step 4: Implement Policy Requirements in the Business Web Service

In the sample solution, the security token service provider is implemented in the same Web service project as the business Web service itself, which contains the service methods that are of interest to the client.

All of the work to obtain a security context token will be wasted if you do not implement and enforce a policy requirement in the business Web service to ensure that all incoming requests are signed and encrypted. You also have to ensure that outgoing responses back to the client are properly signed and encrypted. In the case of a secure conversation, the signing and encryption is accomplished with a security context token. However, the implementation code is generically written for all security scenarios, so you will be covered for standard security tokens, as well as secure context tokens. (Recall that all security tokens derive from the same base class.)

Listing 8-5 demonstrates how to implement checks for digital signatures and encryption on incoming service requests to a business Web method called RequestQuote. It also shows how to implement digital signing and encryption on outgoing responses back to the client.

Listing 8-5. The RequestQuote Method with Request and Response Encryption

```
public Quote RequestQuote(string Symbol)
{
    // Reject any requests which are not valid SOAP requests
    SoapContext requestContext = RequestSoapContext.Current;
    if (requestContext == null)
    {
        throw new ApplicationException("Only SOAP requests are permitted.");
    }

    // Check if the Soap Message is Signed.
    SecurityContextToken sct = GetSigningToken(requestContext) as ➥
        SecurityContextToken;
    if (sct == null)
    {
        throw new ApplicationException("The request is not signed with an SCT.");
    }
```

```
// Check if the Soap Message is Encrypted.
if (!IsMessageEncrypted(requestContext))
{
    throw new ApplicationException("The request is not encrypted.");
}

// Use the SCT to sign and encrypt the response
SoapContext responseContext = ResponseSoapContext.Current;
responseContext.Security.Tokens.Add(sct);
responseContext.Security.Elements.Add(new MessageSignature(sct));
responseContext.Security.Elements.Add(new EncryptedData(sct));

// Step 2: Return a Quote object, with example data
Quote q = new Quote();
if (Symbol.ToUpper() == "MSFT")
{
    q.Symbol = Symbol; // Sample Quote
    q.Company = "Microsoft Corporation";
    q.DateTime = "11/17/2003 16:00:00";
    q.Last = 25.15;
    q.Previous_Close = 25.49;
    q.Change = -0.36;
    q.PercentChange = -0.0137;
}
return q; // Return a Quote object
}
```

Notice that the RequestQuote method uses two helper methods to verify digital signatures and encryption on an incoming service request:

- **GetSigningToken:** Retrieves the security token from a signed incoming service request

- **IsMessageEncrypted:** Verifies whether an incoming service request is encrypted

Listing 8-6 displays the code listing for the GetSigningToken method. Listing 8-7 displays the code listing for the IsMessageEncrypted method.

Listing 8-6. Code Listing for the GetSigningToken Method

```
using Microsoft.Web.Services2;
using Microsoft.Web.Services2.Security;
using Microsoft.Web.Services2.Security.Tokens;

private SecurityToken GetSigningToken(SoapContext context)
{
    foreach ( ISecurityElement element in context.Security.Elements )
    {
        if ( element is MessageSignature )
        {
            // The given context contains a Signature element.
            MessageSignature sig = element as MessageSignature;

            if ((sig.SignatureOptions & SignatureOptions.IncludeSoapBody) != 0)
            {
                // The SOAP Body is verified as signed.
                return sig.SigningToken;
            }
        }
    }
    return null;
}
```

Listing 8-7. Code Listing for the IsMessageEncrypted Method

```
using Microsoft.Web.Services2;
using Microsoft.Web.Services2.Security;
using Microsoft.Web.Services2.Security.Tokens;

private bool IsMessageEncrypted(SoapContext context)
{
    foreach (ISecurityElement element in context.Security.Elements)
    {
        if (element is EncryptedData)
        {
            EncryptedData encryptedData = element as EncryptedData;
            System.Xml.XmlElement targetElement = encryptedData.TargetElement;

            if ( (targetElement.LocalName == Soap.ElementNames.Body) && ➥
                 (targetElement.NamespaceURI == Soap.NamespaceURI) && ➥
                 (SoapEnvelope.IsSoapEnvelope(targetElement.ParentNode)))
            {
```

```
                // The SOAP Body element is verified as Encrypted.
                return true;
            }
        }
    }
    return false;
}
```

Step 5: Implement Policy Verifications

The STS provider must verify that incoming requests for security context tokens are signed, in order to verify that the request has not been tampered with by an unauthorized party. At a minimum, you should implement a custom token manager, as outlined in Step 3 previously. Alternatively, you can implement a policy file for the receive operation, and have the WSE infrastructure automatically validate the policy requirement for you.

You have also seen that the business Web service involved in a secure conversation with a client has its own set of policy requirements. One is that incoming service requests must be signed and encrypted. The other is that the Web service must sign and encrypt outgoing responses back to the client. You can implement a policy file for the Web service to enforce these send and receive operations.

Build the Client

The client is implemented as a console application, and it includes three methods that work together to request a stock quote over a secure conversation channel:

- **RequestSecurityContextToken:** Encapsulates the code for requesting a security context token via the STS provider's proxy class

- **AssignSecurityContextToken:** Encapsulates the code for assigning a security context token to the SOAP request envelope

- **RequestSecureStockQuote:** Encapsulates the code for requesting a stock quote via the Web service's proxy class

Listing 8-8 displays the code listing for the console application's Main method, showing how the methods are called. Notice that the Web service proxy file is instantiated directly in the Main method and then passed into the two methods.

Listing 8-8. The Client Console Application

```
class StockTraderClient
{
    private string SCTID = "";

    [STAThread]
    static void Main(string[] args)
    {
        StockTraderClient client = null;

        try
        {
            client = new StockTraderClient();

            // Create an instance of the Web service proxy (for the token provider
            // and Web service)
            StockTraderServiceWse serviceProxy = new StockTraderServiceWse();

            // Request the security context token
            SecurityContextToken sct = ➡
                client.RequestSecurityContextToken(serviceProxy, client);

            // Assign the security context token to the SOAP request envelope
            client.AssignSecurityContextToken(serviceProxy, sct);

            // Request a stock quote
            client.RequestStockQuote(serviceProxy);
        }
    }
}
```

Now let's look at the code listing in more detail, broken out according to the logical steps outlined previously for building a secure conversation client.

Step 1: Generate a Security Token for Signing the Upcoming Service Token Request

The request to the service token provider must be signed with a valid security token. You can choose any supported token type, including UsernameToken and X509 security tokens. Listing 8-9 shows a basic code listing to generate a UsernameToken security token.

Listing 8-9. Generating a UsernameToken Security Token

```
private SecurityToken GetSTSRequestSigningToken()
{
    // Generate a security token to sign the request for the security context token
    SecurityToken token = new UsernameToken( username, password, ➡
        PasswordOption.SendHashed );
    return token;
}
```

The UsernameToken security token is also factored into generating the security context token, which the token service provider will generate. So it serves a dual purpose of both signing the request to the service token provider, and being used to generate the security context token.

Step 2: Set a Reference to the Security Token Service Provider

In order for the client to access the STS provider, it must use a specialized proxy class, which is initialized using an endpoint Uniform Resource Indicator (URI), which documents where the provider is located. Because this information may be dynamic, the client typically sets a configuration entry with the URI information for locating the provider's endpoint.

Listing 8-10 shows how you can set a reference to the STS provider's client proxy class.

Listing 8-10. Creating a Client Proxy Class for the Security Token Service Provider

```
// Create a SecurityContextTokenServiceClient (STSClient) that will
// get the SecurityContextToken
string secureConvEndpoint = ConfigurationSettings.AppSettings["tokenIssuer"];
SecurityContextTokenServiceClient STSClient = ➡
    new SecurityContextTokenServiceClient(new Uri( secureConvEndpoint ));
```

Listing 8-11 shows one example of a URI configuration setting for the STS provider, which will be stored in the client's app.config file (in the case of the sample client, which is implemented as a console application).

Listing 8-11. The app.config Setting for the STS Provider's URI

```
<appSettings>
    <add key="tokenIssuer"
        value="http://www.bluestonepartners.com/WSSecureConvService/
        StockTrader.asmx" />
</appSettings>
```

Step 3: Issue a Signed Request to the Provider for a Security Context Token

The client issues a request to the STS provider for a security context token using a proxy class method called IssueSecurityContextTokenAuthenticated. Listing 8-12 shows a modified code listing for the RequestSecurityContextToken method, which encapsulates all of the details for generating a security context token. This code listing is included in the sample solution, within the WSSecureConvClient project. For clarity, I have omitted try-catch exception blocks, exception handling, and caching code, which I will discuss later in the chapter.

Listing 8-12. Generating a Security Context Token Using the STS Provider's Client Proxy Class

```
private SecurityContextToken RequestSecurityContextToken( ➥
    StockTraderServiceWse serviceProxy, StockTraderClient client)
{
    // Step 1: Create a signing (security) token to use as
    // the base for the security context token
    // The security context token (SCT) will be issued later
    // by the security token service (STS)
    SecurityToken token = client.GetSTSRequestSigningToken();

    // Step 2: Create a SecurityContextTokenServiceClient (STSClient)
    // that will get the SecurityContextToken
    string secureConvEndpoint = ConfigurationSettings.AppSettings["tokenIssuer"];
    SecurityContextTokenServiceClient STSClient = ➥
        new SecurityContextTokenServiceClient(new Uri( secureConvEndpoint ));

    // Step 3: Retrieve the server certificate, to include in the signed request
    // to the security token service (STS)
    SecurityToken issuerToken = client.GetServerToken();

    // Step 4: Request the security context token, use the client's
    // signing token as the base
    SecurityContextToken sct = ➥
        STSClient.IssueSecurityContextTokenAuthenticated(token, issuerToken);

    return sct;
}
```

The STS provider's proxy method IssueSecurityContextTokenAuthenticated requires two security tokens: a token to sign the request (token), and a token to encrypt the request (issuerToken). The STS provider generates a security context token, which factors in the client's security token (token) that signs the STS provider request.

The IssueSecurityContextTokenAuthenticated method may be called synchronously (as shown in Listing 8-12) or asynchronously. The synchronous method is preferable because the Web service calls will not be able to proceed anyway in the event that a security context token is not returned. So it is best to wait for the synchronous call to complete, and then to branch directly to an error handler in the event there is a problem.

Step 4: Add Security Elements to Sign and Encrypt Upcoming Web Service Requests Using the New Security Context Token

The security context token works like any other security token, which means that you can use it to sign and encrypt request messages to the Web service. Listing 8-13 illustrates how to apply the security context token to a Web service request.

Listing 8-13. Applying a Security Context Token to a Web Service Request

```
private void AssignSecurityContextToken( ➥
    StockTraderServiceWse serviceProxy, SecurityContextToken sct)
{
    // Use the security context token to sign and encrypt
    // a request to the Web service
    SoapContext requestContext = serviceProxy.RequestSoapContext;
    requestContext.Security.Tokens.Add( sct );
    requestContext.Security.Elements.Add( new MessageSignature( sct ) );
    requestContext.Security.Elements.Add( new EncryptedData( sct ) );
}
```

Security context tokens generate a smaller message payload than standard security tokens when they are used to sign and encrypt SOAP messages. This is an added advantage when you need to make multiple requests within a secure conversation session.

Step 5: Proceed to Call the Web Service As Usual

At the very end of the client code listing, you will find that very little has changed. Once the security code has been implemented, the Web service call can proceed as usual, as shown in Listing 8-14.

Listing 8-14. The Client's RequestStockQuote Method

```
public void RequestStockQuote(StockTraderServiceWse serviceProxy)
{
    // Call the Web service RequestQuote() method
    Console.WriteLine("Calling {0}", serviceProxy.Url);
    Quote strQuote = serviceProxy.RequestQuote("MSFT");

    // Results
    Console.WriteLine("Web Service call successful. Result:");
    Console.WriteLine( "Symbol: " + strQuote.Symbol );
    Console.WriteLine( "Price:   " + strQuote.Last );
    Console.WriteLine( "Change: " + strQuote.PercentChange + "%");
}
```

Listing 8-15 summarizes the complete code listing for the Web service client as it would appear within a single method called SecureConversationRequest. Note that you will not find this method in the sample solution. Instead, this large listing is broken out into several smaller code listings, just as you have seen in the chapter so far. Listing 8-15 is presented so that you can get a clear start-to-finish view of how to implement a secure conversation solution within a client.

Listing 8-15. Implement a Secure Conversation Solution Within a Client

```
using System;
using System.Configuration;
using Microsoft.Web.Services2;
using Microsoft.Web.Services2.Policy;
using Microsoft.Web.Services2.Security;
using Microsoft.Web.Services2.Security.Policy;
using Microsoft.Web.Services2.Security.Tokens;
using Microsoft.Web.Services2.Security.X509;

public void SecureConversationRequest()
{
    // Step 0: Create an instance of the Web service proxy
    StockTraderServiceWse serviceProxy = new StockTraderServiceWse();

    // Step 1: Get our security token to sign the request
    string username  = Environment.UserName;
    byte[] passwordBytes = System.Text.Encoding.UTF8.GetBytes( username );
    Array.Reverse( passwordBytes );
    string passwordEquivalent = Convert.ToBase64String( passwordBytes );
    SecurityToken token = new UsernameToken( ➥
        username, passwordEquivalent, PasswordOption.SendHashed );
```

```
if (token == null)
    throw new ApplicationException("Unable to obtain security token.");

// Step 2: Create a SecurityTokenServiceClient that will
// get the SecurityContextToken
string secureConvEndpoint = ConfigurationSettings.AppSettings["tokenIssuer"];
SecurityContextTokenServiceClient STSClient = ➥
    new SecurityContextTokenServiceClient(new Uri( secureConvEndpoint ));

// Step 3: Retrieve the issuerToken (the server certificate
// from the client's CurrentUserStore)
X509SecurityToken issuerToken = null;
string ServerBase64KeyId = "bBwPfItvKp3b6TNDq+14qs58VJQ=";

// Open the CurrentUser Certificate Store
X509CertificateStore store;
store = X509CertificateStore.CurrentUserStore( X509CertificateStore.MyStore );

// Place the key ID of the certificate in a byte array
// This KeyID represents the Wse2Quickstart certificate included with
// the WSE 2.0 Quickstart samples
X509CertificateCollection certs = store.FindCertificateByKeyIdentifier( ➥
    Convert.FromBase64String( ServerBase64KeyId ) );

if (certs.Count > 0)
{
    // Get the first certificate in the collection
    issuerToken = new X509SecurityToken( ((X509Certificate) certs[0]) );
}

// Step 5: Request the security context token, use the client's
// signing token as the base
SecurityContextToken sct = ➥
    STSClient.IssueSecurityContextTokenAuthenticated(token, issuerToken);

// Step 6: Use the security context token to sign and encrypt a request
// to the Web service
SoapContext requestContext = serviceProxy.RequestSoapContext;
requestContext.Security.Tokens.Add( sct );
requestContext.Security.Elements.Add( new MessageSignature( sct ) );
requestContext.Security.Elements.Add( new EncryptedData( sct ) );

// Step 7: Call the Web service RequestQuote() method
Console.WriteLine("Calling {0}", serviceProxy.Url);
Quote strQuote = serviceProxy.RequestQuote("MSFT");
```

```
// Step 8: Display the results
Console.WriteLine("Web Service call successful. Result:");
Console.WriteLine( " " );
Console.WriteLine( "Symbol: " + strQuote.Symbol );
Console.WriteLine( "Price:  " + strQuote.Last );
Console.WriteLine( "Change: " + strQuote.PercentChange + "%");


// Step 9: Execute a second stock quote request
Quote strQuote = serviceProxy.RequestQuote("INTC");
}
```

Listing 8-15 should provide you with a unified view of all of the code presented in Listings 8-1 through 8-14. The code listings should remain conceptually clear when you reference them in conjunction with the architecture diagrams in Figure 8-1. Listing 8-15 closes out the major discussion on implementing a secure conversation solution. However, I will close out this chapter with a discussion on the advanced topic of caching security context tokens for use in long-running client-service communications.

Cache Security Context Tokens for Long-Running Communications

The sample solution for this chapter uses a simple console application client that executes two back-to-back stock quote requests. Once the second request is complete, the console application closes down, and the secure conversation terminates.

However, if the client were a Web application, then it is likely it would execute several discontinuous requests separated by inactive time between requests. If you were to implement this chapter's code listings in the Web application client, then you would find that the client would request a new security context token with every new request. This of course would defeat the purpose of a secure conversation, which aims to reuse the same security token for the entire duration of the communication between a client and a service.

The way to reuse the same security token is to store it in a global cache when it is first generated. Then on subsequent client requests you can pull the token out as needed. Security tokens are identified by a unique, GUID-based ID. Here is an example of a security context token ID:

SecurityToken-22d4c3d1-7e13-4543-a02c-4c4e6f3a5c3b

You need to track the token ID that applies to your current secure conversation because it is possible that other security tokens will be stored in the global cache. If you pull the wrong one out of the cache, then the next request in your secure conversation will fail.

With caching it also becomes possible for a client to initiate more than one secure conversation with multiple services. The wires will not cross as long as the client tracks which security token applies to which secure conversation.

Listing 8-16 is a rewrite of Listing 8-12, which factors in the global cache. I have added bold formatting to the code that directly relates to the cache implementation. The RequestSecurityContextToken method is responsible for retrieving a security context token for use in a secure conversation. Previously, it would automatically generate the token from scratch. Now it first attempts to retrieve a valid token from the global cache based on a specific token ID that is stored in a client global variable.

Listing 8-16. The RequestSecurityContextToken Method Including Caching

```
using System;
using System.Configuration;
using Microsoft.Web.Services2;
using Microsoft.Web.Services2.Policy;
using Microsoft.Web.Services2.Security;
using Microsoft.Web.Services2.Security.Policy;
using Microsoft.Web.Services2.Security.Tokens;
using Microsoft.Web.Services2.Security.X509;

string SCTID; // Client global variable to track the current token ID

private SecurityContextToken RequestSecurityContextToken( ➥
    StockTraderServiceWse serviceProxy, StockTraderClient client)
{
    // Purpose: Return a security context token
    // Note: This function looks for a valid token in the global cache
    // before automatically requesting a new one
    SecurityContextToken sct = null;
    try
    {
        // Look for a specific security token in the global cache,
        // before requesting a new one
        if (client.SCTID.Length > 0 && ➥
            PolicyEnforcementSecurityTokenCache.GlobalCache.Count > 0)
        {
            sct = RetrieveSecurityContextTokenFromGlobalCache(client.SCTID);
        }

        // Request a new security context token if one was not available
        // from the global cache
        if (sct == null)
        {
```

```
                        // Create a security token to use as the base for the
                        // security context token (SCT), which will be issued
                        // later by the security token service (STS)
                        SecurityToken token = client.GetSTSRequestSigningToken();

                        // Create a SecurityContextTokenServiceClient (STSClient)
                        // that will get the SecurityContextToken
                        string secureConvEndpoint = ➥
                            ConfigurationSettings.AppSettings["tokenIssuer"];
                        SecurityContextTokenServiceClient STSClient = ➥
                            new SecurityContextTokenServiceClient(new Uri( secureConvEndpoint ));

                        // Retrieve the server certificate, to include in the signed request to
                        // the security token service (STS)
                        SecurityToken issuerToken = client.GetServerToken();

                        // Request the security context token, use the client's
                        // signing token as the base
                        sct = STSClient.IssueSecurityContextTokenAuthenticated( ➥
                            token, issuerToken);

                        // Cache the security context token in the global cache for
                        // future requests. You must cache this token if you will be making
                        // multiple distinct requests. Otherwise, you will continue to generate
                        // new security context tokens.
                        PolicyEnforcementSecurityTokenCache.GlobalCache.Add(sct);

                        // Cache the security context token ID for future retrieval
                        client.SCTID = sct.Id;

                    }

                }
                catch
                {}
                return sct;
            }
```

At the beginning of Listing 8-16, the method attempts to retrieve an existing security context token from the global cache using a method called RetrieveSecurityContextTokenFromGlobalCache. Listing 8-17 provides the code listing for this method.

Listing 8-17. The RetrieveSecurityContextTokenFromGlobalCache Method

```
private SecurityContextToken ➥
    RetrieveSecurityContextTokenFromGlobalCache(string SCTID)
{
    // Purpose: Retrieve a security context token from the global cache
    SecurityContextToken sct = null;
    try
    {
        // Loop through the collection of security context tokens
        System.Collections.IEnumerator enmTokens = ➥
            PolicyEnforcementSecurityTokenCache.GlobalCache.GetEnumerator();

        SecurityContextToken token;

        while (enmTokens.MoveNext())
        {
            token = (SecurityContextToken)enmTokens.Current;
            if (token.Id == SCTID)
            {
                sct = token;
                break;
            }
        }
    }
    catch
    {}
    return sct;
}
```

The RetrieveSecurityContextTokenFromGlobalCache method enumerates through all available security tokens in the global cache, and looks for a match against a specific token ID. If no match is found, or if tokens are no longer available in the cache, then the method simply returns null, which triggers the RequestSecurityContextToken method to generate the security context token from scratch. Notice that Listing 8-16 automatically adds new security context tokens to the global cache. The method is implemented in such a way as to avoid the possibility of adding duplicate security context tokens to the global cache.

As an exercise, you can implement the client as a Windows Forms application, rather than as a console application, and provide buttons on the form that call different methods in the StockTrader Web service. For example, one button would call the RequestQuote method, while another would call the PlaceTrade method. You can request the security context token in the form's initialization code, and then store the token in the global cache. You can then retrieve this token every time the user clicks a button on the form to make a new request to the Web service.

As a final note, this chapter describes a number of code-intensive steps for implementing secure conversation. In reality, several of these steps can be handled automatically for you by using policy frameworks, such as the checks for digital signatures and encryption on incoming and outgoing messages. Chapter 7 describes policy frameworks in detail.

Summary

The WS-Secure Conversation specification provides a token-based, session-oriented, on-demand, secure channel for communication between a Web service and client. WS-Secure Conversation is analogous to the Secure Sockets Layer protocol that secures communications over HTTP.

WSE 2.0 provides support for implementing secure conversation in the following ways:

- It provides a prebuilt assembly for the security token service provider.

- It provides a UsernameTokenManager class for processing a signed request from the client to initiate the secure conversation.

- It provides a specialized proxy class for the client to request a security context token from a provider.

- It provides a dedicated global cache for storing security context tokens.

In the next chapter, I will shift the focus to SOAP messaging, and the collection of support specifications that includes WS-Addressing and WS-Referral. The discussion on WSE 2.0 support for SOAP messaging will bring you back full circle to where the book began, with the discussion on the importance of messages in service-oriented applications.

CHAPTER 9

Design Patterns for SOAP Messaging with WS-Addressing and Routing

TRADITIONAL WEB SERVICES are built on the HTTP Request/Response model. This is fine for some applications, but is limiting for others. WSE 2.0 provides a messaging framework that expands the supported transport protocols to include TCP and an optimized in-process transport protocol, in addition to HTTP. These protocols are not natively tied to a Request/Response communications model, so you can implement alternative models, such as asynchronous messaging solutions.

This chapter will focus on working with the WSE 2.0 implementation of the WS-Addressing specification and with messaging and routing. Together, these specifications and features provide support for

- Several transport protocols, in addition to HTTP, including TCP and an optimized protocol called In-Process for clients and services that reside on the same domain

- True asynchronous communication using TCP

- SOAP messages that contain their own addressing headers and endpoint reference information

- Automatic routing and referral for SOAP messages

- Custom SOAP routers

The WSE 2.0 messaging framework is designed to give you more control over the transport and processing of SOAP messages. Of course, WSE 2.0 does not force you to leverage any of its messaging capabilities. You can continue to write traditional HTTP-based Web services if you prefer. But this design pattern is only suitable if you need to implement a Request/Response communication design, and if you want to host your service within a virtual directory.

There are three transport channel protocols that are supported by the WSE 2.0 messaging framework out of the box: HTTP, TCP, and an optimized mode called In-Process, for Web services and clients that reside within the same process. In addition, WSE 2.0 provides framework support for implementing your own custom transport protocols. For example, a number of developers are experimenting with integrating SOAP with Microsoft Message Queuing (MSMQ). Microsoft themselves are actively working towards creating an MSMQ transport channel, with the larger goal in mind of implementing the WS-Reliable Messaging specification.

Communication Models for Web Services

Before starting a discussion on WS-Addressing and messaging, we need to step back and take the big picture view, starting with a review of how Web services communicate with clients. Traditional Web services communicate over the HTTP protocol and use a traditional Request/Response communication pattern, in which a client request results in a synchronous, direct service response. Unfortunately, this model is very limiting because it does not accommodate long-running service calls that may take minutes, hours, or days to complete. A typical synchronous Web service call will time out long before the response is ever delivered.

There are five generally accepted communication design patterns, or models, that govern the exchange of SOAP messages between a service and its client (or between two services):

1. **Request/Response (classic):** The service endpoint receives a message and sends back a correlated response message immediately, or within a very timely fashion.

2. **Request/Response with Polling:** The client sends a request message to a service endpoint and immediately returns a correlation message ID to uniquely identify the request. The service takes a "significant" amount of time to process the request, meaning more than you would expect if you were receiving a timely response message. Knowing this, the client must periodically poll the service using the correlation ID to ask if a response is ready. The service treats this query as a standard request/response, and replies in the negative, or in the affirmative (with the actual response message). So this model involves two pairs of correlated request/response messages.

3. **Request/Response with Notification:** The client sends a request message to a service, and the service takes a "significant" amount of time to process the request, meaning more than you would expect if you were receiving a timely response message. The service does not reply back to the client until the processing of the request is complete. The client is responsible for waiting for the response. This model describes classic asynchronous communication. It also describes what I call the pseudo-asynchronous communication that is supported by standard ASP.NET Web services. (I will provide more discussion on this issue later in this chapter.)

4. **One-way, or Notification:** The service endpoint receives a request message, but does not generate a response message. This model is not widely used.

5. **Solicit/Response:** The reverse of Request/Response, whereby the service endpoint sends the client a solicitation request and receives a response. This model is not widely used.

Standard ASP.NET Web services, which you build by default in VS .NET, give you the illusion that they support an asynchronous communication pattern. The Web service's WSDL document contains asynchronous versions for each operation, and the auto-generated proxy class also dutifully provides asynchronous method calls. Listing 9-1 shows a comparison between synchronous and asynchronous versions of the same Web method, as they appear in an auto-generated proxy class.

Listing 9-1. The Proxy Class for a Traditional XML Web Service

```
public class StockTraderServiceWse : ➡
    Microsoft.Web.Services2.WebServicesClientProtocol
{
    public Quote RequestQuote([System.Xml.Serialization.XmlElementAttribute(
        Namespace="http://www.asptechnology.net/schemas/StockTrader/")]
        string Symbol)
    {
        object[] results = this.Invoke("RequestQuote", new object[] {Symbol});
        return ((Quote)(results[0]));
    }

    public System.IAsyncResult BeginRequestQuote(string Symbol, ➡
        System.AsyncCallback callback, object asyncState)
    {
        return this.BeginInvoke("RequestQuote", new object[] {Symbol}, ➡
            callback, asyncState);
    }
```

```
public Quote EndRequestQuote(System.IAsyncResult asyncResult)
{
    object[] results = this.EndInvoke(asyncResult);
    return ((Quote)(results[0]));
}
}
```

The two callback functions BeginRequestQuote and EndRequestQuote give you the illusion of asynchronous communication, but you cannot truly disconnect the calling thread once the request message has been sent out. And the burden falls on the client to manage the wait time for a response.

A true asynchronous method call completely releases the thread that is used for the request, and then later creates a new thread to receive the response. The limitation here is not with .NET per se, it is with the HTTP-based response/request model. Simply spacing out the request and the response does not equate to an asynchronous call. The solution is to drop HTTP and to use a different protocol such as TCP. Unfortunately, the architecture of your solution will also need to change. How you do so is a central focus of this chapter.

Overview of WS-Addressing

The WS-Addressing specification enables messages to store their own addressing information, so that the source, destination, and reply URI locations are self-contained within the message. This allows a message to hop across multiple endpoints without losing information about the source of the original request. And it allows intermediate services to route and refer the message across multiple endpoints until eventually a response is sent back to the specified reply location.

If you are writing a very basic Web service that uses the HTTP transport protocol, you are implementing a classic Request/Response model in which the client issues a request and the service is expected to issue a direct response. In this scenario, it is unnecessary for the message to contain its own addressing information. But the need changes in other scenarios, such as a message that hops across multiple endpoints over the TCP transport protocol.

WS-Addressing is not interesting in and of itself because it is a support specification that plays an essential support role for other important specifications such as WS-Reliable Messaging. Still, it is important to understand the WS-Addressing constructs and how they are written to a SOAP message. Without WS-Addressing, it would not be possible for messages to travel anywhere other than within the well-established HTTP-based Request/Response model. Nor would it be impossible to write truly asynchronous Web service calls.

Overview of the WS-Addressing Constructs

The WS-Addressing specification supports two types of constructs:

1. Message information headers

2. Endpoint references

These constructs are closely tied to elements that you find in a WSDL document, such as operations, ports, and bindings. The WS-Addressing constructs are a complement to the WSDL document, not a replacement, although it is likely that future versions of the WSDL specification will evolve in conjunction with the WS-Addressing specification. Let's consider each of the constructs in turn.

Message Information Headers

These are the most intuitive addressing headers because they work in a similar fashion to e-mail message addresses, which provide a set of headers including From, To, and ReplyTo. Of course, SOAP message information headers include additional entries that are SOAP-specific and have no relation to e-mail. For example, the Action header stores the XML qualified name of the operation that the SOAP message is intended for.

Table 9-1 provides a summary of the available message headers, including their XML representations.

Table 9-1. XML Elements for Message Information Headers

Header	Type	Description
To	URI	The destination URI for the message (required).
Action	URI	The SOAP action for the message (required). The action identifies the specific endpoint operation that the message is intended for.
From	Endpoint Ref	The source of the message (optional). At a minimum, the From header must provide a URI, if it is specified. But you can also add more complex endpoint reference information (optional).
ReplyTo	Endpoint Ref	The reply to destination for the message response. This may be different from the source address (optional).
Recipient	Endpoint Ref	The complete endpoint reference for the message recipient (optional).

Continued

Table 9-1. XML Elements for Message Information Headers (continued)

Header	Type	Description
FaultTo	Endpoint Ref	The endpoint that will receive SOAP fault messages (optional). If the FaultTo endpoint is absent, then the SOAP fault will default to the ReplyTo endpoint.
MessageID	Endpoint Ref	The message ID property (optional). The ID may be a GUID identifier, or it may be a qualified reference, for example, a UDDI reference.

The only required message headers are To and Action, although if you expect a response, then you will also need to set the From or ReplyTo headers. Table 9-1 shows you the type that the header supports. Notice that the majority of the headers require endpoint references.

Listing 9-2 shows you how message information headers appear within a SOAP message.

Listing 9-2. A SOAP Message with Message Information Headers

```
<S:Envelope xmlns:S="http://www.w3.org/2002/12/soap-envelope"
    xmlns:wsa="http://schemas.xmlsoap.org/ws/2003/03/addressing"
    xmlns:st="http://www.bluestonepartners.com/schemas/StockTrader">
  <S:Header>
      <wsa:MessageID>uuid:7ae86g-95d...</wsa:MessageID>
      <wsa:ReplyTo>
          <wsa:Address>http://investor123.com/client</wsa:Address>
      </wsa:ReplyTo>
      <wsa:FaultTo>
          <wsa:Address>http://investor123.com/faults</wsa:Address>
      </wsa:FaultTo>
      <wsa:To S:mustUnderstand="1">http://stocktrader.com/StockTrader</wsa:To>
      <wsa:Action>http://stocktrader.com/StockTrader#RequestQuote</wsa:Action>
  </S:Header>
  <S:Body>
      <st:RequestQuote>
          <Symbol>MSFT</Symbol>
      </st:RequestQuote>
  </S:Body>
</S:Envelope>
```

Listing 9-2 is a SOAP message that is being sent from a client at investor123.com, to a stock trading service at stocktrader.com. The client is requesting a stock quote, using the RequestQuote operation. This operation is described in the StockTrader schema, as referenced in the envelope header. Note that the StockTrader schema is qualified using the XSD namespace reference `http://www.bluestonepartners.com/schemas/StockTrader`.

This simple code listing displays the best aspect of SOAP messages: that they are fully qualified and self-describing. Every element in this SOAP message is qualified by a specific XML namespace. And the addressing information for the message is self-contained. Nothing that is included in a SOAP message is allowed to exist in a vacuum.

Endpoint References

Endpoint references are a little less intuitive than addressing headers, and they are more akin to the WSDL <service> tag. Think of endpoint references as complex XML data types that provide a collection of child elements to describe the various facets of the type. Endpoint references provide both addressing and SOAP binding information.

Recall from Chapter 2 that the <service> element provides port information and binding information combined. The <service> element describes the operations that are available at a service endpoint, and also provides you with a message protocol–specific binding address. The only message protocol we are really focused on here is SOAP. So, to be more specific, an endpoint reference tells you what operations are supported at a given port, and also how you should address SOAP messages to that port.

Listing 9-3 shows an example of an endpoint reference as it is included within a SOAP message. Compare this with Listing 9-2, which uses message information headers. Notice that the endpoint reference stores the addressing destination information in a different tag, and that it also contains dynamic reference information (such as AccountID) that is specific to the endpoint reference.

Listing 9-3. Endpoint Reference XML

```
<wsa:EndpointReference>
    <wsa:Address>soap.tcp://stocktrader.com/StockTrader</wsa:Address>
    <wsa:ReferenceProperties>
        <st:AccountID>123A</st:AccountID>
    </wsa:ReferenceProperties>
    <wsa:PortType>st:StockTraderSoap</wsa:PortType>
    <wsp:Policy />
</wsa:EndpointReference>
```

Endpoint references do not replace message information headers because they are focused on describing binding information for the endpoint, not specific operation information. You do not get to choose between using message information headers versus endpoint references. Message information addressing headers may include endpoint references for the destination elements in the message. But from a conceptual perspective, you can draw a distinction between the two constructs. Message information headers are a general construct for storing addressing information, for both the sender and the receiver. Endpoint references are more complex and dynamic, and include SOAP binding information to the specific endpoint that the SOAP message is intended for. Luckily, WSE 2.0 sets up the classes so that the constructs can be kept distinct from a programming perspective.

As with all the WS-specifications, you can drill down as far as you want to go and dive into increasing complexity. Inevitably, if you drill down far enough, then you will discover a rich interaction between the specification elements, and the overall conceptual picture will begin to blur. My goal here is to keep the conceptual discussion clear, and to provide you with a solid grounding so that you can continue to explore on your own.

WSE 2.0 Implementation for WS-Addressing

WSE 2.0 implements the full WS-Addressing specification, in a dedicated namespace called Microsoft.Web.Services2.Addressing. Table 9-2 summarizes some of the important WS-Addressing classes (each of which corresponds to an XML element in the WS-Addressing specification).

Table 9-2. Classes in the WSE 2.0 Addressing Namespace

Class	Description
Action	Specifies the XML qualified name of the operation that the SOAP message is intended for.
Address	Stores a binding-specific address, and may be assigned to other classes, including To, From, and ReplyTo. The properties of the Address class correspond to classes that are based on endpoint references. For example, the Address.To property corresponds to the WS-Addressing To class, which is an endpoint reference.
AddressingHeaders	Indicates the collection of properties that address a message, including To, From, ReplyTo, and MessageID.
AddressingFault	Occurs when there is an invalid header in the message, or when an exception occurs along the message path.
EndPointReference	Stores endpoint reference information, which is binding information for a service.

Continued

Table 9-2. Classes in the WSE 2.0 Addressing Namespace (continued)

Class	Description
ReferenceProperties	Indicates the collection of properties that add additional description elements for an endpoint.
To	Stores the source address as an endpoint reference.
From	Stores the destination address as an endpoint reference.
ReplyTo	Stores the reply to address for the response as an endpoint reference.

There are three interesting things to note about the Addressing classes:

1. Most of the Addressing classes derive from XML and SOAP base classes, which reflect their obvious close ties to these specifications. (In fact, the majority of WSE 2.0 specification classes have similarly close ties to XML and SOAP base classes.)

2. You will not often need to instance these classes directly. Instead, it is more likely that you will access them via properties on other classes. For example, the SoapEnvelope class (in Microsoft.Web.Services2) provides a Context.Addressing property that exposes the AddressingHeaders class. Here, you can directly set message addressing information, such as From, To, ReplyTo, and Action properties.

3. The Addressing classes are independent of the underlying transport protocol. It does not matter if the addressed SOAP message is transported over HTTP, TCP, or SMTP. The addressing headers and references will apply, regardless of how the message is transported.

The two more important classes in the Addressing namespace are the AddressingHeaders class and the EndpointReference class. These correspond to the two main constructs in the WS-Addressing specification: message information headers and endpoint references. Your SOAP messages may use one or the other, depending on how you prefer to set addressing to service endpoints. In the future it is likely that most addressing will be done in terms of endpoint references, particularly as the WSDL specification evolves, and as the WS-Addressing specification becomes more established and refined.

> **NOTE** *Do not confuse the message protocol with the transport protocol. SOAP is a message protocol that provides a specification for constructing messages. HTTP, TCP, and SMTP are transport protocols, which are different specifications for transporting messages. SOAP messages may be delivered using all of these transport protocols.*

Security Considerations for WS-Addressing

Addressing information can be sensitive, especially when it contains port numbers and references to qualified endpoints. We are used to thinking of this information as being public because Web services are often publicly accessible. But with WS-Addressing, this information is attached to the SOAP message header directly. You typically do not want the body of the SOAP message to be tampered with or viewed by unauthorized parties. In the same way, you should feel equally protective about the SOAP message headers.

Another sensitive case is when messages are routed between multiple endpoints, each of which writes additional WS-Addressing information to the message header. The additional endpoints may not be designed to handle direct service requests from outside clients. Their addressing information needs to be kept protected.

There are three recommended options for securing the contents of a message that contains addressing headers:

1. Digitally sign the message, including the body and header information.

2. Encrypt the message headers.

3. Add a message ID.

Digital signing allows you to detect whether a message has been tampered with or compromised. Digital signing alone will not encrypt or hide the contents of the message, but it will ensure that a tampered message will be automatically rejected by the receiving Web service.

Encrypting the message headers will clearly protect its contents, but this approach works best if the message is not being routed or referred to another Web service endpoint. Intermediary Web services will need access to the addressing header information, so there is an additional burden on the developer to ensure that the intermediaries can encrypt the message header contents.

The message ID (<wsa:MessageID>) is important because it allows you to design against replay attacks, whereby a client repeatedly resends the same message to a Web service endpoint in order to overwhelm the service and to bring down its host server. The receiving Web service simply needs to cache this message ID, and then ignore additional requests that come in.

NOTE *Refer to Chapter 6 for a detailed discussion on replay attacks and how to prevent them.*

There is no right way to implement security to protect addressing headers. Each of these options are recommended, rather than required. You need to make an individual determination as to whether security measures are required for your service-oriented application.

At this point, you should be more comfortable with the concepts behind WS-Addressing, but you are probably still wondering exactly how to put these concepts, and the code, into action. Remember that WS-Addressing is a support specification that is built for messaging. The next section on messaging will provide you with the context for addressing by showing you the important role that addressing plays for messaging.

Overview of Messaging

WSE 2.0 includes support for messaging, which provides developers with a new range of features for transporting and processing SOAP messages. Traditional XML Web services support the HTTP transport protocol only, which limits the client and server to communicating with a synchronous, Request/Response design pattern.

WSE 2.0 messaging continues to support the HTTP protocol, but it also adds support for two additional transport protocols:

- **TCP:** A low-level protocol that communicates across processes and domain boundaries. Instant messenger and chat applications use the TCP protocol.

- **In-Process:** This protocol is designed for communications between components within the same application domain. It is an optimized, low-level protocol that provides the flexibility of TCP.

In addition, WSE 2.0 provides classes that allow you to custom implement additional transport protocols, such as SMTP and MSMQ.

Comparing Messaging with the HTTP and TCP Protocols

Services that communicate over HTTP must reside on a Web server in order for their endpoints to be accessible. However, services that communicate over TCP are accessible over a direct port, without requiring a virtual directory. Here is an example of an HTTP endpoint:

```
http://www.bluestonepartners.com/StockTrader.asmx
```

And here is an example of the equivalent TCP endpoint:

```
soap.tcp://216.70.214.118/StockTrader
```

The HTTP and TCP protocols have one thing in common, which is that they both enable messaging between remote components that are running on separate processes and on separate domains. TCP is a lower-level protocol that operates on a port rather than a virtual directory, which is a higher-level abstraction of a port.

HTTP is designed for Request/Response messaging patterns, meaning that a request generates a direct response. TCP is designed for decoupled messaging patterns whereby a sender and a receiver communicate, but not necessarily as a two-way conversation. TCP enables asynchronous messaging, whereby the sender releases its calling thread as soon as the message has been delivered to the receiver. By extension, TCP also enables one-way messaging, because once a sender mails out a message, its resources are released, and the sender suffers no resource or scalability problems waiting for a response that will never come. This is the beauty of the decoupled TCP protocol: You can implement a Request/Response messaging pattern if you want to, but unlike with HTTP, you do not have to.

NOTE *Technically, the HTTP protocol does support one-way messaging. The response will generate an HTTP 202 status code, and no SOAP message will be returned.*

Representing SOAP Messages in the WSE 2.0 Messaging Framework

The Microsoft.Web.Services2 namespace provides a class called SoapEnvelope, which you use for generating SOAP messages in code. The SoapEnvelope class derives from the System.Xml.XmlDocument class, not surprisingly, and so it supports XML document loading, so that you can load preformatted SOAP messages into a SoapEnvelope object. Alternatively, you can construct the SOAP message from scratch by setting properties on the SoapEnvelope object.

Table 9-3 highlights important members of the SoapEnvelope class. Listing 9-4 shows you how to construct a SOAP message in code for requesting a stock quote from the RequestQuote operation.

Table 9-3. The SoapEnvelope Class

Property	Type	Description
Envelope	XmlElement	The envelope is the root element of the message XML. It contains the message body and message header elements.
Body	XmlElement	The body element is required for all SOAP messages. It contains qualified XML for the request and response messages.
Header	XmlElement	The header contains optional extended information for the SOAP message. The WS-Specification settings are stored in the header.
Fault	Exception	Retrieves the SOAP fault from the envelope, if there is one, and returns an Exception class.
Context	SoapContext	The Context property enables you to modify the SOAP message contents within a custom WSE filter; or to process the SOAP message contents within a SoapReceiver processing class.

Listing 9-4. Constructing a SOAP Message in Code for the RequestQuote Operation

```
public SoapEnvelope CreateSoapMessage()
{
    SoapEnvelope message = new SoapEnvelope();

    RequestQuote q = new RequestQuote();
    RequestQuote.Symbol = "MSFT";

    message.SetBodyObject(q);

    // Assign the addressing SOAP message headers
    message.Context.Addressing.Action = new Action( ➡
        "http://www.bluestonepartners.com/schemas/StockTrader/RequestQuote");
    message.Context.Addressing.From = new From(fromUri);
    message.Context.Addressing.ReplyTo = new ReplyTo(fromUri);

    return message;
}
```

Listing 9-4 illustrates several important points:

SOAP messages cannot be empty, because their purpose is to communicate requests or responses. Here, the SOAP message is designed to transmit a stock quote request. It uses the RequestQuote class to generate a correctly formatted request. Recall that RequestQuote is defined in an interface definition file that provides class representations for all of the StockTrader custom data types.

The SoapEnvelope's SetBodyObject method automatically generates the SOAP message body for the RequestQuote object.

The SOAP message headers store addressing information directly, using the WSE 2.0 addressing classes. The Action property is required, and must reflect the operation that the sender is calling. If it calls a Web service that supports multiple operations, then the Action property enables the service to differentiate incoming requests, and to process them correctly.

NOTE *Refer back to Chapter 3 for a detailed discussion on the StockTrader XML schema. This chapter shows you how to build the StockTrader XML schema from scratch, and also shows you how to generate an interface definition file of classes based on the schema.*

SOAP Senders and SOAP Receivers

We are all familiar with two common messaging modes: Peer-to-Peer (e.g., chat applications) and Request/Response (e.g., Internet browsing). With SOAP messaging, the concept of clients and services does not really apply, because this implies a fixed communication pattern (meaning that the client always initiates the request, and then the service responds). With SOAP messaging, it is more accurate to refer to senders and receivers, which implies roles rather than functions. A given service may function as a message receiver in some cases, and as a message sender in others.

The WSE 2.0 messaging framework provides dedicated classes for the sender and receiver roles. The SoapSender class sends a message out to a specified endpoint (URI). The class is straightforward to use, as shown in Listing 9-5.

Listing 9-5. The SoapSender Class

```
SoapSender soapSender = new SoapSender(toUri);
soapSender.Send(message);
```

The SoapReceiver class is abstract and must be implemented in a custom class that is assigned to receive the corresponding response for a message request. In a sense, this custom SOAP receiver class acts like a callback function, in that it is called when a response is ready. But unlike a traditional callback function, the custom SOAP receiver class is decoupled from the request.

There are three steps to implementing a custom SOAP receiver class:

1. Create a custom class that implements the SoapReceiver abstract class.

2. Override the Receive method with a custom implementation for processing the incoming response message.

3. Register the custom receiver class so that the messaging framework knows it is the handler for the incoming response message.

Listing 9-6 shows you these three steps in code.

Listing 9-6. Implementing a SOAP Message Receiver

```
class StockTrader
{
    public void SendSoapMessage(SoapEnvelope message)
    {
        // Register the response receiver
            SoapReceivers.Add(fromUri, typeof(StockTraderResponseReceiver));

        // Send the SOAP request message
        SoapSender soapSender = new SoapSender(toUri);
        soapSender.Send(message);
    }
}

public class StockTraderResponseReceiver : SoapReceiver
{
    protected override void Receive( SoapEnvelope message )
    {
        // Process the incoming message...
    }
}
```

Listing 9-6 is implemented in the sender component, to process incoming response messages. It turns out that the receiver component implements very similar code, but this time to process incoming request messages. This is the important point: The SoapReceiver class does not care whether it is implemented in a sender or receiver component. It is agnostic in this regard. Its purpose is to support the processing of incoming SOAP messages, regardless of whether they originate from a sender or a receiver component.

Listing 9-7 shows you how to process an incoming message. This listing is taken from the receiver component, which processes the RequestQuote SOAP request message. The receiver needs to do the following:

1. Deserialize the SOAP message body.

2. Examine the SOAP message Action to determine how to process the incoming SOAP message. The SoapReceiver must be able to correlate the incoming message body to a qualified data type, in this case, the StockTrader Quote type.

3. Process the RequestQuote operation.

4. Generate a response message based on the Quote type, which is the output type from the StockTrader's RequestQuote operation. Inherent in this step is the fact that the SoapReceiver must correlate this outgoing response message with the incoming SOAP request message.

5. Send the response message back to the sender.

Listing 9-7. Generating a SOAP Message Response

```
public class StockTraderRequestReceiver : SoapReceiver
{
    protected override void Receive(SoapEnvelope message)
    {
        if(message.Context.Addressing.Action.Value.EndsWith("RequestQuote"))
        {

            // Retrieve the body of the SOAP request message
            // Since we have screened the Action, we know what class to look for
            RequestQuote request = ➥
                (RequestQuote)message.GetBodyObject(typeof(RequestQuote));
            string symbol = request.Symbol;
```

```
        // Call the RequestQuote() method: delegate the call
        // to a business assembly
        Quote q = RequestQuote(symbol);

        // Transform the result into a SOAP response message
        SoapEnvelope response = new SoapEnvelope();
        response.SetBodyObject(q);

        // Create the URI address objects for send and receive
        // Note, instead of hardcoding the URIs, we will pull them from
        // the original request message
        // Send response to the request message's ReplyTo address
        Uri toUri = (Uri)message.Context.Addressing.ReplyTo;
        // Return response from the request message's To address
        Uri fromUri = (Uri)message.Context.Addressing.To;

        // Assign the addressing SOAP message headers
        response.Context.Addressing.Action = new Action( ➥
    "http://www.bluestonepartners.com/schemas/StockTrader/RequestQuote#Quote");
        response.Context.Addressing.From = new From(fromUri);
        SoapSender soapSender = new SoapSender(toUri);

        // Send the SOAP request message
        soapSender.Send(response);
    }
}

// Implementation for RequestQuote()
private Quote RequestQuote(string Symbol)
{
    // Create a new Quote object
    Quote q = new Quote();

    // Retrieve the stock quote (code not shown)

    // Return the Quote
    return q;
}

}
```

Listing 9-7 highlights the following important points:

This code is contained in a separate component from the sender, running on a separate process. However, both the sender and receiver components must have the same understanding of the StockTrader custom types, including RequestQuote and Quote. They can accomplish this in two ways: They can generate an interface definition file of classes directly from the XSD schema, or they can each implement a reference assembly of types, similar to the StockTraderTypes assembly that is used throughout the sample solutions.

The receiver component implements business processing logic for the RequestQuote method. The sender component simply knows how to construct a qualified RequestQuote message. However, the receiver component must know how to process the operation. (Alternatively, the receiver component could call a dedicated business assembly, which centralizes all of the StockTrader processing. This approach is presented in Chapter 4.)

The receiver component constructs a new response message with its own addressing headers in order to return the stock quote result to the sender. The receiver component uses the same SoapSender class to actually send the message out to the specified endpoint.

> **NOTE** *The StockTraderTypes interface definition file used here is based on the StockTraderWithOperations.xsd schema file from Chapter 3, which includes complex elements to represent each of the four supported Web service operations. Please refer to Chapter 3 if you require more information.*

Implement a Windows Forms–Based Receiver

The receiver component must be up and running to respond to incoming request messages. To illustrate this, the sample solutions include a stand-alone Windows Forms–based receiver called StockTraderSoapReceiver. Figure 9-1 shows the Solution Explorer for this solution.

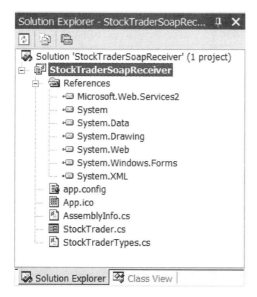

Figure 9-1. Solution Explorer for the StockTraderSoapReceiver solution

The receiver references the Microsoft.Web.Services2 and System.Web assemblies. The startup code for the form registers the custom SoapReceiver class that will handle the incoming request message, as shown in Listing 9-8.

Listing 9-8. Registering a Custom SoapReceiver Class

```
public class StockTrader : System.Windows.Forms.Form
{
    class StockTrader()
    {
        // Use TCP
        receiverUri = new Uri(String.Format( ➡
            "soap.tcp://{0}/StockTraderSoapReceiver", System.Net.Dns.GetHostName()));

        // Register the SOAP receiver objects
        StockTraderRequestReceiver request = new StockTraderRequestReceiver();
        SoapReceivers.Add(receiverUri, request);
    }
}
```

Listing 9-7 provides the code for the custom SoapReceiver class, called StockTraderRequestReceiver.

The StockTraderSoapReceiver project acts as a listener when it is compiled and run. Figure 9-2 shows the form interface when the project is running.

Figure 9-2. The TCP-based receiver component

This approach is a good shortcut for ensuring that the receiver component stays up and running. In a production setting you should implement the listening receiver component as a Windows Service component.

The Interface Definition File and WSDL

The StockTraderTypes.cs class file in the sample receiver project provides the interface definition file (IDF) that provides class representations of the StockTrader custom data types. This type information must be available to both the sender and the receiver, so it is best to compile a dedicated StockTraderTypes assembly, and to reference it from both the sender and receiver solutions. The IDF is included as a class file in the sample so that you can more easily inspect its contents. Listing 9-9 shows an excerpt from the StockTraderTypes.cs file.

Listing 9-9. The StockTraderTypes Interface Definition File

```
using System;
using System.Xml.Serialization;

namespace StockTraderTypes
{
    [System.Xml.Serialization.XmlTypeAttribute(Namespace=
        "http://www.bluestonepartners.com/schemas/StockTrader/")]
    public class RequestQuote
    {
        public String Symbol;
    }

    [System.Xml.Serialization.XmlTypeAttribute(Namespace=
        "http://www.bluestonepartners.com/schemas/StockTrader/")]
    public class Quote
```

```
{
    public string Symbol;
    public string Company;
    public string DateTime;
    // Additional properties are not shown (e.g, Open, Last, etc.)
}
}
```

Since you are no longer working with the XML Web service project type, you have lost your shortcut for generating a WSDL document directly from an .asmx service file. The StockTraderTypes.cs file can in fact be generated directly from the StockTrader XSD schema file, which you are guaranteed to have, so technically you can do without a WSDL file when building a decoupled, TCP-based sender-receiver solution. But a WSDL file contains essential metadata information that is stored according to an established specification. You cannot build a WS-I–compliant service without including a WSDL file.

So by no means am I advocating that you build services without WSDL files. You cannot, because the service must be compliant with established specifications. If it is not compliant, then it is effectively unusable, because the WSDL file stores essential metadata information on the service that is required for widespread use by different clients. However, I am pointing out that if you bypass building a traditional .asmx Web service, then you will be forced to manually generate the WSDL file. I expect that future releases of the .NET Framework will include alternate utilities for generating WSDL files. These will have to be made available once non-HTTP-based Web services become a common service type as XML Web services are today.

Traditional XML Web Services vs. SOAP Messaging over HTTP

Traditional XML Web services are conveniently implemented using the HTTP protocol, and as a developer you never need to interact with the SOAP messages directly. In fact, prior to WSE 2.0, if you needed to interact with the SOAP message directly during processing, then you had to write a custom HTTP handler to intercept the messages. You also needed to manually implement most of the plumbing for parsing, modifying, and generally interacting with the SOAP message.

WSE 2.0 does not require you to use its messaging framework if you are transporting SOAP messages over HTTP. But you will want to if you need to perform custom processing on these SOAP messages. With WSE 2.0 you do not have to write an HTTP handler yourself because one is already provided for you. All you have to do is to implement the processing code for the message itself. All of the plumbing code has already been taken care of for you.

Let's assume that the sender, or client, is a Windows Forms–based application, and that the receiver, or service, is enabled for HTTP. There are three steps for implementing the service as an HTTP-enabled SOAP receiver:

1. Create a custom SoapReceiver class in the receiver component.

2. Register the custom SoapReceiver class as an HTTP handler in the web.config file (see Listing 9-10).

3. Create a virtual directory to host the service (e.g., HttpMessagingService).

Listing 9-10 shows how you register a custom SoapReceiver class in the web.config file, so that it is automatically enabled for the HTTP protocol. Listing 9-7 provides an example of a custom SoapReceiver class. Although Listing 9-7 was developed for the TCP protocol, all you need to do to enable it for HTTP is to modify the URI of the SoapReceiver response endpoint, from soap.tcp://{endpoint} to http://{virtual directory}.

Listing 9-10. Registering a SoapReceiver Class Using the HTTP Protocol

```
<configuration>
    <system.web>
        <httpHandlers>
            <add verb="*" path="receiver.ashx" type="MyNamespace.MyReceiver,
                MyAssemblyName" />
        </httpHandlers>
    <system.web>
<configuration>
```

Based on the earlier Listing 9-7, the type name of the HTTP handler would be

```
type="StockTrader.StockTraderRequestReceiver, StockTraderSoapReceiver"
```

Note that the <add /> section must be formatted as a single line in the web.config file, or it will generate parsing errors at runtime.

The client application calls the HTTP-enabled service using a standard HTTP link, which includes the name of the virtual directory that hosts the service and the name of the standard HTTP handler. For this example, the link is

```
http://localhost/HttpMessagingService/receiver.ashx
```

The WSE 2.0 messaging framework makes it easy for you to continue working with the HTTP protocol, while at the same time making it much easier for you to manually process SOAP request and response messages.

Properties of Message-Enabled Web services

Traditional XML Web services are very limiting compared to the new capabilities provided by WSE 2.0 messaging. As you explore WSE 2.0 in general, and the new messaging capabilities in particular, you should clearly notice that

Web services are about both SOAP *and* XML.

SOAP messages are the key technology in a service-oriented architecture. XML is essential because the SOAP and WSDL specifications are XML-based, but without SOAP there would be no messages, and therefore no purpose for Web services.

SOAP messages are advanced communication instruments.

Previously, SOAP messages were limited to relatively simple constructs, and could not be secured. But the WS-Specifications now enable SOAP messages to record their own addressing information, and to be digitally signed and encrypted (both in the header and the body). SOAP messages have become advanced instruments for communication.

SOAP messages are composable and have unlimited extensibility.

Technically, a Web service is what is composable, not a SOAP message. But it is the message itself that must store and carry the required WS-specification elements (specifically, the SOAP header block). When you apply a communications trace, you are doing so on the exchanged SOAP messages, not on the endpoints themselves. SOAP messages are tailored to reflect the policies of their endpoints, and must correctly incorporate the cumulative set of required custom elements. SOAP messages are composable and have unlimited extensibility.

SOAP senders and receivers replace traditional clients and services.

We are all familiar with two modes of remote transport: Peer-to-Peer (e.g., chat applications) and Request/Response (e.g., Internet browsing). With SOAP messaging, the concept of clients and services does not really apply because this implies a fixed communication pattern (meaning that the client always initiates the request, and then the service responds). With SOAP messaging, it is more accurate to refer to senders and receivers, which implies roles rather than functions. A given service may function as a message receiver in some cases, and as a message sender in others.

Overview of Routing and Referral

SOAP message routing is a topic that follows very naturally from the discussions presented so far in this chapter. Routing allows you to set up a virtual network for processing incoming SOAP messages, by enabling the flexible redirection of SOAP messages to alternate servers that are not directly accessible by the original sender. I use the term *virtual network* because the routing may only take place on a subset of the actual physical network.

There are three main virtual network design models for routing:

Load Balancing: This model routes SOAP messages from a logical endpoint on to one server within a cluster of back-end servers that are running the same services. This routing pattern overlaps what is provided by established network load balancing (NLB) solutions, including Cisco LocalDirector and Microsoft Network Load Balancing Services.

Chain: This model routes SOAP messages through a chain of so-called SOAP intermediaries, which are intermediate services that process a SOAP message on the way to its ultimate receiving endpoint.

Content-Based: This model routes SOAP messages based on header-specific content.

Figure 9-3 provides schematic views of each of these patterns. Notice that each of them defines a common entity called the *SOAP router*. This is the immediate destination endpoint for an incoming SOAP request message. In the Load Balancing model, the SOAP router does no direct message processing; its sole purpose is to redirect the message to alternate servers for processing. However, in the other models the SOAP router may process the SOAP message in addition to routing it.

Chain Routing

Load Balancing and Content Routing

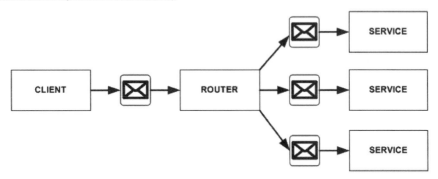

Figure 9-3. Network design patterns for SOAP message routing

WSE 2.0 provides an elegant implementation of routing and WS-Referral for the Load Balancing model that does not require you to write any code in the SOAP router. Everything is driven by configuration file settings that reflect the routing model that you want to put in place. WSE 2.0 is generally good about saving you from writing code. But with routing, this is even truer since you do not need to modify the core business logic in the receiving services. However, if you are implementing the chain routing model, or the content-based routing model, then the intermediary services will need to update addressing headers on the message to reflect the next destination in the chain.

WSE 2.0 provides out-of-the-box support for routing and WS-Referral using the HTTP protocol only. In theory, the specifications can apply to other transport protocols as well, such as TCP and SMTP. However, the WS-Addressing specification provides a more efficient routing and referral implementation for these protocols. In addition, WS-Addressing may be more efficient for implementing the chain routing model. For more on this, refer to the section "Routing vs. WS-Addressing" later in this chapter.

Now let's look at an example of how to build a SOAP router that implements a combination of the Chain and Load Balancing routing models.

Build a SOAP Router for the Load Balancing Routing Model

This example SOAP routing solution is included in the sample files as SOAPRouter.sln. It consists of three projects, as shown in Figure 9-4.

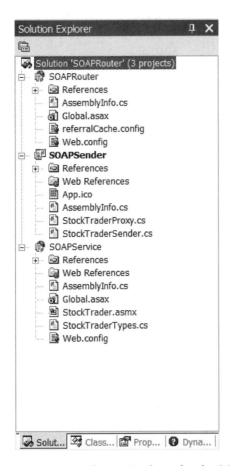

Figure 9-4. Solution Explorer for the SOAPRouter sample solution

The three projects are

1. **SOAPRouter:** A Web service-based SOAP router application

2. **SOAPSender:** A console-based client application

3. **SOAPService:** A Web service application that processes stock quotes and trades

These projects continue to use the StockTrader application that you have seen developed throughout the book. I renamed the projects using clear names so that there is no ambiguity about the purpose of each project. Technically, this solution is a combination of the Chain and Load Balancing routing models because it contains only one referral Web service.

Let's discuss each of the solution projects in turn.

Overview of the SOAP Sender

The SOAP sender application requests stock quotes from the SOAP service using two possible internal method calls:

- **SendUnsignedRequest:** Sends an unsigned stock quote request to the SOAPService RequestQuote operation.

- **SignRequestUsingX509Certificate:** Sends a digitally signed stock quote request to the SOAPService RequestQuote operation. The digital signature is based on an X.509 certificate.

Each of these method calls invokes the same proxy class. The difference between the two methods is simply whether the request message will be sent out as signed or not.

The Web service proxy class provides two possible URIs for requesting a stock quote, as shown in Listing 9-11. One URI requests the quote directly from the Web service, while the other URI requests the quote via the SOAP router, which provides an .asmx file of the same name, although the virtual directory name is different.

Listing 9-11. Service Endpoints for the SOAPSender Application

```
public StockTraderServiceWse()
{
    // Note to user: toggle between each of these URLs
    // 1. SOAPService goes directly to the service
    //this.Url = "http://localhost/SOAPService/StockTrader.asmx";
    // 2. SOAPRouter goes to the service via a router
    this.Url = "http://localhost/SOAPRouter/StockTrader.asmx";
}
```

Of course, in a production setting, the SOAPService would not be directly accessible from outside clients. Instead, they would be forced to route their request through the SOAPRouter.

Overview of the SOAP Service

The implementation code for the SOAP service RequestQuote method is shown in Listing 9-12. The listing checks for the presence of a digital signature, and validates it if it is present. However, the most important aspect of this code listing is the SoapActor attribute, which decorates the Web service class (shown in bold).

This attribute designates the specific recipient of the message response, in this
case, the SOAP router, which will in turn pass the response back to the original
sender. If the SoapActor attribute is not provided, then the Web service request
will generate an addressing error upon receipt, because the most recent sender
of the request (the SOAP router) will not match the first sender and ultimate
recipient of the response (the SOAP sender). The SoapActor attribute allows for
messages to be accepted by services after passing through intermediaries.

Listing 9-12. The SOAPService RequestQuote Method

```
using Microsoft.Web.Services2;
using Microsoft.Web.Services2.Security;
using Microsoft.Web.Services2.Security.Tokens;
using Microsoft.Web.Services2.Messaging;

[SoapActor("http://localhost/SOAPRouter/StockTrader.asmx")]
public class StockTraderService : Microsoft.Web.Services2.WebService
{
    public Quote RequestQuote(string Symbol)
    {
        // Step 1: Verify the signature on the Web service request to this method
        bool SignatureIsValid = true;

        // Code to verify that the request is digitally signed
        SoapContext requestContext = RequestSoapContext.Current;

        foreach (ISecurityElement objElem in requestContext.Security.Elements)
        {
            if (objElem is MessageSignature)
            {
                Signature clientSignature = (MessageSignature)objElem;

                if (clientSignature.SecurityToken is X509SecurityToken)
                {
                    SignatureIsValid = true;
                }
                else
                {
                    SignatureIsValid = false;
                }
            }
        }

        // Step 2: Create a new Quote object, but only populate it
        // if the signature is valid
```

```
        Quote q = new Quote();
        if (SignatureIsValid)
        {
                return q; // Return a populated Quote object
        }

    }
}
```

The validation portion of this code listing may seem a step backward given that Chapter 7 shows how to accomplish the same validation using policy expression files. The code is presented this way for illustrative purposes only.

Listing 9-13 shows you what the SOAPService's web.config file should look like.

Listing 9-13. The SOAPService web.config File

```
<configuration>

    <configSections>
        <section name="microsoft.web.services2"
            type="Microsoft.Web.Services2.Configuration.WebServicesConfiguration,
            Microsoft.Web.Services, Version=2.0.0.0, Culture=neutral,
            PublicKeyToken=31bf3856ad364e35" />
    </configSections>

    <system.web>
        <webServices>
            <soapExtensionTypes>
                <add type="Microsoft.Web.Services2.WebServicesExtension,
                    Microsoft.Web.Services2, Version=2.0.0.0, Culture=neutral,
                    PublicKeyToken=31bf3856ad364e35" priority="1" group="0" />
            </soapExtensionTypes>
        </webServices>
    </system.web>

    <microsoft.web.services2>
        <diagnostics />
        <security>
            <x509 storeLocation="LocalMachine" allowTestRoot="true"
                allowRevocationUrlRetrieval="false" verifyTrust="false" />
        </security>
    </microsoft.web.services2>

</configuration>
```

Recall from Chapter 6 that no additional code is required to verify the incoming digital signature, since WSE performs this validation automatically before the method is called. However, you do need to add an <x509> element to the SOAPService's web.config file.

Overview of the SOAP Router

The SOAP router implements a configuration file called the *referral cache*, which stores destination endpoints for the message to be routed to. Listing 9-14 provides an example of a referral cache for a chain SOAP router that forwards incoming messages on to a single back-end service.

Listing 9-14. The Referral Cache Configuration File

```
<?xml version="1.0" ?>
<r:referrals xmlns:r="http://schemas.xmlsoap.org/ws/2001/10/referral">
    <r:ref>
        <r:for>
            <r:exact>http://localhost/SOAPRouter/StockTrader.asmx</r:exact>
        </r:for>
        <r:if />
        <r:go>
            <r:via>http://localhost/SOAPService/StockTrader.asmx</r:via>
        </r:go>
        <r:refId>uuid:fa469956-0057-4e77-962a-81c5e292f2ae</r:refId>
    </r:ref>
</r:referrals>
```

This configuration file is stored as a separate configuration file within the SOAP router project. In order to find it, you also need to update the project's web.config or app.config configuration files to point to the location of the referral cache file. Listing 9-15 provides an example of how to update the web.config file.

Listing 9-15. Storing the Location of the Referral Cache File in web.config

```
<microsoft.web.services2>
    <referral>
        <cache name="referralCache.config" />
    </referral>
</microsoft.web.services2>
```

Note that referral cache files are cached in memory, just as web.config files are. The referral cache file will refresh in the cache whenever it gets updated.

> **CAUTION**   *You* must *give the ASP.NET worker process read-write access permissions to the referral cache configuration file. Browse to the file location using Windows Explorer, right-click the file properties, and switch to the Security tab. Add the ASP.NET worker process account (by default, [MachineName]\ASPNET), and set read-write permissions. If you do not take this step, then you will get an exceedingly ugly SOAP exception call stack!*

Send a Stock Quote Request Using the SOAP Sender

Now all that is left is to execute the project. First verify that the SOAP sender proxy class is pointing to the SOAP router URI. Then start the SOAPSender project, and test out each of the two possible request calls:

- SendUnsignedRequest

- SignRequestUsingX509Certificate

Each method call returns a successful stock quote result. This result is so uneventful that you would be forgiven for wondering whether the SOAP router actually did anything. You can quickly put these doubts to rest by renaming the referral cache configuration file, so that it cannot be loaded at runtime. This will generate a SOAP exception back to the client indicating that the configuration file could not be loaded.

What is remarkable about this code example is that the destination Web service, SOAPService, does not complain when it receives a digitally signed SOAP message from the SOAPRouter, rather than from the SOAPSender, which originally signed and sent the request. The routing and WS-Referral infrastructure automatically handles this contingency, and prevents you from receiving exceptions about an invalid digital signature.

In summary, chain SOAP routers give service providers flexibility to implement an optimum service processing solution for incoming SOAP messages. Load balancing SOAP routers help network administrators maintain service networks. As servers are taken offline for maintenance, the information in the referral cache can be updated to remove the server from the list of available referral servers. Finally, content-based SOAP routers make strategic routing decisions based on the contents of the SOAP message headers.

> **NOTE** *The sample project SOAPSender.csproj (contained within the solution SOAPRouter.sln) allows you to toggle between a direct Web service call and an indirect one via a SOAP router (see StockTraderProxy.cs, Line 38). If you modify the URL for the Web service request, then you must also modify the SoapActor attribute on the target Web service method to reflect the same target URL (see StockTrader.asmx, Line 33, in the SOAPService project). If you do not, then you will receive addressing errors because the <to> header on the request must match the Actor attribute on the receiver. The sample projects contain clear notes describing how to toggle the SoapActor attribute, in response to a different target URL from the sender.*

Routing vs. WS-Referral

As we talk about routing, we are actually talking about both routing and referral. The term *routing* refers to the infrastructure that enables SOAP messages to be forwarded on to other destination endpoints. The term *referral* describes the physical act of forwarding a message on. It is common practice to use the term *routing* to describe the combined process of routing and referral.

Routing and Security

Remember that all Web service specifications are composable. Routing does not implement any kind of security for referred messages. However, you can use WS-Security in conjunction with routing to provide a security solution for the referred messages. For example, you can digitally sign or encrypt incoming messages, as you saw in the SOAPSender solution. Note that encrypted messages can pass through intermediary routers even if those routers do not know how to decrypt the message. Routing configuration is separate from the message contents. The intermediary only needs to decrypt the message if this is required in order to make a specialized routing decision. But in most cases this will not be necessary. If the routers do need to decrypt the message and you use X.509 certificates for encryption, then you must ensure that each of the intermediary services has access to the necessary keys. In fact, this applies whenever you use an X.509 certificate, whether for digital signatures or encryption.

In a Chain routing model, it is likely that intermediary services will modify the contents of an incoming SOAP request message. If the incoming SOAP message is digitally signed, then the intermediary service will need to resign the message before forwarding it on to the next service. However, as the SOAPSender solution showed you, digital signature validation will not fail if the SOAP router simply passes on the SOAP message to a destination endpoint, without altering the message contents.

There is no question that routing solutions add an administrative and development burden to implementing a service-oriented architecture. And when you add security policies into the mix, the burden will become even greater. It is likely that future releases of WSE will include provisions to address this issue. To this date, subsequent releases of WSE have always managed to reduce complexity compared to earlier releases of the same features.

Routing vs. WS-Addressing

My first thought when I saw the WSE 2.0 WS-Addressing implementation was whether it overlaps with the pre-WSE 2.0 releases for routing and WS-Referral. There is no definitive answer to this question, but it seems very likely that the WS-Addressing specification does indeed supercede the WS-Routing and WS-Referral specifications for all SOAP routing models other than perhaps the Load Balancing model.

The reason is that WSE 2.0 currently implements routing for the HTTP transport protocol only. This model requires the service endpoints to be .asmx service files or custom SOAP handlers. Either way, you need to configure a virtual directory to host the service. This can be a significant administrative burden if your virtual network infrastructure includes multiple chained services. By comparison, the WS-Addressing specification is implemented for non-HTTP protocols, such as TCP, which does not require you to configure a virtual directory.

> **NOTE** *WSE 2.0 supports routing for HTTP only due to a technical issue with the Request/Response model and TCP. With the TCP protocol, the intermediary does not know whether to hold a thread open to wait for a response. With HTTP, the intermediary either receives a response or receives an HTTP 202 error. TCP-compliant intermediaries must be custom written.*

Perhaps the clearest indication for potential overlap between routing and WS-Addressing is the fact that WSE 2.0 continues to implement routing for the HTTP transport protocol only. I believe this was a purposeful decision to avoid implementing overlapping specifications that accomplish the same thing. In this scenario, one specification will always be more efficient than the other.

You can further enhance your productivity with WS-Addressing by using classes called SoapClient and SoapService, which are higher-level classes than their counterparts SoapSender and SoapReceiver. The SoapClient and SoapService classes automatically handle much of the plumbing code that SoapSender and SoapReceiver require you to write for processing SOAP messages. I will not be discussing these higher-level classes here, because they shield details that are important to understanding how SOAP messaging actually works. In addition, these classes are very easy to understand once you are comfortable with the lower-level SoapSender and SoapReceiver classes. But once you find yourself writing the same kind of messaging code over again, then by all means use these classes and avoid some manual coding.

> **NOTE** *WSE 2.0 provides support for routing, but does not implement the WS-Routing specification. This is because the WS-Addressing specification supercedes the WS-Routing specification. (The WS-Referral specification is orthogonal to the WS-Routing specification.)*

Integrate Web Services and MSMQ

This chapter ends with a bonus section that shows you one possible approach for integrating Web services and message queuing (with MSMQ). I should quickly point out that I am not going to show you how to create an MSMQ custom transport channel. Instead, I am going discuss how to configure a message queue, and then access it from a Web service using the System.Messaging namespace.

WSE 2.0 does not implement reliable messaging, nor does it provide any kind of support for managing message delivery. If you want to implement this capability today, then you will need to custom build the support infrastructure using MSMQ (or another middleware product such as MQSeries).

Use MSMQ for Reliable Messaging

Consider the following application design for a StockTrader application for mutual fund trades, which cannot be executed until after the stock exchange closes for the day. Clients can send trade requests to their broker, but they will be stored and processed later, once the stock exchange is closed. Here is the workflow between the client and service:

1. A client decides that they want to place a mutual fund trade.

2. The client formats an XML message with the details of the trade and sends it to the StockTrader Web service.

3. The StockTrader Web service receives the message but does not process the trade immediately. Instead, the Web service drops the message into a queue for later processing.

4. The StockTrader Web service formats an acknowledgment response message to the client to let them know that the trade request has been received, and that it will be processed shortly.

5. The client receives the response message.

Let's implement this workflow using a TCP-based StockTrader Web service that integrates with a message queue on its host server.

Create a Message Queue Trigger

Our first step is to create the message queue using MSMQ, and then to create a message queue trigger, which will respond to incoming messages. MSMQ is available with the Windows 2000 operating system and higher. If you do not have MSMQ installed then, you can add it using the Control Panel ➤ Add or Remove Programs option (select Add/Remove Windows Components from the selection screen).

MSMQ is included under the Computer Management MMC snap-in, as shown in Figure 9-5.

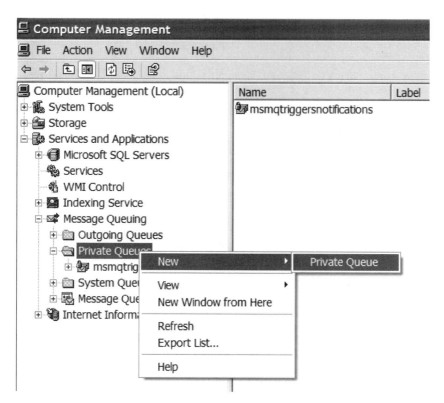

Figure 9-5. The Computer Management MMC snap-in, including MSMQ

To create a new private queue, expand the Message Queuing node and right-click the Private Queues subfolder. Expand and select the New ➤ Private Queue menu option. Enter a name for the queue (I used wsmessaging) and click OK. You will see the new queue listed under the Private Queues subfolder.

Next, expand the wsmessaging node, right-click the Triggers node, and select the New ➤ Trigger menu option. You will see a property page, shown in Figure 9-6. Enter the configuration information as shown, selecting the Retrieval processing type.

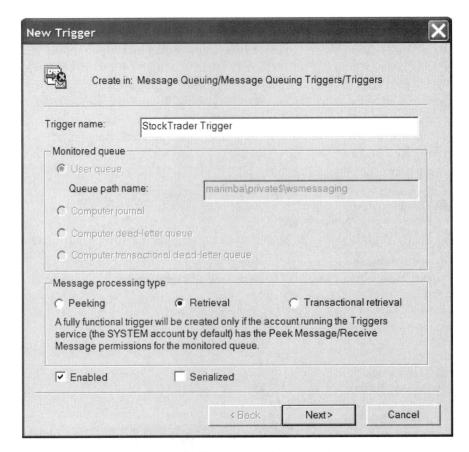

Figure 9-6. Creating a new MSMQ message trigger

Note that you are not creating a fully functional trigger that will fire off a process when a message is received. Instead, you will allow the message to sit in the queue so that you can examine its contents manually.

Create a Web Service That Uses MSMQ

The Web service is written as a TCP-enabled service, and is included in a sample solution called StockTraderMSMQReceiver.sln. The solution includes a reference to the System.Messaging assembly, which is not included with WSE 2.0, but is instead a separate assembly within the .NET Framework.

The Web service provides a Receive method that examines incoming SOAP request messages. All messages with an action value of PlaceTrader are dropped into the message queue. Listing 9-16 provides the code listing for the Receive method and a helper method called AddSoapMessageToQueue.

Listing 9-16. A Web Service That Uses MSMQ

```
// This class represents the Request Receiver (i.e., the service)
public class StockTraderRequestReceiver : SoapReceiver
{
    protected override void Receive(SoapEnvelope message)
    {
        if(message.Context.Addressing.Action.Value.EndsWith("PlaceTrade"))
        {
            bool status = false;

            // Drop the incoming SOAP message to a queue, for later processing
            status = AddSoapMessageToQueue(message);

            // Generate a return status message
            AcknowledgeMessage a = new AcknowledgeMessage();
            a.AcceptedToQueue = status;

            // Transform the result into a SOAP response message
            SoapEnvelope response = new SoapEnvelope();
            response.SetBodyObject(a);

            // Create the URI address objects for send and receive
            // Do not hardcode the URIs, pull them from original request message

            // Send response to the request message's ReplyTo address
            Uri toUri = (Uri)message.Context.Addressing.ReplyTo;

            // Return response from the request message's To address
            Uri fromUri = (Uri)message.Context.Addressing.To;

            // Assign the addressing SOAP message headers
            response.Context.Addressing.Action = new Action( ➡
    "http://www.bluestonepartners.com/schemas/StockTrader/RequestQuote#PlaceTrade");
            response.Context.Addressing.From = new From(fromUri);
            SoapSender soapSender = new SoapSender(toUri);

            // Send the SOAP request message
            soapSender.Send(response);
        }
    }
```

```
private bool AddSoapMessageToQueue(SoapEnvelope message)
{
    bool status = true;
    MessageQueue mq;

    // Verify that the Queue exists
    if (MessageQueue.Exists(@".\private$\wsmessaging"))
    {
        // Assign a reference to the queue
        mq = new MessageQueue(@".\private$\wsmessaging");

        // Drop the incoming message to the queue
        mq.Send((SoapEnvelope)message, ➥
            message.Context.Addressing.MessageID.Value.ToString());
    }
    else
    {
        // Error condition if queue does not exist
        status = false;
    }
    return status;
}

}
```

Notice that the Receive method formats an acknowledgement message that corresponds to a custom data type called AcknowledgeMessage, which is included in both the Web service XML schema file and client proxy class file, and is also shown in Listing 9-17.

Listing 9-17. The AcknowledgeMessage Custom Data Type

```
[System.Xml.Serialization.XmlTypeAttribute(Namespace=
    "http://www.bluestonepartners.com/schemas/StockTrader/")]
public class AcknowledgeMessage
{
    public bool AcceptedToQueue;
}
```

The sample project does not include code for processing the message because this is beyond what I am trying to show. If you open the message queue in the MMC console, you will see a new message in the queue. Figure 9-7 shows an example of what the message body looks like. The property page displays both the byte array and the readable message body. Notice the SOAP contents on the right side of the figure.

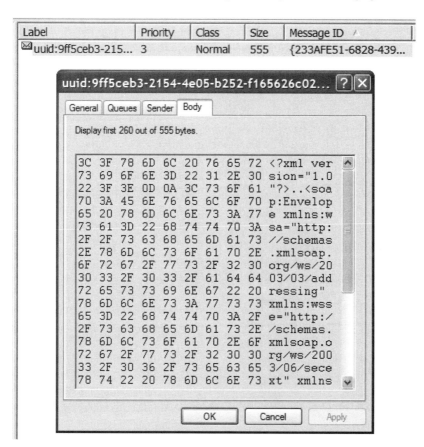

Figure 9-7. The body contents for an MSMQ message

Implement the Web Service Client

The Web service client is written as a TCP-enabled console application, and is included in a sample solution called StockTraderMSMQClient.sln.

The Web service client sends out a trade request and provides a Receive method that examines incoming SOAP response messages. All messages with an action value of PlaceTrader are dropped into the message queue. Listing 9-18 provides the code listing for the Receive method, showing how the client processes the acknowledgement message.

Listing 9-18. A Web Service Client That Processes an Acknowledgement Message

```
// This class represents the Response Receiver (i.e., the client)
public class StockTraderResponseReceiver : SoapReceiver
{
    protected override void Receive( SoapEnvelope message )
```

```
    {
        if (message.Fault != null)
        {
            Console.WriteLine(message.Fault.ToString());
        }
        else
        {
            if (message.Context.Addressing.Action.Value.EndsWith( ➥
                "RequestQuote#PlaceTrade"))
            {
                // Deserialize the message body into an AcknowledgeMessage object
                // Since we have screened the Action, we know
                // what class to look for
                AcknowledgeMessage a = ➥
                  (AcknowledgeMessage)message.GetBodyObject( ➥
                     typeof(AcknowledgeMessage));
                if (a.AcceptedToQueue)
                {
                Console.WriteLine("Your trade will be processed at 4PM EST today.");
                }
                else
                {
                    Console.WriteLine("Your trade can't be processed at this time.");
                }
            }
        }
    }
}
```

This concludes the discussion on the WSE 2.0 messaging framework, and the discussion of one approach for integrating MSMQ with Web services.

Summary

The most challenging aspect of understanding the WSE 2.0 messaging framework is in the concepts, not in the code. The code is straightforward, but the concepts are difficult if you are used to working with the familiar HTTP Request/Response model. The key to understanding messaging is to stop thinking in terms of fixed clients and services and to instead think in terms of flexible sender and receiver roles.

I began this chapter by reviewing several communication models for Web services beyond classic Request/Response. I then discussed the WS-Addressing specification, which provides important support functionality for Web services that communicate over alternate transport channels, such as TCP.

Next I discussed the messaging, and showed you how to implement truly asynchronous client-service communication using SOAP over TCP and the WSE 2.0 messaging framework classes. WSE 2.0 provides both lower-level and higher-level classes that provide a consistent messaging framework independent of the transport channel. The framework classes shield developers from the underlying complexities of the transport layer, which increases productivity and makes it relatively easy to implement a wider range of service-oriented solutions.

Next, you saw the routing and WS-Referral specifications, which provide support for messages that are referred between multiple endpoints. I noted that there is some overlap between the routing and addressing specifications.

Finally, I provided one example of how to integrate message queuing with Web services. This approach does not implement MSMQ as an alternative transport channel, but it is a good first step towards implementing reliable messaging.

The central focus of this book is to make you rethink what Web services are all about, and nowhere is this more apparent than with the WSE 2.0 messaging framework. This chapter marks the end of the discussion on WSE 2.0. Service-oriented architecture is constantly evolving, so in the next chapter I will focus beyond WSE 2.0, and show you what specifications and technologies are in store for the near future.

CHAPTER 10

Beyond WSE 2.0: Looking Ahead to Indigo

TODAY, WEB SERVICES ENHANCEMENTS (WSE) 2.0 is the easiest way to implement selected WS-Specifications in your .NET Web services and service-oriented applications. WSE 2.0 provides developer support for building service-oriented applications and infrastructure support for running them. Web services and service-oriented applications require a lot of support to build and run. Developers require classes that make it easier to work with messages without having to interact with the raw SOAP. In addition, they require infrastructure support to make it easier to run service-oriented applications. WSE 2.0 provides all of these levels of support by providing

- A rich class framework for implementing important WS-Specifications such as WS-Security and WS-Addressing.

- Infrastructure support, in the form of the WSE pipeline, which automatically intercepts and processes incoming and outgoing SOAP messages.

- Infrastructure support for common service requirements, such as policy verification (using WS-Policy). For example, WSE 2.0 automatically processes XML-based policy framework files, which saves you from needing to write additional processing code in both the service and the client.

WSE is very good at implementing discrete WS-Specifications such as WS-Security and WS-Policy, which can be boiled down to a set of specific operations. But where WSE falls short is in being able to provide the infrastructure support for broad-based WS-Specifications such as WS-Reliable Messaging, which provide service guarantees for message delivery.

This is where Indigo and Longhorn (the next version of the Microsoft Windows operating system) come into play. *Indigo* is the code name for a new unified programming and infrastructure support model for service-oriented applications. It provides built-in support for message-oriented and service-oriented architectures, built of course on the managed .NET Framework. Indigo will greatly enhance developer productivity in these application areas.

There are many reasons why you should start learning about Indigo today. The most important reason in my opinion is that you need to know how relevant your existing service-oriented applications will be with a new support infrastructure such as Indigo. The questions you should be asking yourself are

- How will I build service-oriented applications in the future using Indigo?

- How do I preserve the existing investment that I have made in my XML Web services and .NET Remoting development?

- What current technologies are going to be phased out in Indigo?

- Should I be using Web Services Enhancements (WSE) 2.0 today?

The purpose of this chapter is to give you a preview of Indigo from the perspective of where we are today with WSE 2.0. As you will see, every hour spent learning and working with WSE is a worthwhile investment that is directly applicable to Web service development with Indigo. This should be of no surprise because Indigo is still based on the standards and specifications that we are comfortable with today. Indigo does not reinvent the WS-Specifications, or use exotic transport channels that we have never seen before. Instead, it provides a better support infrastructure for building service-oriented applications that implement today's important standards and specifications, including the WS-Specifications. And best of all, Indigo is strongly oriented towards services and messages.

Overview of Indigo

Indigo is an exciting technology because it unifies all of the concepts that have been presented throughout this book. Developers today must contend with a variety of different technology choices for building distributed applications, including

- XML Web services (.asmx)

- Web Services Enhancements (WSE)

- .NET Remoting

- MSMQ (provided by the .NET Framework System.Messaging namespace)

- Enterprise Services (The .NET Framework namespace for COM+)

These various technologies overlap and complement each other in different ways. In many cases, an application requirement can be fulfilled with two or more of these technologies. Perhaps the clearest example of a potential overlap is with XML Web services and .NET Remoting. Both technologies operate on the same principle, namely that they facilitate remote service invocation over a defined transport channel. .NET Remoting solutions are generally more focused on object invocation using Remote Procedure Calls (RPCs). On the other hand, XML Web service solutions tend to be more focused on invoking services by passing message-based requests. But these differences are simply a function of what the technologies are best at today. With today's technology, you do have flexibility and a choice on whether to deploy .NET Remoting versus XML Web services for the same application solution. And where you do not, it is fair to ask why the technologies should have different capabilities. After all, they are based on the same concept: allowing remote service calls over a defined transport channel.

Figure 10-1 illustrates the high-level architecture for Indigo. Note that this diagram is adapted from a January 2004 *MSDN Magazine* article on Indigo (see the Appendix for detailed reference information).

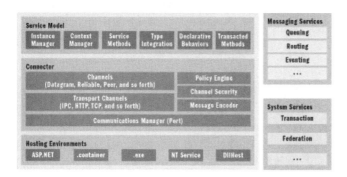

Figure 10-1. The high-level Indigo architecture (adapted from MSDN Magazine, *January 2004)*

There are five major areas within the Indigo architecture:

The Indigo service model: Provides general support for services and messages. The service model provides programming and infrastructure support for implementing and managing code as a message-oriented service.

The Indigo connector: Provides communications support for services and messages, including multiple transport channels, ports, and built-in support for reliable message delivery. The connector provides the infrastructure that allows your service to exchange messages with the outside world in a secure, reliable fashion.

Hosting environments: Provides support for several different hosting environments for message-oriented services, including traditional IIS-based ASP.NET hosting.

Messaging services: Provides support for managing messages, including message queuing and routing. Messaging services provides the functionality that we currently associate with MSMQ.

System services: Provides support for transactions and other low-level system support infrastructure that is complex and which needs to be managed by the framework on behalf of the service.

Let's review each of these areas in more detail.

The Indigo Service Model

The Indigo service model provides a wide range of support for service-oriented Web services, including

- Associating Web methods with incoming service messages

- Session management for Web services

- Transaction management for Web services

- Support for security and policy

- Support for reliable message exchange

Indigo contains built-in support for many of the tasks that are currently handled by Web Services Enhancements 2.0. In a sense, WSE 2.0 is a prerelease of the Indigo service model. Of course, WSE 2.0 is not completely built out, and certain tasks still require you to write manual code. Indigo will integrate the WSE 2.0 functionality in a much tighter way. But there is no better preparation for Indigo than to start working with WSE 2.0 and all of the subsequent releases leading up to the release of Indigo (as part of the Longhorn operating system).

Indigo associates Web methods with incoming service messages using a set of declarative attributes. The service model operates in a similar way to .asmx files, which allow you to declaratively mark up methods and to associate them with incoming Web requests. Today, .asmx files provide a [WebMethod] attribute for marking methods. Tomorrow, Indigo will provide a [ServiceMethod] attribute for marking up methods.

The qualified data types that are used by Web services can be represented as typed objects, and manipulated directly in code, without having to process the raw SOAP and XML directly. Listings 10-1 and 10-2 illustrate this point with a custom data type called Trade. Listing 10-1 displays the qualified XML for the data type, while Listing 10-2 displays its object representation.

Listing 10-1. XML for the Trade Custom Data Type

```
<?xml version="1.0" encoding="utf-8" ?>
<xs:schema id="StockTrader"
    targetNamespace="http://www.bluestonepartners.com/Schemas/StockTrader/"
    elementFormDefault="qualified"
    xmlns="http://www.bluestonepartners.com/Schemas/StockTrader/"
    xmlns:mstns="http://www.bluestonepartners.com/Schemas/StockTrader/"
    xmlns:xs="http://www.w3.org/2001/XMLSchema" version="1.0">
    <xs:complexType name="Trade">
      <xs:sequence>
          <xs:element name="TradeID" type="xs:string" />
          <xs:element name="Symbol" type="xs:string" />
          <xs:element name="Price" type="xs:double" />
          <xs:element name="Shares" type="xs:int" />
          <xs:element name="tradeType" type="TradeType" />
          <xs:element name="tradeStatus" type="TradeStatus" />
          <xs:element name="OrderDateTime" type="xs:string" />
          <xs:element name="LastActivityDateTime" type="xs:string" />
      </xs:sequence>
    </xs:complexType>
</xs:schema>
```

Listing 10-2. Object Representation for the Trade Custom Data Type

```
[System.Xml.Serialization.XmlTypeAttribute( ➥
    Namespace="http://www.bluestonepartners.com/schemas/StockTrader/")]
public class Trade {
    public string TradeID;
    public string Symbol;
    public System.Double Price;
    public int Shares;
    public TradeType tradeType;
    public TradeStatus tradeStatus;
    public string OrderDateTime;
    public string LastActivityDateTime;
}
```

Today, ASP.NET gives you the flexibility to work with raw SOAP and XML directly, or to interact with object representations instead. Indigo will continue to support this approach, allowing you to work with either. Not only are typed objects easier to work with, but they are also managed, custom .NET class framework types, which means that you get all the support of the managed .NET runtime, including trustworthy compilation. If you interact with the raw XML directly, then you lose this automatic verification that you are using the custom data type correctly.

In service-oriented architecture, Web services provide WSDL-based interfaces, and all of the nonstandard data types are represented by qualified XML schemas. Even the interface methods themselves can be described using XML, and can be included in a reference schema file for the Web service. I focused on this in great detail in Chapters 3 and 4.

To use SOA terminology, service-oriented components support and conform to contracts. The term *contract* implies a formal, established agreement between two or more parties. Indigo formalizes data constructs and message constructs as contracts, and defines them as follows:

Data contracts: These are analogous to XML schema files, and they document the data types that a Web service supports and exchanges.

Service contracts: These are analogous to WSDL document definitions, specifically the <portType> and <message> sections of the WSDL document. Service contracts document the messages that a Web service supports, both for request and response messages.

Listing 10-3 illustrates a portion of the StockTrader Web service WSDL file, showing the <portType> and <message> definitions related to the PlaceTrade Web method.

Listing 10-3. Excerpt from the StockTrader Web Service WSDL File Showing the <portType> and <message> Definitions

```
<portType name="StockTraderServiceSoap">
    <operation name="PlaceTrade">
        <input message="tns:PlaceTradeSoapIn" />
        <output message="tns:PlaceTradeSoapOut" />
    </operation>
</portType>

<message name="PlaceTradeSoapIn">
    <part name="Account" element="s0:Account" />
    <part name="Symbol" element="s0:Symbol" />
    <part name="Shares" element="s0:Shares" />
```

```
    <part name="Price" element="s0:Price" />
    <part name="tradeType" element="s0:tradeType" />
</message>

<message name="PlaceTradeSoapOut">
    <part name="PlaceTradeResult" element="s0:Trade" />
</message>
```

The purpose of Listings 10-1 through 10-3 is ultimately to show you that the service-oriented concepts you have learned in this book apply to Indigo, and that Indigo implements very familiar service-oriented concepts, despite supporting a very different class framework than the current ASP.NET class framework.

The Indigo service model will end up being where you as a developer spend much of your time working because it provides the programmatic classes and the declarative attributes for your service-oriented applications.

The Indigo Connector

The Indigo connector provides transport-independent support for message-based, service-oriented applications. Recall Chapter 2, where I discussed WSDL elements such as ports and bindings. These elements play an important role in the Indigo connector because they govern how services provide endpoints for message requests.

The three most important Indigo connector elements are

Ports: These provide URI-accessible endpoints for delivering messages to a service.

Transport channels: These provide a way to deliver messages, and they are based on established protocols, including HTTP, TCP, and IPC.

Message channels: These channels operate in conjunction with the transport channels, and provide additional message delivery support, including reliable message delivery.

Security support for message-oriented communications is provided throughout the Indigo framework, including within the Indigo connector. Indigo provides three types of security support for messages:

Session-based security: Session-based support uses an on-demand session key to provide encryption and digital signatures. This mode closely follows the approach taken by the WS-Secure Conversation specification, which is discussed in detail in Chapter 8.

Message-based security: Provided for reliable messaging scenarios where the receiver may not be online at the time that the message is received. Message-based security ensures that message integrity and security are provided during asynchronous communication between a sender and receiver.

Transport-level security: Using a direct security protocol such as Secure Sockets Layer (SSL) which automatically provides message encryption and signatures, based on digital certificates.

As with the Indigo service model, WSE 2.0 and today's ASP.NET Web services clearly prepare you for working with the future Indigo connector. Make sure that you understand the concepts that are presented in Chapter 2 on the WSDL document. The Indigo connector rolls up all of these concepts and more, including transport and communication channels, and message security.

Hosting Environments

ASP.NET Web services must currently be hosted within a virtual directory managed by Internet Information Service (IIS), and they will only communicate over HTTP. With WSE 2.0 you have additional messaging capabilities, so you can build TCP-based services in addition to HTTP-enabled services. TCP-enabled services do not have to be hosted by IIS, although they must be running at all times and listening on a defined port. WSE 2.0 also provides the Interprocess Communication (IPC) transport protocol.

Indigo expands the number of available hosting options for services, and also introduces on-demand services. These are activated by the Indigo framework when it identifies a targeted incoming service request message that is intended for a specific service. The other available hosting options in Indigo are not necessarily new, but the difference is that Indigo provides a good level of automated support for different hosting environments, which makes it easier for you to deploy your services. Here are some examples of hosting environments that Indigo supports:

- **ASP.NET:** Traditional IIS-based, HTTP-enabled hosting environment

- **Windows Service:** A hosting environment for TCP-enabled services

- **DLLHost:** A hosting environment for IPC-enabled services

This list is not comprehensive; it represents just some of the available hosting environments and just some of the possibilities for using them.

It is important to note that the hosting environment is independent of a Web service's data and service contracts. As a developer, you can create your Web services and service components independently of the intended hosting environment. Indigo will relay messages across to your services equally well in all of the supported environments.

Messaging Services

Today, MSMQ-based applications support message queues for reliable message delivery, and they also support a trigger-based event model that fires up the application code when an incoming message is received. Today, messaging applications that are built around MSMQ are almost considered to be a nonstandard type of application. If they were standard, then all of us would be incorporating message queues into every application that we built. Of course this is not the case, largely because it creates a level of overhead that is considered unnecessary for many applications.

But in service-oriented applications, reliable message delivery is not an abstract concept; instead, it represents a quality of service expectation on the part of your clients. Message delivery and the potential for message loss are critically important to service-oriented applications. Indigo provides built-in messaging support, including message queues and events, and makes it easier for you to implement reliable messaging in your service applications. Indigo will provide a set of classes for interfacing with the messaging infrastructure.

Today's WSE 2.0 does not natively integrate with MSMQ, which is essentially just an alternate transport channel for messages. With some effort, you could custom integrate MSMQ with WSE today as a transport channel, although this is an advanced programming task. Alternatively, you could take a simpler approach and have your service simply interact with an MSMQ queue that you configure separately. The .NET Framework provides a namespace called System.Messaging, which allows you to interact with an MSMQ queue.

You can expect that a future version of WSE will support MSMQ as a new integrated transport channel. It is very likely that this will happen because of the fact that reliable message delivery is so important to service-oriented applications.

System Services

This category represents a catch-all of features, many of which provide infrastructure-level support that may be fully out of direct sight, but which is working on your behalf nonetheless. The System services includes infrastructure-level support for transactions (via a distributed transaction coordinator) and security. The security portion of the System services are expected to support the WS-Federation specification, which allows you to set up and manage trusted communications across application and domain boundaries. This is not the same thing as the WS-Secure Conversation specification, which I discussed in Chapter 8. However, there are shared concepts between the two specifications.

Understanding Indigo Web Services

One of my first thoughts when I heard about Indigo was whether Indigo Web services would be different compared to ASP.NET Web services. And if so, how would they differ? The good news is that while Indigo Web services are different, they still retain the core characteristics of a traditional ASP.NET Web service, but with even more functionality and flexibility. Indigo Web services support the standard WSDL and SOAP specifications, in addition to the extended WS-specifications.

What Is an Indigo Web Service?

Traditional .ASMX pages can still be used within Indigo, which will interoperate with them in addition to supporting a newer form of Web service. ASP.NET-style Web services will continue to be limited within Indigo to simple HTTP-based Request/Response message patterns. However, Indigo Web services will provide all of the extended communication capabilities that WSE 2.0 provides (and more) including alternate transport protocols and true asynchronous and one-way communications.

The characteristics of an Indigo Web service are documented in the Longhorn SDK as follows:

- Secure communication across any number of intermediaries, including firewalls.

- Participate in widely distributed transactions.

- Encapsulate two way conversations that allow clients and servers to send messages in both directions.

- Provide guarantees about the reliability of message delivery.

- Support situations requiring scalability, such as Web service farms.

- Support advanced features even with participants that are not built on Microsoft platforms.

- Enable developers familiar with the .NET Framework to build messaging applications without knowing anything about XML or SOAP.

- Enable developers familiar with XML Web services to leverage their XML, WSDL, and SOAP knowledge to work with XML messages described by XSD.

- Support smooth management of deployed applications.

Indigo Web Services vs. Indigo RemoteObjects

The two types of distributed objects that you can build with Indigo are Web services and so-called RemoteObjects. Both service types provide the same benefits of Indigo: secure, reliable, transacted message delivery and processing.

RemoteObjects are the functional equivalent of .NET Remoting solutions; namely, they are RPC-style distributed objects that can communicate across a small or large domain area, from an intranet to an internet. The important limitation with RemoteObjects is that Indigo must be installed both at the sender and at the receiver. If type fidelity is important, then you should choose to build RemoteObjects. This is because RemoteObjects can serialize and transport objects exactly. In contrast, Web services must approximate their data types using XML schema files, which are accurate for standard data types and for custom data types that are a compilation of standard data types. However, XML schema files will not accurately represent more exotic data types such as specific integer and floating point data types.

For interoperability, you should always choose Indigo Web services over Indigo RemoteObjects. Indigo Web services do not require both the sender and the receiver to have Indigo installed, although they do require that both sender and receiver conform to standard WS-I specifications, including SOAP and WSDL.

Security-wise, Web services are more secure than RemoteObjects across application domains that cross trust boundaries (meaning that you do not have a trusted or established relationship with the other party). This is because Web services implement advanced specifications, including WS-Security and WS-Secure Conversation. In addition, Web services work with digital certificates (and other security tokens) very easily. You can certainly leverage these in RemoteObjects as well, but the supporting infrastructure is not as well developed, and you will need to write much more manual code compared with the limited amount of support coding required in Web services.

Scalability-wise, RemoteObjects are optimized for communications within the same process, or across different processes that are on the same computer. Traditional ASP.NET Web services are built for interoperability more than for scalability. It remains to be seen what performance advances Indigo Web services have made by comparison.

Web services and RemoteObjects preserve similar clear choices to what we have today with ASP.NET Web services and .NET Remoting.

Understanding Indigo Applications and Infrastructure

Indigo applications decouple the messaging and transport layer from the service layer, which allows you as the developer to focus on programming the service without having to worry about implementing the lower-level communications infrastructure. The service layer is built using the class framework that is provided by the Indigo service model. It includes classes that allow you to interact programmatically with the messaging layer.

In this section, I will review five important aspects of Indigo that provide support for managing and processing service-oriented applications:

- The Indigo service layer

- Ports

- Typed channels

- Service managers

- Transports and formatters

The Indigo Service Layer

Figure 10-2 illustrates the high-level schematic architecture for a typical message-based, service-oriented application that you might build using Indigo.

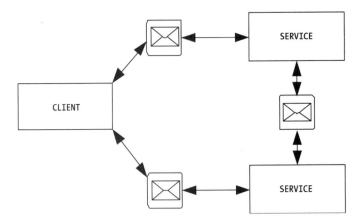

Figure 10-2. High-level schematic architecture for an Indigo application

The application architecture uses arrows to describe the path that a message takes between service endpoints. Although they are not shown in the diagram, the service endpoints are located where the arrow head contacts the client or service. Another interesting aspect of this diagram is the chained path that the messages take. Indigo supports this level of complex message pathways because of its infrastructure-level support for addressing and routing specifications. Finally, the diagram makes no mention of a specific transport channel. This implicitly emphasizes Indigo's most important advantage of not having to factor in the transport and messaging infrastructure into the application design. In contrast, today's ASP.NET Web services that leverage WSE 2.0 still require the developer to write manual code that is specific to alternate transport channels, such as TCP.

In Indigo, the service is the basic component of an application, and it supports a special kind of object called a *typed channel* that is equivalent to today's proxy objects for Web service clients. The typed channel provides an interface for sending and receiving messages between service components. Indigo provides a utility called *WSDLgen.exe*, which is similar to today's wsdl.exe utility, and which allows you to generate proxy class files for clients to use for accessing your service.

Typed channels are independent of the actual objects that process the service request. Indigo employs Service Manager objects that are responsible for mapping typed channels to their associated business objects, including the DialogManager and ListenerManager objects.

The Indigo service layer automatically handles the receiving, processing, and sending of messages, including all of the serialization work that is required to build and process a message. This is very similar to the way that the ASP.NET infrastructure processes messages that are received and sent via an .asmx Web page. Indigo provides the Service object for its services, which is conceptually equivalent to the ASP.NET WebService object. The Service object provides you with programmatic access to the underlying messaging and transport infrastructure.

The Indigo service layer also supports a special kind of service called RemoteObjects, which is functionally equivalent to today's .NET Remoting–enabled solutions in that it allows you to invoke remote distributed objects, while preserving object type fidelity during transport. RemoteObjects uses RPC-style communications, and like .NET Remoting, it can be used for both interprocess communications and internet communications that operate across different application domains.

Ports

Service-oriented applications send and receive messages to SOAP endpoints. In Indigo, the Port object defines two things:

1. Service layer information, including the operations that the service supports, and

2. The supported transport mechanisms and wire formats (e.g., SOAP 1.2 encoding over HTTP)

As I have done throughout this chapter, I want to emphasize the tie-in between Indigo technology and today's technology. The Indigo Port object is equivalent to a WS-Addressing construct called the *endpoint reference*. In Chapter 9, I discussed endpoint references, which are equivalent to the <service> element in the WSDL document, and which provide both addressing and binding information for a Web service. Listing 10-4 provides an excerpt from the StockTrader WSDL document showing how the <service> and associated <binding> tags work together to document the location of a service, and the operations that it provides.

Listing 10-4. Excerpt from the StockTrader Web Service WSDL File Showing the <service> and <binding> Definitions

```
<service name="StockTraderService">
    <port  name="StockTraderServiceSoap" binding="tns:StockTraderServiceSoap">
        <soap:address location="http://localhost/StockTrader/StockTrader.asmx" />
    </port>
</service>

<binding name="StockTraderServiceSoap" type="tns:StockTraderServiceSoap">
    <soap:binding transport="http://schemas.xmlsoap.org/soap/http"
        style="document" />
    <operation name="RequestAllTradesSummary">
        <soap:operation
            soapAction="http://www.bluestonepartners.com/schemas/StockTrader/
            RequestAllTradesSummary" style="document" />
            <input>
                <soap:body use="literal" />
            </input>
            <output>
                <soap:body use="literal" />
            </output>
    </operation>
<!- Additional operations are not shown ->
    <operation />
</binding>
```

The WS-Addressing specification takes this concept one step further by encapsulating addressing, binding, and security policy information within a single reference, as shown in Listing 10-5.

Listing 10-5. Endpoint Reference XML

```
<wsa:EndpointReference>
    <wsa:Address>soap.tcp://stocktrader.com/StockTrader</wsa:Address>
    <wsa:ReferenceProperties>
        <st:AccountID>123A</st:AccountID>
    </wsa:ReferenceProperties>
    <wsa:PortType>st:StockTraderSoap</wsa:PortType>
    <wsp:Policy/>
</wsa:EndpointReference>
```

You can clearly see how the Indigo Port object maps to familiar constructs such as endpoint references and the WSDL <service> and <binding> definitions.

The Indigo Port object is tied into an extended processing pipeline that supports common message-processing features, including security, policy, routing, and transactions. When you write a service method, you need to add attributes for each of the specifications that you want to implement; for example, you can specify authorization access for a specific user or role. Assuming that the incoming message includes the right specification information, it will be routed through the Port object and into an extended processing pipeline. You can programmatically control the processing further by modifying property settings on one or more dedicated manager objects. For example, security processing is handled by the SecurityManager object.

Listing 10-6 provides a very simple example of an Indigo service method, showing the annotations that you require for specifying basic authorization security processing.

Listing 10-6. An Indigo Service Method Specifying Authorization Security Processing

```
[DatagramPortType(Name="PlaceTrader", ➥
    Namespace="http://www.tempuri.org/quickstarts")]
public class Hello
{
    [ServiceSecurity(Name = "Brokerage", Role = "Traders") ]
    [ServiceMethod]
    public string PlaceTrade(string Account, string Symbol, int Shares, ➥
        System.Double Price, TradeType tradeType)
    {
        // Code to execute trade not shown
        return ("Your confirmation code is: " + TradeID);
    }
}
```

This service must still implement a policy framework file to specify authentication security, such as encryption and digital signature requirements.

Typed Channels

A typed channel is similar to a Web service proxy object, which provides a typed object representation of the Web services WSDL interface. In a similar fashion, an Indigo typed channel provides a typed object reference to a messaging endpoint and its associated operations.

In order to create a typed channel, you need to first create the Web service and define its methods. This in turn defines a WSDL interface, which you can then extract automatically (for example, you can append ?WSDL to the Web service URI, in order to review the WSDL document). Finally, you can use a code-generation tool to generate a proxy class based on the WSDL file. Today, we have a utility called wsdl.exe. Indigo ships with an equivalent utility called WSDLgen.exe.

The output of the code-generation utility is the typed channel, which provides a proxy representation of the WSDL interface as a managed object.

Service Manager

The Service Manager objects do all of the heavy lifting in processing messages and providing the support infrastructure for managing communications. Table 10-1 summarizes the important Service Manager objects and their purpose.

Table 10-1. The Indigo Service Manager Objects

Service Manager	Description
ListenerManager	Used by user-mode listener implementation to handle Listener messages and perform the appropriate actions on the router, service environment
PolicyManager	Provides support for consuming, applying, processing, and generating policy on a specific port
RemotingManager	Manages the Indigo remoting infrastructure
RequestReplyManager	Creates SendRequestChannel objects through which messages can be sent and replies received
RoutingPolicyManager	Controls the consumption and application of routing and transport policy
RuleManager	Represents the factory for rules, and through its namespace hierarchy, the associated properties

Continued

Table 10-1. The Indigo Service Manager Objects (continued)

Service Manager	Description
SecurityManager	Controls application security requirements either programmatically or using application and machine configuration files
ServiceManager	Manages the associations between communication channels and service instances; registers services; and produces typed channels to make requests of other services
TransactionManager	Represents the base class for a transaction manager
DialogManager	Manages creation and deletion of the participants in a dialog

The Service Manager objects work with the Port object as extensions into a processing pipeline for incoming and outgoing messages. Service Managers automatically process messages as long as the associated service method has the appropriate annotations. Figure 10-3 shows the architecture of the port processing pipeline, including Service Managers.

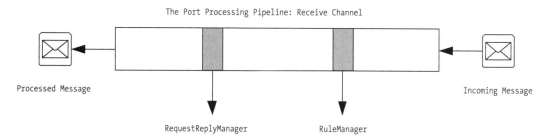

Figure 10-3. The port processing pipeline architecture

Transports and Formatters

The transport and formatter layer is the low-level infrastructure that sits below the activity that is occurring in the port processing pipeline. You will rarely need to interact with the transport and formatter layer directly, beyond specifying what the service will support. You can also specify directional message transport information, such as whether a service is receive-only or is enabled for both send and receive operations.

The transport and formatter layer is what enables messages to be moved across the wire. Indigo supports a wide range of transport protocols, as shown in

Table 10-2, which indicates the associated Indigo object that abstracts the transport protocol information.

Table 10-2. Indigo-Supported Transport Protocols

Protocol	Indigo Object
HTTP	HttpTransport
POP3	Pop3Transport
SMTP	SmtpTransport
SOAP	SoapTransport
TCP	TcpTransport
InProc	InProcessTransport (on the same machine)
CrossProc	CrossProcessTransport (on the same machine)

The transport and formatter layer delegates message serialization (and deserialization) to a dedicated object called the MessageFormatter, which is responsible for translating a byte stream between a formatted message and an in-memory Message object representation of the message.

How to Get Ready for Indigo

Most developers are understandably ambivalent about a major upcoming release like Indigo. On the one hand, we welcome advancements in technology and the improvements in functionality and productivity that it will hopefully bring. On the other hand, we dread having to learn a new way of doing things, and we wonder whether we will be able to migrate our existing code to the new infrastructure.

These are valid concerns, especially with Indigo. But the issue is less about Indigo changing things than it is about things needing to change. Developers today are faced with multiple and often competing technologies for building distributed applications, including the classic choice between XML Web services versus .NET Remoting. Certainly, there are cases where there is no overlap and no ambivalence, and where one technology is clearly the better choice than another. But these technologies share too much in common to be treated differently. They are simply variations of the same technology. In the case of XML Web services and .NET Remoting, they are both concerned with remote, distributed object and service invocation over a defined transport channel.

Microsoft is starting to address developer concerns by providing guidelines for how to get ready for Indigo. They are already making sure to bring this topic up at professional conferences, and they will certainly continue to do so until the release of Indigo. There has simply been too much investment in existing technologies for them not to.

Indigo is obviously not a replacement for the entire set of .NET Framework functionality. Instead, it is focused on supporting distributed, service-oriented applications with security, transaction support, and reliable messaging. Indigo primarily extends five core technologies that are available today:

- ASP.NET Web services (built with .asmx pages)

- Web Services Enhancements (WSE)

- .NET Remoting

- System.Messaging

- System.EnterpriseServices

Microsoft has stated that they will make the migration to Indigo from current technologies a straightforward process. Here are some guidelines on how to get ready for Indigo today, based on professional conferences, published whitepapers, and conversations with members of product development teams:

- Build services using .asmx pages.

- Use WSE 2.0 for additional, extended functionality, including security, policy, and secure conversation.

- Build qualified XML schema files for all custom data types used by the service.

- Use managed framework classes for integrating your services with MSMQ message queues, and with COM+ components. Use the managed System.Messaging namespace for MSMQ, and the System.EnterpriseServices namespace for COM+ components.

- Avoid using the HTTP Context object in your .asmx pages.

- Avoid using .NET Remoting sinks and channels.

Given that WSE 2.0 is such an important part of this book, let's look in more detail at how you can use the toolkit to prepare for Indigo.

WSE 2.0 and Indigo

WSE 2.0 allows developers to become early adopters of the next generation of service-oriented application technology. Every hour that you spend working with WSE 2.0 is an hour that you have contributed towards Indigo. Applications that are built using WSE should migrate smoothly to the Indigo framework, with only minor modifications required. The caveat is that WSE is expected to undergo several revisions and releases prior to the release of Indigo. If you choose to implement WSE today, then you should expect to accommodate changes to WSE between now and the release of Indigo. For this reason, WSE 2.0 should not be used as the basis for production-level applications unless you are prepared to make multiple revisions.

The one thing lacking with WSE 2.0 is that it does not provide wide system-level or infrastructure-level support for the enterprise aspect of service-oriented applications. Specifically, it does not provide support for transactions or reliable messaging. Certainly, WSE 2.0 provides many of the required parts, but it does not provide the whole. For example, WSE 2.0 provides support for message addressing, and it also integrates with MSMQ via the System.Messaging namespace classes. So WSE 2.0 gives you the ability today to custom build a service-oriented application that implements "reliable" messaging (via MSMQ) and which can process message addressing information and provide message correlation. But this is not the same as a built-in support infrastructure that manages these tasks for you.

These limitations are not a weakness of the WSE 2.0 technology. They simply underscore two things:

1. Infrastructure support for message-based, service-oriented architecture is most effectively handled at the operating system level. This level of support must wait until a future release of the operating system (i.e., Longhorn).

2. WSE 2.0 allows early adopters to start designing and building their code for the future Indigo infrastructure. More importantly, it gets developers thinking about application design in new ways. There is a large conceptual jump between traditional RPC-based applications and message-based, service-oriented applications.

With this being said, let's review the major feature areas of WSE 2.0 (which you should by now feel very familiar with) and explain where they fit within the Indigo framework:

Security and policy specifications: The WS-Security and WS-Policy specifications are supported by the Indigo connector.

Messaging specifications: Indigo provides Messaging services that subsume the functionality currently provided by MSMQ. In addition, it provides support for reliable messaging. WSE does not currently provide comprehensive support for the WS-Reliable Messaging specification, but it does provide some of the component parts that you can cobble together to approximate the specification. Specifically, WSE includes support for WS-Addressing, and it integrates with MSMQ via the managed System.Messaging namespace.

Routing and referral specifications: Indigo includes these within its Messaging services functionality.

Alternate transport channels: Indigo provides support for several transport channels, including HTTP, TCP, and IPC. WSE 2.0 currently provides support for the same three channels, so you can begin coding with them today.

In closing, I hope that this book has ultimately convinced you of three important things:

1. Message orientation and service orientation are the way to go.

2. Indigo provides a welcome level of support for this technology, which will increase developer productivity and minimize confusion by unifying today's disparate technologies.

3. WSE 2.0 is an excellent way for developers to become early adopters for Indigo.

Good luck with your future adventures in service-oriented architecture!

Summary

Indigo provides infrastructure and programming support for service-oriented applications. It is focused on messages, and provides support for creating messages, for delivering messages, and for processing messages. With Indigo, there is less ambiguity in your services: The infrastructure forces you to be message oriented, and to work with well-qualified XML-based data types.

Indigo is built on five major areas:

- **The Indigo service model:** Provides support for processing incoming service request messages

- **The Indigo connector**: Provides support for communicating with services reliably and securely

- **Hosting environments**: Provides several different hosting options for services

- **Messaging services**: Provides reliable messaging support

- **System services**: Provides a wide range of support infrastructure, including for transactions and trusted communications

WSE 2.0 allows early adopters to start building service-oriented applications today, using the next generation of service-oriented and message-oriented technologies. Working with WSE 2.0 provides you with excellent preparation for Indigo. In addition, you should be familiar with Microsoft's guidelines for how to tailor today's development to be more compatible with Indigo-based applications in the future.

References

HERE IS A SELECTION of references that you will find useful for learning more about service-oriented architecture, the WS-I Basic Profile, the WS-Specifications, and Web Service Enhancements. The references are broken out by topic. Note that Web services standards and specifications evolve quickly, so some of the specification references that are listed here will be superceded in future months by others.

Service-Oriented Architecture (General)

Application Architecture for .NET: Designing Applications and Services

Patterns & Practices, Microsoft Corporation

Whitepaper (December 2002)

Located at MSDN Home ➤ MSDN Library ➤ Enterprise Development ➤ Application Architecture ➤ Microsoft patterns and practices for Application Architecture and Design

```
http://msdn.microsoft.com/library/default.asp?url=/library/en-us/
dnbda/html/distapp.asp
```

Building Interoperable Web Services: WS-I Basic Profile 1.0

Patterns & Practices, Microsoft Corporation

Whitepaper (August 2003)

Located at MSDN Home ➤ Web Services Home ➤ Building ➤ .NET Framework and Visual Studio .NET ➤ Designing .NET Web Services

```
http://msdn.microsoft.com/webservices/building/frameworkandstudio/
designing/default.aspx?pull=/library/en-us/dnsvcinter/html/wsi-bp_
msdn_landingpage.asp
```

The Evolution of Web Services—Part 2

Adnan Masood

Whitepaper (September 2003)

http://www.15seconds.com/issue/030917.htm

Java modeling: A UML workbook, Part 4

Granville Miller

Whitepaper (April 2002)

Provides a discussion of the Service Façade design pattern

Located at IBM developerWorks ➤ Java Technology ➤ Web services

http://www-106.ibm.com/developerworks/java/library/j-jmod0604/

XML Schemas and SOAP

Understanding SOAP

Aaron Skonnard

Whitepaper (March 2003)

Located at MSDN Home ➤ Web Services Home

http://msdn.microsoft.com/webservices/default.aspx?pull=/library/
en-us//dnsoap/html/understandsoap.asp

XML Schemas and the XML Designer

MSDN Articles

Located at MSDN Home ➤ MSDN Library ➤ .NET Development ➤
Visual Studio .NET ➤ Visual Basic and Visual C# ➤ Accessing Data ➤
XML Schemas and Data

http://msdn.microsoft.com/library/default.asp?url=/library/en-us/
vbcon/html/vborielementattributecreation.asp

A Quick Guide to XML Schema

Aaron Skonnard

MSDN Magazine (April 2002)

Located at MSDN Home ➤ MSDN Magazine ➤ April 2002

```
http://msdn.microsoft.com/msdnmag/issues/02/04/xml/default.aspx
```

Place XML Message Design Ahead of Schema Planning to Improve Web Service Interoperability

Yasser Shohoud

MSDN Magazine (December 2002)

Located at MSDN Home ➤ MSDN Magazine ➤ December 2002

```
http://msdn.microsoft.com/msdnmag/issues/02/12/WebServicesDesign/
```

RPC/Literal and Freedom of Choice

Yasser Shohoud

Web Services Developer Center whitepaper (April 2003)

Located at MSDN Home ➤ Web Services Home ➤ Understanding Web Services ➤ Web Service Basics

```
http://msdn.microsoft.com/webservices/understanding/webservicebasics/
default.aspx?pull=/library/en-us/dnwebsrv/html/rpc_literal.asp
```

Web Services Encoding and More

Aaron Skonnard

MSDN Magazine (May 2003)

Located at MSDN Home ➤ MSDN Magazine ➤ May 2003

```
http://msdn.microsoft.com/msdnmag/issues/03/05/XMLFiles/
```

SOAP is Not a Remote Procedure Call

Ingo Rammer

Ingo Rammer's Architecture Briefings (October 2003)

```
http://www.thinktecture.com/Resources/ArchitectureBriefings/
SoapIsNotARemoteProcedureCall.pdf
```

WS-Specifications (General)

IBM developerWorks: Links to original standards and specifications documents

Located at IBM developerWorks ➤ Web services ➤ Technical Library

http://www-106.ibm.com/developerworks/views/webservices/standards.jsp

Secure, Reliable, Transacted Web Services: Architecture and Composition

Donald F. Ferguson (IBM), Tony Storey (IBM), Brad Lovering (Microsoft), John Shewchuk (Microsoft)

Whitepaper (September 2003)

Located at MSDN Home ➤ Web Services Home ➤ Understanding Web Services ➤ Advanced Web Services

http://msdn.microsoft.com/webservices/understanding/
advancedwebservices/default.aspx?pull=/library/en-us/dnwebsrv/
html/wsoverview.asp

Compare Web Service Security Metrics

Roger Jennings (OakLeaf Systems)

XML & Web Services Magazine (October 2002)

http://www.fawcette.com/xmlmag/2002_10/online/webservices_rjennings_
10_16_02/default.aspx

Installing Certificates for WSDK X.509 Digital Signing and Encryption

Roger Jennings (OakLeaf Systems)

XML & Web Services Magazine (October 2002)

http://www.fawcette.com/xmlmag/2002_10/online/webservices_rjennings_
10_16_02/sidebar1.aspx

Web Services Enhancements 1.0 and 2.0 (General)

Programming with Web Services Enhancements 1.0 for Microsoft .NET

Tim Ewald (Microsoft)

Whitepaper (December 2002)

Located at MSDN Home ➤ MSDN Library ➤ XML and Web Services

```
http://msdn.microsoft.com/webservices/building/wse/default
.aspx?pull=/library/en-us/dnwebsrv/html/progwse.asp
```

Programming with Web Services Enhancements 2.0

Matt Powell (Microsoft)

Whitepaper (July 2003)

Located at MSDN Home ➤ MSDN Library ➤ XML and Web Services

```
http://msdn.microsoft.com/webservices/building/wse/default
.aspx?pull=/library/en-us/dnwebsrv/html/programwse2.asp
```

WS-Security

Standards Documents: Web Services Security (WS-Security)

OASIS Web Services Security Standards

Specifications (March 2004)

Located at OASIS Web Services Security TC

```
http://www.oasis-open.org/committees/tc_home.php?wg_abbrev=wss
```

Specifications: SOAP Message Security 1.0

OASIS Web Services Security Standards

Specifications (March 2004)

Located at OASIS Web Services Security TC

```
http://docs.oasis-open.org/wss/2004/01/oasis-200401-wss-soap-message-
security-1.0.pdf
```

Understanding WS-Security

Scott Seely (Microsoft)

Whitepaper (October 2002)

Located at MSDN Home ➤ Web Services Home ➤ Understanding Web Services ➤ Advanced Web Services

```
http://msdn.microsoft.com/webservices/understanding/
advancedwebservices/default.aspx?pull=/library/en-us/dnwssecur/
html/understw.asp#understw_topic3
```

WS-Security Drilldown in Web Services Enhancements 2.0

Don Smith (Microsoft)

Whitepaper (August 2003)

Located at MSDN Home ➤ MSDN Library ➤ XML Web Services

```
http://msdn.microsoft.com/library/default.asp?url=/library/en-us/
dnwebsrv/html/wssecdrill.asp
```

(Note: This reference is cross-listed under WS-Secure Conversation.)

WS-Security Authentication and Digital Signatures with Web Services Enhancements

Matt Powell (Microsoft)

Whitepaper (December 2002)

Located at MSDN Home ➤ Web Services Home ➤ Building ➤ Web Services Enhancements (WSE)

```
http://msdn.microsoft.com/webservices/building/wse/default
.aspx?pull=/library/en-us/dnwssecur/html/wssecauthwse.asp
```

Building Secure Web Services (Patterns & Practices Chapter 12)

J.D. Meier, Alex Mackman, Michael Dunner, Srinath Vasireddy, Ray Escamilla, and Anandha Murukan

Patterns & Practices whitepaper (June 2003)

Located at MSDN Home ➤ MSDN Library ➤ .NET Development ➤ .NET Security ➤ Improving Web Application Security

```
http://msdn.microsoft.com/library/default.asp?url=/library/en-us/
dnnetsec/html/THCMCh12.asp
```

Encrypting SOAP Messages Using Web Services Enhancements

Jeannine Hall Gailey

Whitepaper (December 2002)

Located at MSDN Home ➤ MSDN Library ➤ XML and Web Services

```
http://msdn.microsoft.com/library/default.asp?url=/library/en-us/
dnwse/html/wseencryption.asp
```

Web Services Security: Moving up the Stack

Maryann Hondo (IBM), David Melgar (IBM), and Anthony Nadalin (IBM)

Whitepaper (December 2002)

Located at developerWorks ➤ Web services

```
http://www-106.ibm.com/developerworks/library/ws-secroad/
```

Web Services Security UsernameToken Profile

Chris Kaler (Microsoft, editor) and Anthony Nadalin (IBM, editor)

Working draft (August 2003)

```
http://www.oasis-open.org/committees/wss/documents/WSS-Username-11.pdf
```

Web Services Security Kerberos Binding

Giovanni Della-Libera (Microsoft), Brendan Dixon (Microsoft), Praerit Garg (Microsoft), Maryann Hondo (IBM), Chris Kaler (Microsoft), Hiroshi Maruyama (IBM), Anthony Nadalin (IBM), and Nataraj Nagaratnam (IBM)

Web Services Developer Center whitepaper (December 2003)

Located at MSDN Home ➤ Web Services Home ➤ Understanding Web Services ➤ Specifications

```
http://msdn.microsoft.com/webservices/understanding/specs/default
.aspx?pull=/library/en-us/dnglobspec/html/ws-security-kerberos.asp
```

WS-Policy

Specification: Web Services Policy Framework (WS-Policy)

Chris Kaler (Microsoft, editor) and Maryann Hondo (IBM, editor)

Specification (May 2003)

Located at IBM developerWorks ➤ Web services

http://www-106.ibm.com/developerworks/library/ws-polfram/

Understanding WS-Policy

Aaron Skonnard

Whitepaper (August 2003)

Located at MSDN Home ➤ MSDN Library ➤ XML and Web Services ➤ Specifications

http://msdn.microsoft.com/library/default.asp?url=/library/en-us/ dnwebsrv/html/understwspol.asp

Web Services Policy Assertions Language (WS-Policy Assertions)

Don Box (Microsoft), Maryann Hondo (IBM), Chris Kaler (Microsoft), Hiroshi Maruyama (IBM), Anthony Nadalin (IBM, editor), Nataraj Nagaratnam (IBM), Paul Patrick (BEA), Claus von Riegen (SAP), and John Shewchuk (Microsoft)

Whitepaper (December 2003)

Located at MSDN Home ➤ MSDN Library ➤ XML and Web Services ➤ Specifications ➤ Metadata Specifications Index Page

http://msdn.microsoft.com/library/default.asp?url=/library/en-us/ dnglobspec/html/ws-policyassertions.asp

Using Role-Based Security with Web Services Enhancements 2.0

Ingo Rammer

Whitepaper (September 2003)

Located at MSDN Home ➤ MSDN Library ➤ XML Web Services

http://msdn.microsoft.com/library/default.asp?url=/library/en-us/ dnwssecur/html/wserolebasedsec.asp

WS-SecureConversation

Specification: Web Services Secure Conversation (WS-SecureConversation)

Don Box (Microsoft, editor) and Francisco Curbera (IBM, editor)

Specification (March 2003)

Located at IBM developerWorks ➤ Web services

http://www-106.ibm.com/developerworks/webservices/library/ws-secon/

Specification: Web Services Trust (WS-Trust)

Chris Kaler (Microsoft, editor) and Anthony Nadalin (IBM, editor)

Specification (December 2002)

Located at IBM developerWorks ➤ Web services

http://www-106.ibm.com/developerworks/library/ws-trust/

WS-Security Drilldown in Web Services Enhancements 2.0

Don Smith (Microsoft)

Whitepaper (August 2003)

Located at MSDN Home ➤ MSDN Library ➤ XML Web Services

http://msdn.microsoft.com/library/default.asp?url=/library/en-us/
dnwebsrv/html/wssecdrill.asp

(Note: This reference is cross-listed under WS-Security.)

WS-Addressing

Specification: Web Services Addressing (WS-Addressing)

Don Box (Microsoft, editor) and Francisco Curbera (IBM, editor)

Specification (March 2003)

Located at IBM developerWorks ➤ Web services

http://www-106.ibm.com/developerworks/webservices/library/ws-add/

***Expanding the Communications Capabilities of Web Services
with WS-Addressing; Making Web Services Intermediary-Friendly,
Asynchronous, and Transport-Neutral***

John Shewchuk, Steve Millet, Hervey Wilson (Microsoft)

Whitepaper (October 2003)

Located at MSDN Home

```
http://msdn.microsoft.com/library/default.asp?url=/library/en-us/
dnwse/html/soapmail.asp
```

WS-Messaging

***Asynchronous operations and Web services, Part 1: A primer on asynchronous
transactions***

Holt Adams (IBM)

Whitepaper (April 2002)

Located at IBM developerWorks ➤ Web services

```
http://www-106.ibm.com/developerworks/library/ws-asynch1/index.html
```

***Asynchronous operations and Web services, Part 2: Programming patterns to
build asynchronous Web services***

Holt Adams (IBM)

Whitepaper (June 2002)

Located at IBM developerWorks ➤ Web services

```
http://www-106.ibm.com/developerworks/library/ws-asynch2/index.html
```

Introducing the Web Services Enhancements 2.0 Messaging API

Aaron Skonnard

MSDN Magazine (September 2003)

Located at MSDN Home ➤ Web Services Home ➤ Building ➤ Web
Services Enhancements (WSE)

```
http://msdn.microsoft.com/webservices/building/wse/default
.aspx?pull=/msdnmag/issues/03/09/xmlfiles/default.aspx
```

WS-Routing and WS-Referral

Routing SOAP Messages with Web Services Enhancements 1.0

Aaron Skonnard

Whitepaper (January 2003)

Located at MSDN Home

```
http://msdn.microsoft.com/library/default.asp?url=/library/en-us/
dnwse/html/routsoapwse.asp
```

WS-Reliable Messaging

Specification: Web Services Reliable Messaging Protocol (WS-ReliableMessaging)

David Langworthy (Microsoft, editor) and Christopher Ferris (IBM, editor)

Specification (March 2003)

Located at IBM developerWorks ➤ Web services

```
http://www-106.ibm.com/developerworks/webservices/library/ws-rm/
```

Reliable Message Delivery in a Web Services World: A Proposed Architecture and Roadmap

IBM Corporation and Microsoft Corporation

Whitepaper (March 2003, Version 1)

Located at MSDN Home ➤ Web Services Home ➤ Understanding Web Services ➤ Advanced Web Services

```
http://msdn.microsoft.com/webservices/understanding/
advancedwebservices/default.aspx?pull=/library/en-us/dnglobspec/
html/ws-rm-exec-summary.asp
```

Indigo

A Guide to Developing and Running Connected Systems with Indigo

Don Box (Microsoft)

MSDN Magazine (January 2004)

Located at MSDN Home ➤ Longhorn Developer Center Home ➤
Understanding Longhorn ➤ The Pillars of Longhorn ➤ Indigo

```
http://msdn.microsoft.com/longhorn/understanding/pillars/indigo/
default.aspx?pull=/msdnmag/issues/04/01/Indigo/default.aspx
```

Microsoft "Indigo" Frequently Asked Questions

Whitepaper (October 2003)

Located at MSDN Home ➤ Longhorn Developer Center Home ➤
Support ➤ Longhorn Developer FAQ

```
http://msdn.microsoft.com/Longhorn/Support/lhdevfaq/default.aspx#Indigo
```

Creating Indigo Applications with the PDC Release of Visual Studio .NET Whidbey

Yasser Shohoud (Microsoft)

Whitepaper (January 2004)

Located at MSDN Home ➤ Longhorn Developer Center Home ➤
Understanding Longhorn ➤ The Pillars of Longhorn ➤ Indigo

```
http://msdn.microsoft.com/Longhorn/understanding/pillars/Indigo/
default.aspx?pull=/library/en-us/dnlingo/html/indigolingo01062004.asp
```

Distributed Applications Using "Indigo" Services

Microsoft online documentation (preliminary)

Located at Longhorn SDK ➤ Distributed Programming Distributed
Applications Using "Indigo" Services

```
http://longhorn.msdn.microsoft.com/?://longhorn.msdn.microsoft.com/
lhsdk/indigo/conDistributedApplicationsUsingMessageBusServices.aspx
```

Miscellaneous

PDC 2003 Sessions

Session slides and downloads from PDC 2003

Located at MSDN Home ➤ PDC 2003 - PDC Central ➤ Agenda and Sessions ➤ Sessions

http://msdn.microsoft.com/events/pdc/agendaandsessions/sessions/
default.aspx

List of Books on Building Web Services Using .NET

Web Services Developer Center

This page lists books about Web services in general and about building Web services using .NET in particular.

Located at MSDN Home ➤ Web Services Home ➤ Understanding Web Services ➤ Books

http://msdn.microsoft.com/webservices/understanding/books/default.aspx

Newsgroups Related to Web Services, Web Services Enhancements, and Indigo

microsoft.public.dotnet.framework.webservices

microsoft.public.dotnet.framework.webservices.enhancements

microsoft.public.windows.developer.winfx.indigo

Find more newsgroups at MSDN Home ➤ MSDN Newsgroups.

http://msdn.microsoft.com/newsgroups/default.aspx?dg=microsoft.public
.dotnet.framework.webservices.enhancements

Orchestrating XML Web Services and Using the Microsoft .NET Framework with Microsoft BizTalk Server

Ulrich Roxburgh (Microsoft)

Whitepaper (February 2002)

Located at MSDN Home ➤ MSDN Library ➤ Enterprise Development ➤ Windows Server System ➤ Microsoft BizTalk Server

http://msdn.microsoft.com/library/default.asp?url=/library/en-us/
dnbiz2k2/html/bts_wp_net.asp

Attributes

MSDN Online Articles

Provides an overview of Reflection attributes and custom attributes

Located at: MSDN Home ➤ MSDN Library ➤ .NET Development ➤ Visual Studio .NET ➤ Visual Basic and Visual C# ➤ Reference ➤ Visual C# Language ➤ C# Language Specification

```
http://msdn.microsoft.com/library/default.asp?url=/library/en-us/
cpguide/html/cpconaccessingcustomattributes.asp
```

Index

forums.apress.com

JOIN THE APRESS FORUMS AND BE PART OF OUR COMMUNITY. You'll find discussions that cover topics of interest to IT professionals, programmers, and enthusiasts just like you. If you post a query to one of our forums, you can expect that some of the best minds in the business—especially Apress authors, who all write with *The Expert's Voice*™—will chime in to help you. Why not aim to become one of our most valuable participants (MVPs) and win cool stuff? Here's a sampling of what you'll find:

DATABASES
Data drives everything.

Share information, exchange ideas, and discuss any database programming or administration issues.

PROGRAMMING/BUSINESS
Unfortunately, it is.

Talk about the Apress line of books that cover software methodology, best practices, and how programmers interact with the "suits."

INTERNET TECHNOLOGIES AND NETWORKING
Try living without plumbing (and eventually IPv6).

Talk about networking topics including protocols, design, administration, wireless, wired, storage, backup, certifications, trends, and new technologies.

WEB DEVELOPMENT/DESIGN
Ugly doesn't cut it anymore, and CGI is absurd.

Help is in sight for your site. Find design solutions for your projects and get ideas for building an interactive Web site.

JAVA
We've come a long way from the old Oak tree.

Hang out and discuss Java in whatever flavor you choose: J2SE, J2EE, J2ME, Jakarta, and so on.

SECURITY
Lots of bad guys out there—the good guys need help.

Discuss computer and network security issues here. Just don't let anyone else know the answers!

MAC OS X
All about the Zen of OS X.

OS X is both the present and the future for Mac apps. Make suggestions, offer up ideas, or boast about your new hardware.

TECHNOLOGY IN ACTION
Cool things. Fun things.

It's after hours. It's time to play. Whether you're into LEGO® MINDSTORMS™ or turning an old PC into a DVR, this is where technology turns into fun.

OPEN SOURCE
Source code is good; understanding (open) source is better.

Discuss open source technologies and related topics such as PHP, MySQL, Linux, Perl, Apache, Python, and more.

WINDOWS
No defenestration here.

Ask questions about all aspects of Windows programming, get help on Microsoft technologies covered in Apress books, or provide feedback on any Apress Windows book.

HOW TO PARTICIPATE:
Go to the Apress Forums site at **http://forums.apress.com/**.
Click the New User link.